The Imaginary App

THE
Imaginary
App

edited by **Paul D. Miller**
and **Svitlana Matviyenko**

THE MIT PRESS   CAMBRIDGE, MASSACHUSETTS   LONDON, ENGLAND

MIT Press books may be purchased at special quantity discounts for business or sales promotional use. For information, email special_sales@mitpress.mit.edu.

Set in Chaparral Pro and Helvetica Neue by the MIT Press. Printed and bound in the United States of America.

Library of Congress Cataloging-in-Publication Data

The imaginary app / edited by Paul D. Miller and Svitlana Matviyenko.
    pages cm. — (Software studies)
Includes bibliographical references and index.
ISBN 978-0-262-02748-9 (hardcover : alk. paper) 1. Computers and civilization.
2. Mobile computing—Social aspects. 3. Application software—Social aspects.
I. DJ Spooky That Subliminal Kid. II. Matviyenko, Svitlana, 1976
QA76.9.C66I35 2014
303.48'34—dc23

2013044424

10   9   8   7   6   5   4   3   2   1

Contents

Series Foreword

Software is deeply woven into contemporary life—economically, culturally, creatively, politically—in manners both obvious and nearly invisible. Yet while much is written about how software is used, and the activities that it supports and shapes, thinking about software itself has remained largely technical for much of its history. Increasingly, however, artists, scientists, engineers, hackers, designers, and scholars in the humanities and the social sciences are finding that the questions they face, and the things they want to build, require an expanded understanding of software. For such understanding they can call upon texts in the history of computing and new media, they can take part in the rich implicit culture of software. They also can take part in the development of an emerging and fundamentally transdisciplinary computational literacy.

This series uses and develops cultural, theoretical, and practice-oriented approaches to make critical, historical, and experimental accounts of (and interventions via) the objects and processes of software. It engages and contributes to the research of computer scientists, the work of software designers and engineers, and the creations of software artists. It tracks how software is substantially integrated into the processes of contemporary culture and society, reformulating processes, ideas, institutions, and cultural objects around their closeness to algorithmic and formal description and action. It proposes histories of computational cultures, and it works with the intellectual resources of computing to develop reflexive thinking about its entanglements and possibilities. It does this both in the scholarly modes of the humanities and social sciences and in the software creation/research modes of computer science, the arts, and design.

The Software Studies series aims to publish the best new work in a critical and experimental field that is at once culturally and technically literate, reflecting the reality of today's software culture.

Preface

Paul D. Miller

What happens when you first think of an app? There is an immediate sense of reducing the thoughts at the edge of what you envision to an icon, a logo, a square, a circle, a widget—the basic interpretation of thought into action, of sense into sensation. The logos and icons that symbolize the surface touch of an irresistible logic of late capitalism are all on the surface of a screen that fits in your hand.

Imagine that you have on your screen an icon that was posted on Apple's App Store on August 5, 2008 and removed the next day. Called I Am Rich, it is an iOS Application created by Armin Heinrich. It is what economists call a "Veblen good"—a dematerialized form of commodity named after Thorstein Veblen, the American economist and sociologist who coined the term "conspicuous consumption." I Am Rich, having been presented as a "work of art with no hidden function at all," occupies a fuzzy and imprecise area of economic theory. But so does most art.

Heinrich's creation set the tone for an ecosystem governed by the laws of perception rather than the "bricks and mortar" approach of the norms of economics. It does nothing except display on the screen of your iPhone an icon that suggests that you have wealth and status.

What does a Veblen good have to do with dematerialized stuff like apps? It is all about perception. If everybody has it, it should be free. But the laws of scarcity get turned upside down in the realm of software. Software acquires more utility as more people use it.

An app is a software equivalent of a paradox of value—a kind of pastiche of how we assign meaning in a world where digital currencies like Bitcoin and "status symbols" like painting, sculpture, handbags, cars, and high-end wines hold sway. In fact, these consumer goods are opposite of what the norms of economic theory would convey. Decreasing their price decreases people's desire to buy them, because they are then viewed as "cheap" and no longer "exclusive." They go against the logic of the dictum that demand moves conversely to price. But a painting or a sculpture is a reflection of a collector's impulse to create scarcity. If everyone has a Picasso painting, a Picasso paint-ing isn't very interesting. But if everyone uses Apple's App Store or Google's Play Store to download utilitarian or useless apps, they still create a certain kind of cumulative, incremental value based not on "perceived" value but on the ambiguous numbers of what Pierre Bourdieu liked to call "cultural capital."

I Am Rich is a "conspicuous consumption" app that, when activated, shows a red gem and displays, in large text, this "mantra":

I am rich
I deserve it
I am good,
healthy &
successful

Apple removed it from the App Store after 24 hours. Priced at $999.99 in the United States and €799.99 in Europe, it generated thousands of dollars in sales in those 24 hours.

I like to think of I Am Rich as a perfect example of some of the themes of this anthology. It was fictional, and it served no purpose except to portray a perception of status, but the fact that it was removed and the fact that it left a media trail of articles describing its status after it had been erased point to what André Malraux called *le musée imaginaire*—a museum without walls, a gallery of perceptions connected by algorithms instead of curators. In fact, as longer battery life, low latency response times, and technologies like MIMO Wi-Fi transform the mobile digital media experience into truly immersive ubiquitous computing, issues like this will come to the forefront. That is what *The Imaginary App* is about: giving people tools to navigate the theoretical ter-rains that apps have unleashed.

What exactly is an app? There is a vast distance between what is plausible and what is possible. The measurement between the two is what this col-lection of essays explores. The exponential growth of apps has unleashed a huge wave of creativity—the way apps function has fostered a revolution in almost all aspects of creativity. As of this writing, the iPad has been out only a couple of years, and yet more than 45 billion apps for it have been downloaded from Apple, most of them in 2012. Google Android's Play Store has delivered more than 50 billion downloads. Between the two operating systems, that is more than the number of words humanity has generated in its entire existence as a species. It dwarfs the number of stars in the sky. That is some serious memory.

In 1936, in one of the most prophetic observations of the twentieth cen-tury, Alan Turing wrote "It is possible to invent a single machine which can be used to compute any computable sequence." Apps have inherited the emergent patterns of complexity that Turing anticipated.

On one hand, apps are the end result of work by the engineers and mathematicians who midwifed America's post-World War II technological order. On the other hand, they are uniquely purposed to end users' desires in ways no one could have imagined beyond the realm of either science fiction or that of engineers' esoteric dreams of the 1950s and 1960s. Dynabook (a device, imagined by Alan Kay in 1968, that was essentially the predecessor to the iPad, every Google Android tablet, and even Microsoft's Surface Pro tablet) and Vannevar Bush's Memex (imagined in a 1945 magazine article titled "As We May Think") couldn't have been built at the time they were conceived because the technology that would have made them possible didn't exist.

I wanted to see what would happen if we tried to envision something at the edge of the imagination to see what will be possible, in the manner of the famous philosophy question so many students are asked at the beginning of Philosophy 101. The question: "Why?" The answer: "Why Not?" *The Imaginary App* says "Let us see how that would apply to apps." Every time you touch an app, you are basically just touching a metaphor, a conduit into an operating system linked to more metaphors layered on metaphors about the unfolding equations defining the data you see on the screen in front of you.

As a conduit for digital information to invade every aspect of modern life, apps are scripts that link the way we search for small software solutions to things that we once took for granted, and to the larger issues facing a hypernetworked society on the precipice of total immersion in digital culture. At this point in the evolution of digital media, a song is basically a lot of zeros and ones. So is an app. The codified architecture of the way these scripts interact with mobile devices, and in return condition everything from the way we search for movies to the occasional foray into the darker realms of encrypted info dumps such as Wikileaks app being banned from the iTunes App Store. The App Store is such a closed environment, but with sites like Cydia you can easily re-route and "jailbreak" your iPad and iPhone to move away from the approved apps such as "Wiki offline lite—a Wikipedia experience" to more dynamic software like CyanogenMod on Google Android, or Ubuntu and Firefox operating systems that layer over Linux and Unix. After all, Clay Shirky, the author of *Here Comes Everybody*, likes to say "Communications tools don't get socially interesting until they get technologically boring." So let us think of the metaphors that apps convey—a phone icon (Text Plus App), a Green Elephant (Evernote app), a green, yellow, and blue triangle (Google Drive), and others—as a kind of disambiguation, a type of analogy closely related to the technological rhetoric of our era that has achieved its effects on our culture via association, comparison, or resemblance. These icons and logos represent an ambiguous category that includes allegory, hyperbole, and simile, but does not exclude willful playfulness. As a matter of fact, you can think of an app as a kind of dynamic tension between code and culture.

An amusing example is the Japanese Vocaloid character Hatsune Miku, which comes from the term merging the Japanese words for "first" (*hatsu*), "sound" (*ne*), and "future" (*miku*). Hatsune is a holographic animated projection fully owned by Crypton Future Media Corporation. A crowdsourced virtual idol, she has had number-one hit songs—sold online, they have generaed millions of dollars, and they are among the most requested karaoke downloads in Asia. On top of that, she (that is, the software program) promotes Toyota in TV commercials, and she gives holographic concerts. She is a voice in music synthesizer software. Her users have created a totally crowdsourced celebrity that reflects the dynamics of "the social" in media and the value of collaborative creativity. She, of course, is now an app.

"The world of the future," according to Norbert Wiener's 1950 book *The Human Use of Human Beings*, "will be an even more demanding struggle against the limitations of our intelligence, not a comfortable hammock in which we can lie down to be waited upon by our robot slaves." Hatsune Miku embodies this to the point where you can plausibly argue that the idea of a person, the idea of an app, and the distance between the two have vanished into the quantum realm of the networks that hold the modern information economy together. The question that arises is "Are we working for technology, or is technology working for us?" Think of that phenomenology next time you touch a screen and expect to see software respond. It is not a secret that the desktop experience of digital media is in terminal decline. Let us push it into an early grave and see if zombies rise from its coffin.

The processors in every tablet, iPad, laptop, cell phone, and router can still be traced back to some of the debates between John von Neumann and Alan Turing, between Lady Ada Lovelace and Charles Babbage, and between al-Khwarizmi and Stephen Wolfram. This volume explores some of the dynamic tensions between their approaches from a modern point of view in which the sampling and the use of "found" sources such as apps have converged in theory and in practice. In a 1954 essay titled "The question concerning technology," Martin Heidegger wrote that his essays were a collection of thoughts on what he simply called an "insight into what is." This volume looks for counterpoints in the algorithmic architecture of the way apps have shaped the emergent patterns of digitality in the twenty-first century. Whereas Heidegger could write about the rapidly evolving world of technology only theoretically, only a short time later von Neumann could seriously say of his computer inventions "What we are creating now is a monster whose influence is going to change history, provided there is any history left." Think of this book as a "jailbroken" cell phone in the middle of a new update that pulls into an allusion of a transcendent and unique theme in modern life. This is a collection of glitches—errors in the codes that define the way we think about apps—that generate new and unexpected approaches to art, aesthetics, and design. That is what this collection of essays evokes. It comprises some of the best thinking about the immense potential apps have in modern life, and the effects they have had on everything. I invite you to use a haptic sensibility to explore the immaterial and ethereal realms it manifests. Press "Play," sit back, read, and immerse.

Acknowledgments

Oscar Wilde once wrote "the difference between literature and journalism is that journalism is unreadable and literature is not read." With *The Imaginary App*, I wanted to create a community of people to riff on some ideas about art, design, and the social process of digital media, and, perhaps, reverse engineer Oscar Wilde's observation from a couple of centuries ago. So it's with great thanks that I extend sincere and heartfelt gratitude to our editor at the MIT Press, Doug Sery, and my co-editor, Svitlana Matviyenko. It couldn't have happened without you!

It's almost one of the most obvious of truisms, but it's one that nevertheless always rings true: no work of literature is created without context. In that light, I'd like to extend my sincere thanks to a group of friends who have supported my work over the years, and who have always been available for criticism and feedback.

SeungJung Kim diligently reading the various essays, giving insight into how to shape and mold the "mega-mix" that this book represents. I also owe a debt of gratitude to Ken Jordan and Erik Davis, who have been sounding boards for the evolution of some of my thoughts on the topic of mobile media and creative design. I'd also like to thank Ken Tanabe for his great sense of nuance when we spoke about the topic of Apps, and Steven Heller and Alice Rawsthorn for feedback about how to think of an anthology as a designed experience. As always, I'd like to thank my Mother, Rosemary Eloise Reed Miller, and my sister, Sabrina Miller, for being my Muses over the years. Last, I reflect on the memory of my father, Paul E. Miller, who passed away many years ago. I work in the shadow of his memory.

—Paul D. Miller a.k.a. DJ Spooky

My deep gratitude goes to Doug Sery of the MIT Press for his generous support of and interest in this project and to Paul Bethge, also of the MIT Press, for his thorough reading of the manuscript. I am especially thankful to Nick Dyer-Witheford for his important suggestions during the book's completion.

I also want to thank Nick and Vincent Manzerolle for giving me the opportunity to test out some ideas related to this project in a lecture form with their students. I owe a lot to Patricia Ticineto Clough, who was with me at the very beginning of my thinking about a potential collection of essays on mobile apps. I really appreciate the help Robbie Cormier, our editorial assistant, offered during the preparation of the volume. Lev Manovich's encouragement was very important to me. I thank all contributors—I learned so much from them. And of course, I thank my co-editor, Paul Miller, for joining this project, thinking it through with me, sharing his fascination with apps and mobile gadgets, and exploring their creative potentials.

I want to extend my gratitude to my friends Ricky Varghese and Umair Abdul, who offered their lovely Toronto apartment as a place for my summer writing retreat. And I thank my mother, Ludmila Karasiuk, for keeping her Skype app always on—for me.

—Svitlana Matviyenko

Introduction

Svitlana Matviyenko

The change has come. There is no search. But there is, there is that hope and that interpretation and sometime, surely any is unwelcome, sometime there is breath and there will be a sinecure and charming very charming is that clean and cleansing. Certainly glittering is handsome and convincing.

—Gertrude Stein, *Tender Buttons*

Advertising rhetoric does not exhaust itself entertaining associations between technology and happiness. "Think appy thoughts," Nokia's app store tells us. Apple's slogan "There's an app for that" sends the same message: "If you have a problem, look for an app, the ultimate solution—always, anytime, anywhere." No matter what one thinks about such marketing propaganda, "(h)appiness" has been delivered and installed on our mobile devices at the tips of our fingers. The goal of this book is to carve a discursive niche that accommodates a variety of multidisciplinary accounts of mobile applications, addressing the expectations, skepticisms, risks, changes, fantasies, and disappointments we face as users, consumers, and developers of mobile apps. By enabling encounters between artists, media analysts, and scholars with backgrounds in philosophy, media studies, information science, psychoanalysis, and sociology, this collection looks at apps through several metaphorical and metonymical descriptions in order to discuss the mechanisms and ideologies that shape the "complicated relationship" with apps by which we now connect with one another and orient within our habitat.

When the App Store was launched in July 2008, it was meant to be a "wow factor" to compensate for the minimal hardware upgrades of the second-generation iPhone 3G released a month earlier. But for the majority of users, the new signifier "app" became known only around 2009 when it quickly gained popularity after Apple's iPhone 3G ad campaign remembered for the slogan "There's an app for that" which Apple subsequently trademarked. An app is an abbreviated software application—figuratively and literally, linguistically and

Figure I.1

"Think appy thoughts,"
a promotional image from
Nokia's website.

technically: apps are small programs—pieces of software designed to apply the power of a computing system for a particular purpose. While elegance in code has always been a preoccupation for the information-technology community, app designers made elegance a priority in order to use of the limited space on their devices more effectively while also tailoring the utility of those devices to their specific personal and professional needs. An app, itself an assemblage, also enters other technological assemblages. It requires certain operating-system specifications in order to function properly. The operating system mediates between hardware and apps by means of the set of system interfaces, which enables apps to run on the devices with different hardware capabilities. Depending on the operating system, separate components of the app such as activities, services, content providers, and broadcast receivers, performing different functions in the work of the application, can be activated separately from other components.[1] In order to run, some apps require a network connection; others are constantly available to the user. Some apps work on their own; others enter into temporary relations with other technologies by synchronizing the user's data with other applications on the device or between paired devices. In a time of location-based media capable of receiving content, processing content, and sending content anywhere at any time, apps have become synonymous with mobility[2] and with the ubiquity of computing—to a larger extent than the hardware devices that carry them.

In comparison with a Web browser, an app is a short-cut that guarantees direct and immediate access to the information stored in a database on the cloud. Yet the attractive side of apps as a new technique of mobile computing is often overshadowed by challenges they pose. The ongoing debate on advantages and disadvantages of apps has been unfolding for quite some time. In 2010, *Wired* magazine published an essay, titled "The Web is dead, long live the Internet,"[3] in which Chris Anderson and Michael Wolff announced the decline of the World Wide Web caused by the growing popularity of cloud computing and mobile apps. In their analysis of the decline of the Web, Anderson held responsible "us," users and consumers, while Wolff blamed "them," media moguls. The new demands and expectations of high functionality and operability of mobile gadgets that have been often fetishized by advertising campaigns have a big influence on users' preference for apps. According to Anderson, "much as we love freedom and choice, we also love things that just work, reliably and seamlessly."[4] In his critique of users' fascination with slick technologies at the cost of freedom, Anderson drew on Jonathan Zittrain's argument, in his 2008 book *The Future of the Internet and How to Stop It*, that cloud computing marks the loss of open standards and services of the free Internet as it was envisioned by its creators.[5] Zittrain described a new model of computing based on tethered appliances as the shift from "a generative Internet that fosters innovation and disruption, to an appliancized network that incorporates some of the most powerful features of today's Internet while greatly limiting its innovative capacity—and, for better or worse, heightening its regulability."[6] The latter concerned Zittrain because the new model of computing opened up possibilities for exercising micro control on a macro scale. "The prospect of tethered appliances and software as service," he maintained, "permits major regulatory intrusions to be implemented as minor technical adjustments to code or requests to service providers."[7] Geert Lovink, who is critical of Zittrain's "foundational myth" of the free Internet, challenges Zittrain's nostalgia and emphasizes that the Internet has never been free from the start: it has been "a closed world, only accessible to (Western) academics and the U.S. military."[8] Whereas Lovink is right about the free Internet being almost a romantic fantasy about a new frontier "naturally independent of the tyrannies," as John Perry Barlow proclaimed in 1996,[9] back then no one could imagine the exposure of users that cloud computing has enabled. Now that information about users is basically always already in possession of the cloud owners, in contrast to protected corporate and governmental data, we are witnessing unprecedented abuse of users' rights.[10]

Several things have to be said about the cloud. First of all, it is an operating system—more precisely, the Internet Operating System (IOS)—that runs as a Web browser and, therefore, allows users to move information from the datacenters onto computational devices almost instantaneously. It is quick at booting, it is easy to use, and its hardware requirements are low because applications and information that users move back and forth are stored on the Internet and not on the users' devices.[11] Rob Coley and Dean Lockwood describe the cloud as "the coalescence of processing power into an instantly available utility, ready for any eventuality."[12] The origin of the term "cloud" for this "systematized virtualization of data storage and access"[13] can be traced back to 1996. According to *MIT Technology Review*, it was coined inside the Houston offices of Compaq Computer.[14] Another possible source is a paper about the Internet as a unified and coordinated system in which Sharon Gillett and Mitchell Kapor mentioned the "cloud" of intermediate networks operated by a common protocol.[15] For the next twenty years, the term was used mainly inside the IT community. Then, in 2006, at a conference held by Google, that company's CEO, Eric Schmidt, re-introduced the term for "an emergent new model" of computing based on accessing and using data remotely.[16] As the term implies, cloud computing is based on invisible connectivity, which Mark Weiser, the father of ubiquitous computing, believed to be an important property not only of a new paradigm of pervasive computing but of any "good tool." In a 1994 article titled "The world is not a desktop," Weiser argued that "a good tool is an invisible tool."[17] By "invisible" he meant that the tool "does not intrude on [one's] consciousness," so that a user can focus on the task rather than on the tool. In his 1991 article "The computer for the 21st century," Weiser had stated that "the most profound technologies are those that disappear," and that "they weave themselves into the fabric of everyday life until they are indistinguishable from it."[18] Since our tools have become so "good" that we truly do not think of how they work, until they malfunction, new questions should be asked about the consequences of such invisibility.

After we download apps and grant them access to our private information, they share that information with other apps, and with advertisers (especially when apps are free), in a way that those without control over the distributed network (which means all regular users) are unable to trace. In this sense, mobile apps function as lures. By making computing seamless and making the media environment subliminal, apps trick users and draw their attention from the network's algorithmic architecture to entertaining and user-friendly opaque screens.[19] As Wendy Chun points out, "software offers us an imaginary relationship to our hardware"[20] by means of very selective graphical representations that show only those elements of computing that the user is allowed to see. Of course, such interfaciality is typical of computing, mobile or not; in the end, the purpose of the graphical user interface (GUI) was to mediate between a user and a technology. In the case of cloud computing, interfaciality contributes to the consumer myth of weightless, safe, cheap, easy, fun-to-use, and helpful apps. Not only are users offered an imaginary relationship with their hardware; in addition, seamless computing sets users in an imaginary relationship with the entire distributed network. At the same time, it strengthens the channels of access to users' private information and engages them in producing more of free data without knowing that they are being exploited for the sake of establishing control and generating profit: for those who harvest data—if their processing algorithms are good—no data are bad or useless. Any information about users, even if it is trivial, can be monetized. Apps make it fun for users to produce data, appealing to their desire to be organized, productive, or creative. In 2009, Andrew Blumberg and Peter Eckersley expressed concerns about the loss of locational privacy. In a report on mobile platform design and privacy policy, they noted that "modern cryptography actually allows civic data processing systems to be designed with a whole spectrum of privacy policies: ranging from complete anonymity to limited anonymity to support law enforcement." "But we need to ensure," they insisted, "that systems aren't being built right at the zero-privacy, everything-is-recorded end of that spectrum, simply because that's the path of easiest implementation."[21] Not only is it the path of easiest implementation; apparently it is the most profitable for the cloud's owners. That "everything is recorded" is the selling point of Google Glass and its apps, in which this feature is taken to the extreme.

It has been argued that peer-to-peer monitoring when surveillance and control are disseminated within the network has replaced the top-down form of control and surveillance usually associated with the panoptic principle. However, cloud computing and networking demonstrate that the top-down model of control has not disappeared. The top-down model exists not only along with but *because of* effective peer-to-peer horizontal monitoring. Although there is no such thing as a "complete user profile," some consistency could be assumed or algorithmically calculated on the basis of the user's multiple online real or fake presences. This is a rather disturbing and dangerous scenario when users' digital footprint collected via users' and their peers' digital exchanges gives enough of information for generating any narrative that can be easily used against users. Drawing on a Massachusetts Institute of Technology study, Jay Stanley and Ben Wizner[22] address the dangers of the access to users' information by using the notion of "metadata": "if the 'data' of a communication is the content of an email or phone call, this is data *about* the data—the identities of the sender and recipient, and the time, date, duration and location of a communication. This information can be extraordinarily sensitive." This is why, they explain, "the 'who,' 'when' and 'how frequently' of communications are often more revealing than what is said or written. Calls between a reporter and a government whistleblower, for example, may reveal a relationship that can be incriminating all on its own."[23]

While many consider the dangers of such exposure, Google Glass' commercial promises an accurate and complete record of one's daily performance to feed the customers' appetites for both—the spectacle of others' privacy and the desire to expose oneself to the networks of anonymous users. Black Mirror, a 2011 British mini-series about the risks and challenges of living with such technology comes to mind. An episode titled "The Entire History of You" tells the story of a couple named Liam and Ffion who live in a time when everyone has a device implanted behind one ear. The device makes an accurate record of the person's daily routine available for playback and review, either in front of person's eyes or projected on a screen. The characters' already complicated relationship is continually challenged by the technological possibility of accessing one another's daily record. The more accurate data is obtained, the easier to confuse it with 'the truth' and to forget that the reality cannot be substituted with a representation. The difference between this and the Google Glass scenario is that in Black Mirror the characters are left alone in their drama, whereas Glass, in addition to making it Google's property, discloses such a record of a person's life for the whole network. When we download apps, it is hard not to notice how much access to our information they demand. One may only wonder, for example, why QR Code Scanner app needs access to your location and to such personal information as your use of a browser, your bookmarks, and your contact data. It is obvious that colonizing and monetizing users' individual experience are the primary goals of many apps.

The notion of "cloud computing" responds to the question of how mobile computing operates: it describes the *relocation* of computational resources from local machines to a distributed network accessed with weightless and quick-functioning apps from any platform, anywhere, at any time. However, "cloud" is also a metaphor; it is loaded with meanings, as is any other metaphor, and that has contributed to a misunderstanding of *what* cloud computing is. For obvious reasons, the "cloud" metaphor supports the myth of its imaginary *immateriality*. This may explain why the materiality of datacenters is a relatively new concern. In 2012 this topic got public attention after Google released photographs of the interior and the exterior of its datacenter in The Dalles, Oregon. "The cloud is a building. It works like a factory,"[24] as Andrew Blum reminds us in *Tubes*. Or, as Bratton says, "the Cloud is heavy."[25] Now Google's website invites you to visit the eight places "your computer has already been." The visitors are offered a series of utterly beautiful images where the huge physical constructions that presumably consume enormous

amounts of energy and cause environmental pollution are shown in the context of vast natural surroundings. The visual rhetoric of the photographs
appeals to the myth of the "American technological sublime," that David E.
Nye defines as the overpowering sense of awe and disorientation in the presence of machines or any technological constructions. On this photographs,
the technological sublime is reinforced by the boundlessness and overwhelm-
ing sense of landscape. On the micro-level of the interior, the aesthetically
pleasing images of the blue, green, yellow, and red tubes, the installations of
multiple cords in thoroughly arranged metal frames suggest the complexity
of Google's organization. Despite the claimed "inside view," the photographs
are just another interface that makes "scientific and technical work . . . invisible by its own success," as Bruno Latour defines blackboxing.

Computing has supplanted computers. It a continuous, uninterrupted, and
playful process of switching devices—"platformativity," as Joss Hands calls
it.[26] However, this does not imply the end of a computer; it implies only that
the computer *as we know it* has been replaced by "the invisible computer."[27]
Such invisibility is sustained by a variety of objects, or "everyware," to which
the computing power is distributed."[28] As Adam Greenfield notes, the very
term "user" is no longer suitable for designating a person interacting with
technology: "At the most basic level, one no more 'uses' everyware than one
would a book to read or the floor to stand on. For many of the field's origina-
tors, the whole point of designing ubiquitous system was that they would be
ambient, peripheral, and not focally attended to in the way that something
actively 'used' must be."[29] As an alternative, Greenfield suggests "subject,"
which describes a new user as "someone with interiority, with his or her own
irreducible experience of the world"—as someone who "*has subjectivity*" and
is subjected to law, regulation, and change ("a person without a significant
degree of choice in a given matter").[30] Although Greenfield immediately withdraws the suggestion because "it sounds tinny and clinical,"[31] it is hard to deny
that we now find ourselves *subjected* to "lab experiments" by corporations col-
lecting and storing our data in order to calculate and premediate[32] our desires
and needs. One of our desires—to access and manipulate the surrounding
objects of the world with a double click or a touch of your finger—relies on a
firm distinction between subject and object. Today such a distinction is also
related to the refusal to find oneself in the wilderness or chaos rather than in
what seemed to be the humanist order. The app as a technique for operating
mobile devices has become an imaginary connector between users and the
datacenter of "absolute knowledge." It acts to ensure (or simulate) safety and
comfort by resetting the user's environment from the uncanny mesh to the
Internet of connected and reachable things.[33] In other words, it becomes a

means of experiencing, interacting with, and thinking of (uncanny) *space* in terms of (familiar) *place*.

The notion of "technique," as I use the word in reference to apps, draws on the work of such differing theorists of technology as the French sociologist Jacques Ellul and the German media historian Bernhard Siegert. In 1954, Ellul theorized technique as an invisible but powerful agency, a "complex of standardized means for attaining a predetermined result," an operational "know-how" in the technological society.[34] His Marxist reading of technique as a dominant force is particularly dark. According to Ellul, in technologically dependent society, where technique determines the meaning and conditions of human survival, such things as liberty, choice, and freedom are mere illusions so that "the appearance of a personal life [of an individual] becomes for him the reality of a personal life."[35] As Robert K. Merton comments in his introduction to the English edition, to Ellul the submission to technique is "suicidal": "In Ellul's conception, . . . life is not happy in a civilization dominated by technique. Even the outward show of happiness is bought at the price of total acquiescence. The technological society requires men to be content with what they are required to like; for those who are not content, it provides distractions—escape into absorption with technically dominated media of popular culture and communication."[36] Invisible and "almost completely independent of the machine,"[37] technique is not only a result of blind reliance on technology; it is the major mechanism of delegating work to the machine. Paradoxically, Ellul's intentionally threatening definition of technique is nearly a verbatim description of apps' promotional discourse, minus the warning. In the culture of accelerated mobility, where "software takes command"[38] instead of mechanical machines, the "submission to technique" is propagated by new ideologies as a gain rather than a loss: we are constantly reminded that ubiquitous computing is the only way of "having it all" under control, at the tips of our fingers. What Ellul identifies as "suicidal" is now repackaged as "(h)appy" and sold as the biggest advantage of techno-culture.

For Ellul and Siegert, the notion of "technique" transcends both machines as such and skills related to their usage: it rather concerns the whole systems in which machines exist along with those who operate them, the discourses and ideologies attached to them; in other words, for them, technique concerns the whole actor-network assemblage. But whereas for Ellul technique is the enslaving force within the technologically driven society, Siegert's notion of technique is rather neutral: it is a socially coded physical inclination of doing things in a particular way; in other words, techniques are *cultural*. Siegert believes that techniques expose "operative sequences that historically and logically precede the media concepts generated by them."[39] Cultural

techniques, he writes, "have to be understood as heterogeneous arrangements in which technological, aesthetic, symbolic, and political concepts of
one or more cultures of writing, image, number, line, and body interact."[40]
That notion allows Siegert to think of the materiality of the symbolic realm
as marked or mapped by technical objects, as he demonstrates in his essay on
doors. Like doors in his reading, apps are "not something fully real."[41] Owing
to the ideologies, fantasies, and the power of agency ascribed to them, apps
are also symbolic and imaginary, to use Jacques Lacan's terms that refer to
three intrapsychic realms that constitute the various levels of psychic phenomena. "Doors," Siegert writes, "are operators of symbolic, epistemic, and
social processes that, with help from the difference between inside and outside, generate spheres of law, secrecy, and privacy and thereby articulate
space in such a way that it becomes a carrier of cultural codes."[42] The same
can be said of apps: they participate in generating laws and articulating space.
However, if doors maintain the inside/outside division, apps either entirely
eliminate it in the eyes of users or, at least, make it look flexible and con-
trollable by a subject-with-a-gadget. In a sense, apps make an assault on the
former symbolic order in which "the door and the doorkeeper implement the
differential law of the signifier itself."[43] The new meanings and expectations
expressed in apps as the *it-object* of the commodity economy reveal the collapse of the old relation between time and space that has been constructed
within Western culture for centuries. Nothing, perhaps, demonstrates the
power of the symbolic law in modernism as well as Franz Kafka's parable
about the man who travels a long way but has to stop near the door, waiting
for permission to open it, without knowing that the door is unlocked, until,
full of hesitation, he actually loses the chance to enter. "The waiting of the
man by the door," Siegert comments on Kafka's text, "generates the paradox
that the state of opening has the effect of an interruption. The logic of a door
that is closed while it is opened 'as always' is the logic of the symbolic."[44] Read
with Lacan, Siegert's argument about the materiality of the symbolic mani-
fested in cultural techniques can be extended to the imaginary and the real.
In psychoanalysis, the question of matter is the question of the symptom that
pertains all three realms of psyche: the imaginary, the symbolic, and the real.

A discussion of symptoms related to the new social and technological
arrangements (and, specifically, ubiquitous computing with apps) would
exceed the limits of this introduction. One of these symptoms, however, is
worth a mention: the unbearable feeling now associated with a socially coded
practice of waiting. There is a connection between the pains of waiting and
the new notion of time-space relation regulated by the logics of acceleration and immediacy. Besides, if in the past waiting was associated with the

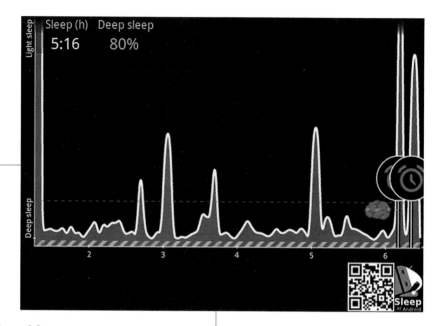

Figure I.2
A record of a sleep cycle made with the Sleep as Android app. Image created by Svitlana Matviyenko. Reproduced with permission of the copyright holder.

practices of obedience and submission forced by the symbolic law, as we see in Kafka's parable, recently the subjects are being persuaded that waiting is not an option, that they have to be able to obtain anything they need in *no time*, and that everything is already *right here* for them—at the tips of their fingers. As far as symptoms are concerned, "nobody knows any longer," Siegert suggests by referring to Lacan, "whether a door opens onto the imaginary or the real. We have all become unhinged."[45] And app technique promises to remove all doors, gates, and their gatekeepers—in order to save us waiting. Or even more so, to save us from waiting.

Psychoanalytically speaking, Luca Bosetti's term "a-(d)diction" captures similarities between drug addiction[46] and the dependency on prosthetics—from antidepressants to gadgets—nurtured and exploited by the ideologies of consumption. Both dependencies are sustained by the subject's refusal to deal with the symptoms directly; both grant the subject immediate access to *jouissance*, the term by which Lacan designated an experience of harmful excessive enjoyment that the subject renounces when she enters the symbolic order and accepts its cultural laws.[47] This double effect of a-(d)diction works perfectly for the capitalist cult of uninterrupted productivity, now also governed by apps.

In his 2013 book 24/7, Jonathan Crary expresses hope that in a time when "most of the seemingly irreducible necessities of human life—hunger, thirst, sexual desire, and recently the need for friendship—have been remade into commodified or financialized forms [s]leep poses the idea of a human need and interval of time that cannot be colonized and harnessed to a massive engine of profitability, and thus remains an incongruous anomaly and site of crisis in the global present." "The stunning, inconceivable reality," Crary believes, "is that nothing of value can be extracted from it."[48] Unfortunately, with apps it is no longer the case: a user doesn't have to be aware of producing data; in fact, she does not have to be awake. Take, for instance, Sleep as Android, an app that "wakes you up gently in light sleep for pleasant mornings." In addition to accessing sensitive log data, phone calls, phone state, and identity—continuously, 24/7, it is an alarm clock with a sleep-cycle tracker that produces a new layer of data by capturing the specifics of user's sleep. Apparently, the very purpose of apps is to carry on the continuity of production, to ensure that there is no rupture in it: users are encouraged to check emails while on the go, to text while walking "without fear," and to spend every spare moment entertaining themselves with games, reading, news, and so on. One falls asleep, but like an *android*, one never stops working: the production of data by a sleeping body continues—until the app calculates the best moment for one to wake up rested and ready for more labor.

There is a way to argue, following Slavoj Žižek, that apps turn on the mechanism of interpassivity,[49] when the app "takes from me, deprives me of, my own passivity, so that it is the object itself which enjoys . . . instead of me, relieving me of the duty to enjoy myself."[50] When users or, indeed the *subjects* of technological unconscious, are engaged in the *interpassive* relation with apps, they do not even come to acknowledge or confront their own needs. With apps, the logic of the problem-solution relation is reversed, and the reversal happens at the level of imperceptibility for a subject-user. Here the mechanism of interpassivity is in accordance with capitalist consumerism. The "needs" come with apps as part of the package, which means the "solutions" are being sold to us along with the "problems" they are meant to resolve. This is why the criticism of "technological solutionism"[51] misses the point when it only exposes the dangers of delegating all *tasks* to technology. What is really disturbing is that we seem to enjoy the idea that the *production of human needs* has been delegated to the machine.

To return to the notion of "appy thought," sold to users by one of the corporations, suggests both happy resolution of problems by means of apps and the impossibility of thought as such without the assistance of technology. I read this notions along with Luciana Parisi's *soft(ware) thought*, or simply, *soft thought*, "defined by the speculative function of algorithms."[52] Soft thought does not come "after" human thought: it is not post-human but subpersonal, "autonomous from cognition and perception,"[53] "nothing more than that numerical and logical mode of thinking which is proper of software itself."[54] The question "Who or what thinks soft thought?" is not relevant. For Parisi, soft thought assumes the full agency: it thinks itself.[55] Here "appy thought" is an avatar of soft thought in the commodity economy of the capitalist machine that thinks—instead of us. Governed by algorithms, it opens for users the potentiality to connect without thinking, immediately and intuitively, which is the very definition of "appiness" in today's technological arrangement. But what about the stubborn letter "h"? Just like Lacanian *letter*, it "always arrives to its destination," even though it is bracketed from the notion. We keep hearing and seeing it—the fossil or the ghostly shadow of *humanness*—there, where it is not.

In a 2009 book titled *Optical Media,* the German media materialist Friedrich Kittler describes the introduction of signal codification and digital image processing as the beginning of the switch from the imaginary to the symbolic regime that "ultimately represents the liquidation of [the] last remainder of the imaginary."[56] And yet, the imaginary persists in the ways worth our attention. One is related to the common users' misconception caused by ubiquitousness of mobile computing, when the "[power of] informatics underlying the apparent simplicity of the experience."[57] Users unfamiliar with the algorithmic structures of the networks treat the symbolic regime, described by Kittler, as the imaginary realm protecting them against the aggressively of the network, against information pollution, and against overload. An app here is the ultimate *imaginary tool* that assists, connects, organizers, and entertains. Eric Kluitenberg also theorizes "the imaginary media" by drawing on Benedict Anderson's notion of "imagined community."[58] For Anderson, the notion of imaginary is very important; it functions to sustain a community of people as one nation, even though in reality they do not know one another. Kluitenberg argues that there is a relation between communities and media in the sense that "media and communities double each other's imaginaries; an imaginary communion is shared via mediating machineries that are believed to be able to transfer more than 'mere' information; feelings rather than signals; meaning rather than data; satisfaction rather than sound, words, images; identity rather than codification of social life."[59] This is the notion that runs through many of the essays in this collection as they address different theoretical and technical aspects of computing as well as the discourses created around the topic of apps—from production and marketing to daily use and fascination with this new digital object.

The essays in part I explore how control and power are distributed and consolidated within software architecture. Benjamin Bratton explores the disciplinary effect of rendering the environment for the user and the user for the environment by means of an app that he describes as an interface between the user and his habitat. Søren Bro Pold and Christian Ulrik Andersen explore the potential risks of cultural computing with new gadgets apps, the tools for filtering and delivering cultural content. Patricia Ticineto Clough engages with object-oriented ontology to respond to concerns about "dangerously obscuring human knowing" by means of blackboxing. By looking at the modularity of the interface, Robbie Cormier, too, discusses apps' complicity with control and offers a detailed reading of Wolfram's research, focusing on a computational knowledge engine Wolfram|Alpha, which Theodore Gray, a founder of Wolfram Research, identifies as a "killer app." Paul Miller interviews Stephen Wolfram about organization, systematization, and accumulation of knowledge in the time when "all is computation."

The essays in part II look at apps' ability to extend or enhance certain human capacities. Nick Srnicek approaches this topic using Deleuze and Guattari's concept of the body without organs and suggests that apps offer themselves as "a non-religious form of experimentation" for exploring the question of "what a body can do" posed outside of mind/body dualism. Dock Currie explores how apps attached to a user attached to a mobile device create the immobile subject within a "spaceless instantaneity" of mobile technology. Eric Kluitenberg focuses on apps as tools beyond their practical purposes that "project imaginary solutions for potentially unattainable aspirations," and by which the lacking subjects displace their anxieties and impossible desires. Anna Munster explores the optical illusion of transparency at the level of hardware and software performed by a new "genre" of augmented reality (AR) apps (i.e., *Type n Walk* and *Transparent Screens*) that, she argues, opens up a possibility for "a novel recomposition of the senses" by means of the sophisticated play between revelation and trickery of phantasmagoria, stage magic, and cinematic illusionism of the late nineteenth century.

The essays in part III analyze how apps as an ideal commodity within capitalist "tyranny of choice"[60] (Renata Salecl). Nick Dyer-Witheford speaks about the allure of apps as a new possibility not only to make living but also to make a fortune. He puts his case study of the emergent "app worker" in the wider context of discussions on immaterial labor in order to raise the questions about the actual incomes and conditions of app workers as well as the dominating discourses of app work. Vincent Manzerolle and Atle Mikkola Kjøsen continue this discussion by looking at the new dynamics of the app economy wherein commodities (apps and the services they deliver) do not just simply attract money, but *stalk* it. Dal Yong Jin and Steven Millward address the specifics of the app economy in South Korea and China, where apps often compensate for the failure to consider the demands of local consumers of mobile technology.

Part IV opens with Lev Manovich's reading of apps (and software in general) as a metamedium[61] in contrast to the modern understanding of an artistic medium, or monomedium, limited by its properties and possibilities. Manovich looks at the process of "softwarization" to demonstrate how media software brings a new set of techniques operating across *all* media. Thierry Bardini questions overrated necessity of apps and their practicality that is often limited to the extent where apps simply sit on our touchscreens, handy and cute, without ever being used. Drawing on François Laruelle's photo-fictional apparatus of non-philosophy, Drew Burk offers his version of a theoretical "photo-fictional" imaginary app. Like a photograph in Laruelle's reading, the app is not "some new technique, but a new description and conception of . . . the practice that arises within it; of its relation to philosophy."[62] Dan Mellamphy and Nandita Biswas Mellamphy engage with Vilém Flusser's work *Vampyroteuthis* to meditate on apps' function within an overconnected environment. Referencing H. P. Lovecraft's 1930 novella *At the Mountains of Madness* and his 1928 short story "The Call of Cthulhu," they draw a Lovecraftian scenario in which a user is captured by a tentacular system of capitalism, apps serving as a trap to appropriate a user's identity or "user-information" such as location, destination, usage-duration, and replication "into the arena and concourse of capitalist coursing or hunting." Also included in part IV are transcripts of my interview of the interactive media artist Scott Snibbe—whose projects include *Gruvilax* and *Bubble Harp* (now available as apps) and the singer Björk's *Biophilia* apps—and of Chris Richards' interview of Ryan and Hays Holladay of the band Bluebrain. The Holladay brothers discuss their use the mobile phone's GPS technology for their location-aware music project, in which various musical passages are geo-tagged to various landmarks and routes, turning passive listening into an adventure of navigating through a musically transformed landscape.[63] By connecting different soundtracks to different geographic locations, Bluebrain's album offers the experience of the "extra dimensionality" of space as one passes through its different sonic "pockets." The location-aware album triggers the permanence of sonic memories and associations attached to certain localities as well as the very sense of awareness of the landscape.

To be fair, apps do open up the possibility of hacking, mostly because of the properties I discussed above: they are small programs, they are easy to write, their technological requirements are low, and they are easy to use. Apps have quickly become a means of political expression. One well-known example is Phone Story, banned by Apple but available for Android. Another hack that attracted a lot of attention was the Transborder Immigrant Tool (TBT), created by Ricardo Dominguez; a group called Electronic Disturbance Theater used it in A Mexico/U.S. Border Disturbance Art Project. The TBT app uses Spatial Data Systems and GPS technology to help immigrants find water stations in the Southern California desert.[64] Also worth mentioning is Drones+, an app designed by a New York University student named Josh Begley that, in addition to challenging the "neutrality" of app stores' regulations, notified users every time the United States carried out a drone strike. "When I started reading all the reports of drone strikes in Yemen, Pakistan, and Somalia," Begley said in an interview for *New York Magazine*, "one thing stood out: the flatness of language. There are words like 'militant' and 'compound' and 'hideout,' which come to mean very little when you read them in such volume. I sincerely didn't know what the contours of our drone war looked like. So I wanted to dig into the data set about every reported U.S. drone attack and try to surface that information in a new way."[65] After banning Drones+ twice for "technical reasons," Apple admitted that the reason for the bans was "objectionable or crude" content. To quote McKenzie Wark: "Just as the situationists imagined a space of play in the interstitial spaces of the policing of the city via the dérive, so too we now have to imagine and experiment with emerging gaps and cracks in the gamespace that the commodity economy has become. The time of the hack, or the exploit, is at hand."[66] Apps are eminently suitable for that.

The color gallery features (as plates 1–15) selected works from the book's sister project, an exhibition called The Imaginary App. Paul Miller and I invited artists and graphic designers to explore users' expectations of technology by designing icons for impossible, imaginary apps and formulating descriptions mocking the standards of the online app stores. Democratic in nature, the exhibition includes works by well-known designers, art students, and even a group of 14–16-year-olds affiliated with Ontario's Museum London, one of the exhibition's venues. I am especially grateful to Executive Director Brian Meehan, to Curator of Art Cassandra Getty, to Curator of Public Programs

Dianne Pearce, to Francisco Gerardo Toledo Ramírez, and to Kadie Ward for their support and help in organizing the exhibition. (Plates 16–18 are images of Scott Snibbe's works.)

Notes

1. See, for example, the description of Android application fundamentals and components at http://developer.android.com/guide/components/fundamentals.html. However, there are iPhone apps that grant no access to individual components of the app.

2. Every new technology adds to our understanding of mobility. For instance, Jason Farman makes a point that "the term 'mobile' has been applied to technologies as early as papyrus, when the written word became transportable across a broad geographic space" (*Mobile Interface Theory: Embodied Space and Locative Media*, Routledge, 2012, 1).

3. Chris Anderson and Michael Wolff, "The Web is dead, long live the Internet," *Wired*, August 2010 (http://www.wired.com).

4. Ibid.

5. Several months later, in an article in *Scientific American* titled "Long live the Web: A call for continued open standards and neutrality," Tim Berners-Lee expressed similar concerns and emphasized the following: "The Web is critical not merely to the digital revolution but to our continued prosperity—and even our liberty. Like democracy itself, it needs defending." See *Scientific American*, November 22, 2010 (http://www.scientificamerican.com).

6. Jonathan Zittrain, *The Future of the Internet and How to Stop It* (Yale University Press, 2008), 8.

7. Ibid., 125.

8. Lovink explains: "Zittrain needs a foundational myth of the Internet in order to praise its past openness and warn for a future lockdown of personal computers and mobile phones. From the ancient world of Theory we know why people invent foundational myths: to protect those in power (in this case US-American IT firms and their academic-military science structures that are losing global hegemony). The Zittrain myth says that, compared to centralized, content-controlled systems such as AOL, CompuServe and Prodigy, the 'generative' Internet of the late 1980s was an open network. But this was simply not the case, it was closed to the general public. This foundational myth is then used to warn the freedom-loving guys for

the Downfall of Civilization." See Lovink, "Zittrain's foundational myth of the open internet" (October 2008) (http://networkcultures.org).

9. John Perry Barlow, "A declaration of independence of cyberspace" (https://projects.eff.org/~barlow/Declaration-Final.html).

10. Recent exposure of the National Security Agency's monitoring of all electronic communications turned old technology-related anxieties into a reality that cannot be dismissed by a careless "I have nothing to hide." As has been recently brought to our attention, online profiles of virtually any user may contain potentially incriminating content; that is why, as Danah Boyd commented, "a surveillance state will produce more suspect individuals," instead of protecting their freedom and rights. The very fact of such monitoring not only violates the presumption of innocence, but on the contrary, it acts upon an assumption that everyone is potentially guilty. Technology, so much ahead of our very ability to process the changes it brings, is especially ahead of law-making critically needed to protect its users and creators. See danah boyd, "Where "nothing to hide" fails as logic," http://www.zephoria.org/thoughts/archives/2013/06/10/nothing-to-hide.html.

11. Daniel van der Velden and Vinca Kruk's two-part essay "Captives of the cloud" (2012) was very helpful in my work on this introduction and the entire project. The essay can be found at http://www.e-flux.com.

12. Rob Coley and Dean Lockwood, *Cloud Time: The Inception of the Future* (Zero Books, 2012), 1.

13. Ibid.

14. Antonio Regalado, "Who coined 'cloud computing'?" *MIT Technology Review*, October 2011.

15. Sharon Gillett and Mitchell Kapor, "The self-governing Internet: Coordination by design," presented at Coordination and Administration of the Internet Workshop at John F. Kennedy School of Government, Harvard University, 1996 (http://ccs.mit.edu/papers/CCSWP197/ccswp197.html).

16. See the conversation with Eric Schmidt hosted by Danny Sullivan at https://www.google.com/press/podium/ses2006.html.

17. Mark Weiser, "The world is not a computer" (www.ubiq.com/hypertext/weiser/AMCInteractions2.html).

18. Mark Weiser, "The computer for the 21st century," *Scientific American* 264 (1991), no. 3: 78–89.

19. In a discussion of universal surveillance and infrastructural imperialism of Google and its collaboration with the product advertisers, Siva

Vaidhyanathan explains that the precision of its processing algorithms is the goal; otherwise it is a waste of money for the corporation. He writes: "Google complicates the ways we manage information about ourselves in three major ways. It collects information from us when we use its services; it copies and makes available trivial or harmful information about us that lies in disparate corners of the Internet; and it actively captures images of public spaces around the world, opening potentially embarrassing or private scenes to scrutiny by strangers—or, sometimes worse, by loved ones. In theory, Google always gives the victim of exposure the opportunity to remove troubling information from Google's collection. But the system is designed to favor maximum collection, maximum exposure, and the permanent availability of everything. One can only manage one's global electronic profile through Google if one understands how the system works—and that there is a system at all. Google is a system of almost universal surveillance, yet it operates so quietly that at times it's hard to discern" (84). See Siva Vaidhyanathan, *The Googlization of Everything (And Why We Should Worry)* (University of California Press, 2011).

20. Wendy Hui Kyong Chun, "On software, or the persistence of visual knowledge," *Grey Room* 18 (2005), winter, 26–51, at 43.

21. Andrew J. Blumberg and Peter Eckersley, "On locational privacy and how to avoid losing it forever" (https://www.eff.org/files/eff-locational-privacy.pdf).

22. Jay Stanley and Ben Wizner, "Why the government needs your metadata," Reuters, June 7, 2013 (http://blogs.reuters.com).

23. Andrew Blum, *Tubes: A Journey to the Center of the Internet* (HarperCollins, 2012).

24. See "The cloud, the state, and the stack: Metahaven in Conversation with Benjamin Bratton" (http://mthvn.tumblr.com/post/38098461078/thecloudthestateandthestack).

25. See the issue of *Culture Machine* 14 (2013) on platforms. Also see Joss Hands, "Politics, power, and 'platformativity,'" http://www.culturemachine.net/index.php/cm/issue/view/25.

26. In *The Invisible Computer* (MIT Press, 1998), Donald Norman argued that in the future technology would be "invisible," hidden from sight.

27. Although I appropriated Levi Bryant's term, in this case it only denotes an equal possibility for different objects to become a computing platform.

28. Adam Greenfield, *Everyware: The Dawning Age of Ubiquitous Computing* (New Riders, 2006), 1.

29. Ibid., 70.

30. Ibid., 71.

31. Ibid.

32. Richard Grusin's term by which he described the way media as part of cultural industries map a plurality of possible futures, see Grusin's book *Premediation: Affect and Mediality After 9/11* (Palgrave Macmillan, 2010).

33. In 1999, Kevin Ashton coined the term "the Internet of Things" for a system in which the Internet is connected to the physical world by means of ubiquitous sensors.

34. Robert K. Merton, "Foreword," in Jacques Ellul, *The Technological Society* (Random House, 1964), vi.

35. Ellul, *The Technological Society* (Random House, 1964).

36. Merton, "Foreword," viii.

37. Jacques Ellul, *The Technological Society*, 4.

38. This is Lev Manovich's rephrasing of the title of Sigfried Giedion's book *Mechanization Takes Command* (Oxford University Press, 1948).

39. Bernhard Siegert, translated by Geoffrey Winthrop-Young, "Cacography or communication? Cultural techniques in German media studies," *Grey Room* 27 (2007): 26–47, at 29.

40. Ibid.

41. Ibid., 10.

42. Ibid., 9.

43. Ibid., 8.

44. Ibid., 10.

45. Ibid., 20.

46. For more on this subject, see *Lacan and Addiction: An Anthology*, ed. Yael Goldman Baldwin, Kareen Malone, and Thomas Svolos (Karnac Books, 2011).

47. For a more detailed discussion of the similarities between addiction and dependence on tools, see Luca Bosetti, "Three questions on prosthetic technology and a-(d)diction," *Paragraph 33.3* (2010).

48. Jonathan Crary, *24/7* (Verso, 2013), 10–11.

49. See Slavoj Žižek, "Is it possible to traverse the fantasy in cyberspace?" in *The Žižek Reader*, ed. Elizabeth Wright and Edmond Wright (Blackwell, 1999), 102–124.

50. Slavoj Žižek, "The interpassive subject: Lacan turns a prayer wheel," in *How to Read Lacan* (http://www.lacan.com/zizprayer.html).

51. Evgeny Morozov, *To Save Everything, Click Here: The Folly of Technological Solutionism* (Public Affairs), 2013.

52. Luciana Parisi, *Contagious Architecture. Computation, Aesthetics, and Space* (MIT Press, 2013), 266.

53. Ibid.,169.

54. Luciana Parisi and Stamatia Portanova, "Soft thought (in architecture and choreography)," *Computational Culture* 1 (2011) (http://computational culture.net/article/soft-thought).

55. "Things (or machines)," Parisi and Portanova explain, "do not think but 'are' thought. They do not simply host thought or become implementations of a predeterminate cognitive structure. Rather, thought results from the modalities or the mannerism of the machine: what thought becomes is how the machine thinks." (Ibid.)

56. Friedrich Kittler, *Optical Media* (Polity, 2009), 226.

57. Greenfield, *Everyware*, 1.

58. Benedict Anderson, *Imagined Communities: Reflections on the Origin and Spread of Nationalism* (Verso, 1983).

59. Eric Kluitenberg, "Second introduction to an archaeology of imaginary media," in *Book of Imaginary Media: Excavating the Dream of the Ultimate Communication Medium*, ed. Eric Kluitenberg (NAi/De Balie, 2006), 5.

60. Renata Salecl, *The Tyranny of Choice* (Profile Books, 2010).

61. "Metamedium" is Alan Kay's term for a computer.

62. François Laruelle, *The Concept of Non-Photography* (Sequence, 2011), 4.

63. See Bluebrain's website: http://www.bluebra.in.

64. For more, see http://post.thing.net/node/1642.

65. Joe Coscarelli, "Tweeting every U.S. drone strike is taking way longer than expected," *New York*, January 8, 2013.

66. McKenzie Wark, "#Celerity: A critique of the manifesto for an accelerationist politics" (http://syntheticedifice.files.wordpress.com/2013/06/celerity.pdf).

I Architectures

1

On Apps and Elementary Forms of Interfacial Life: Object, Image, Superimposition

Benjamin H. Bratton

What are apps? On the one hand, apps are applications, and so operate within something like an application layer of a cloud-to-device software/hardware "stack." But as most of the real information processing is going on in the cloud, and not in the box in your hand, the app on your phone is really more an interface to the real application, which sits in a datacenter, hidden within an anonymous shed or mountain. As an interface, the app connects the single remote device to an ocean of data and brings that data to bear on the user's immediate interests. Further, given that the app may connect the user to his environment and the things within it (looking, writing, subtitling, capturing, sorting, linking, hearing, etc.), the app is also an interface between the user and his habitat. It structures and activates a programmed mediation between user and environment (and therefore cloud and environment) according to a specific program. It renders the environment for the user, and the user for the environment, according to the logics and limits of that programmability, and it does this in ways that are exacting or vague, prescriptive or reactive. This chapter is interested in (and more than a little apprehensive about) this dynamic of prescription, as built into the habitus/habitat dynamic of the geolocative app, particularly those that superimpose descriptive layers upon a device's mobile machine vision capabilities. We should consider with caution (and a bit of awe) how emergent genres of apps that project interfacial elements onto what is seen through the device's camera eye (including augmented reality, or AR) may in effect radicalize and literalize absolutist and fundamentalist dispositions (including but by no means limited to those inspired by Abrahamic monotheisms) in addition to spawning as yet unimagined bizarre new cloud/AR-based politico-theological mutations. In many AR applications, artificial textual annotation of the world is fused with direct perception. Visual symbols are less a reference to something than they are directly laminated onto real things and into real landscapes. How might this collapse of representational distance within the immediate perceptual field transform metaphoricity and referentiality (versus immanence and tactility)?

Does the categorized interface, like a GUI, work differently when it is perceived as a real worldly object, as opposed to a screen event at a distance? Further, when its annotations are labeling and dividing not commodity X and commodity Y, but rather the sacred and the profane, can the primate brain manage to keep open the critical space of metaphor? Does it want to? Are its capacities extended and augmented, or are they synthesized and amputated? What promising accidents are even contained in the later?

Interfaces at Hand: From Object to Sign to Object

With reference to our hands, those prehensile interfaces with which we embody cognition and manipulation, Michel Serres remarks that the hand is never done—unlike animals and their niche, the hand is "de-specialized," adapted not to a specific task like the crab's claw, but open to the limit of the world. The world is the place where hands are usable.[1] Evolutionary biologists may differ, but Serres point is that hands (which are not exclusively human) are—unlike, say, the fur that camouflages a cheetah only in the savannah niche—adaptable to any number of unforeseen environmental and technical challenges. As evolutionary adaptations, hands are general-purpose interfaces; they are machines we came to acquire that allow for the fabrication of all manner of subsequent machines (clothing, shelter, tools, weapons, etc.) which together allowed us accelerate evolutionary advantages by transforming our environment faster that it would be possible to evolve our bodies (capturing and wearing the fur of another animal is more expedient than learning to grow fur, for example).

I have a few photographs of the moment when my then infant son first became interested in a certain remote control that turned an overhead light and fan in our home office on and off. That night he spent at least an hour clicking them on and off in various combinations. He was lost in a new and fundamental discovery about his world: namely, that some things are not like other things, in that some things possess an inscrutable power to affect other things at a distance in predictable and repeatable patterns. He had discovered a basic principle of modern interfaciality, and this was very big news. Like many kids, he entered a phase of button-pushing mania, investigating which objects, surfaces, and icons possess this capacity, serving which effect. He may also have deduced that this interfaciality is not reducible to the physical qualities of any object. A plastic button, by itself, disconnected from any relay, has no interfacial power. Only when embedded in some system of input and output, usually involving waves or wires he soon learns, does the thing become interfacial. But of course his discovery is limited only to particular mechanical and computational interfaces with local, observable cybernetic cycles. We could say that any effective tool has some "interfacial" capacities in that transforms, encodes, or transmits some worldly dynamic in specific ways. Even a rock is an interface if you use it the right way. At the risk of being teleological, the mastery of a tool, which is a kind of embodied internalization of its effects, entails a specific intelligence regarding the mutual interfaciality of objects in the world. A first reflexive knowledge of effects and environments includes understanding the intrinsic and extrinsic interfacialities of available objects.

A "thing" is, at least in the German, a "gathering." Invoking this etymology, Bruno Latour extends Martin Heidegger's fourfoldedness of the thing into new domains. We could say, however, that the interfaciality of a thing inverts the gathering and its network of relations. According to the Latour-Heidegger story, drawn from Heidegger's 1950 essay "Das Ding" and Latour's recent essays on the "parliament of things," a thing is an assemblage or index of those actors and forces that gave rise to it, which are combined and folded within one another in marvelous ways to result in a given thing.[2] The "thing," however stable or temporary, gathers its particular forms and forces of earthly production into itself and presents them (each one of these—sun, water, metal, work—is still present in the thing) toward a new use or encounter. Conversely the interfaciality of a thing inverts the direction of that gathering. In connecting one thing to another by remote control, by action at a distance, the interfacial thing unfolds out toward the world of other things in looping cybernetic circuits of relay and interruption. It doesn't fold in, it explodes out. The unfolding, de-gathering interfaciality of the thing is equal and opposite to its infolding gathering as assemblage.

But what about GUIs? It is a well-understood principle of the language of new media that graphical users interfaces are cinematic in some essence. The Peircean range of the sign—icon, index, symbol, diagram—are all put to use to represent what interfaces do and the machines whose programs they present to us. Instead of manipulating objects as tools, we have learned to manipulate signs which have the technical effects of tools. In the modern history of the graphical user interface as a dominant genre of interfaciality per se, a fantastic conversion takes place in the sense that visual signs and images no longer simply represent other interfaces in the world but are instead tactile technologies which, when activated, cause a real event to occur correspondent with the semantic content of that sign/image. A picture of a bomb is a mere representation, a button with a picture of a bomb on it which causes remote explosions is a weaponized skeuomorphism. Not unlike my infant son, we are all probing our condition, trying to figure out the ultimate ethical and political (not to mention aesthetic) ramifications of a world full of images of things that do (or do not do) the things they visually signify. In the awkward, incomplete (and incompletable) semiotics of interface representability, where the full range of possible causes and effects is reduced to a bounded array of idiomatic and idiotic pictograms, culture becomes interfaces and vice versa. Even a maturing metaphysics of data visualization (serving the ubiquity of time-based diagrams of events and patterns and prototyping what future visual interfaces will look like) does not provide a way out, but it does raise the stakes.[3]

However, at the same time as physical objects are imbued with the intelligences of computational media (storage, calculation, and transmission) we also see a counter-conversion, a reversal even, of the shift from interfacial object to interfacial sign (and now back again). At MIT's Media Lab, Hiroshi Ishii's Tangible Media Group works on Tangible User Interfaces (TUIs) and a future of "radical atoms" based on microscopic computing machines dissolved so to speak into physical matter, while Neil Gershenfeld's Center for Bits and Atoms develops self-assembling microrobotics and a program of "conformal computing" in which artificial and natural information layers interoperate directly. Computation is cast as generic solvent within and between everyday things. In living rooms, Microsoft's Kinect gesture-based gaming interface dispenses with touch altogether and relies upon users natural perceptive and proprioceptive abilities to manipulate physical things and their digital shadows. The expansion of general interfaciality is profound. The GUI largely reduced the hand to a fingertip pointing and selecting among a bounded array of canned options, synthesizing the simulation of tactile craft into a sequence of discrete menu items each executing some sub-routine in the preferred order. But with gestural-tangible-haptic interfaces, we can imagine the possibility of a fully mature interface regime that dispenses almost altogether with the alphanumeric machine of the keyboard and the semiotic machine of the clickable icon. To provide interfacial mediation between mobile primates and environmentally embedded digital information, it would rely instead on the epiphlyogenetic wisdom of spatial-object navigation accumulated over millennia: waving, poking, dancing, stacking, peeling, throwing, and so on.

We might trace a vector from objects as primordial interfaces, shifting then to graphical signs as modern interfaces, then again back to objects, now imbued with the computational intelligence to interpret our gestures. In considering an emergent genre of interfaciality that blends natural and artificial information into composite manipulative substances and habitats, one question to raise, after Serres, is the following: What happens to the hand and its universal flexibility to manipulate the world? For the GUI the hand is trained to sift through menus, windows, and sliders, playing a software application like an musical instrument, but in doing so, its range of machinic expression is focused to the pushing and pulling of signs. But when objects or habitats are programmable to respond to a wide range of gestures and manipulations we imagine that they allow the hand a wider range of expression. There is a co-adaptation of the hand and the programmable object interface, of the grasp and the grasped. As the world meets it more than half-way, the uniqueness of the hand to exceed the accommodation of a niche is made that much less unique, as the niche is programmed to perform specific reactions to whatever the hand commands (or to resist that command and frustrate its intention). When the physical object is programmable in this way and responsive to gestures, or able to make such gestures on its own affecting other objects in its orbit, then the interfacial thing doesn't just un-fold, it aggressively unfurls in an tangle of affect and relay.

Notions on Apps in Worlds (Decks, Platforms, Stacks)

But then within the ecology of interfaces, what are apps? What specific role do they play? What do they want to become? Below are five observations on what apps are and what they do.

An app is tiny. The Google Earth iOS app puts a total geography into your pocket for 29.5 megabytes. It can do this because most of the significant information that the app displays is stored and calculated in the cloud. The app is a thin membrane on top of a vast machine, but one that nevertheless allows its user to pilot (and be piloted by) that machine with the slightest gesture. The app is the intersection point between two far more complex reservoirs of intelligence: the intentional user and the cloud infrastructure upon which the little app is perched. As that tiny membrane, it can synthesize and make useful vast continents of data and computational intelligence gathered for the instance of a single user interaction. As a single piece of code, its utility out-leverages its modest intrinsic complexity.

An app is a layer within a larger stack. Following on this, hardware and software stacks such as TCP/IP or OSI provide a modular architecture for the global Internet and allow innovations to be inserted into complex systems without disrupting embedded technologies. These two network stacks are comprised of sectional layers (seven layers for OSI, merged to four for TCP/IP) such that each layer performs specific, delimited tasks within a technical division of labor. In principle, each layer in turn sends information to and receives information from only the same layer, or the layer directly above or below it, or according to established protocols. An app is a kind of interface layer within a larger global computing stack, somewhere between a user and the networks that link the user to the cloud or to environmentally embedded software. Within the logic of platforms, an app transforms some capacity of the cloud and renders and frames it for the user as an at-hand service. In turn it draws the interactions of the user into a larger aggregation of data (location, path, preference, etc.), capitalizing on their qualities and feeding the updated information back to the user in a virtuous loop.

An app turns a habitat into cloud hardware. In this regard, whatever the app happens to be interfacing (geo-locative routing, portable banking services, stored files, news or music streams, games, etc.) is made available to the user through the app to the extent that it is provided as a cloud-based service. But given that the service is provided to a device user who is in motion, moving through the landscape and encountering different contexts on the go, the app platform provides a provisional link between a physical spatial context and the superimposed cloud service. There is a kind of programmatic blend-ing between the architectural or urban situation through which a user moves and the interactions he may be having with a specific app-mediated cloud platform. A mall becomes a game board. A sidewalk becomes a banking center. A restaurant becomes the scene of the crime in a crowd-sourced recommenda-tion engine. At any given moment, multiple users interacting with different apps in the same place may have enrolled their shared location into very dif-ferent cloud dramas and economies, making the solidarity of the crowd that much more fragmented and its swarming that much more mediated. With billions of users wielding mobile apps at a time, and to varying degrees navi-gating their domains accordingly, it is certain that physical habitats are, to a corresponding degree, recast (re-programmed) as part of a cloud platform. Instead of thinking of the app as a virtual projection onto the un-effected screen of a physical site, better to imagine a blended co-programming of space and software, habitat and habitus. The terrain, in time, comes to modulate itself to the dictates of the navigation tool, in this case the app, the thin, user-facing membrane of a larger cloud platform. The app is the aperture through which the cloud redraws the city.

The app turns the device into modulation of the hand. The platform structure of the app, device, and cloud locates globally effective computing directly in the hand of the ambulatory user. This, not laptops or desktops, is the first and still primary computing experience for most Earthlings. In this, the app-interface on the deck (what some still call a "phone") is an extension and a modulation of the hand. It is a tool for pointing, grabbing, selecting, drawing, mapping, pushing, and pulling. It may also extend the eye, the ear, the voice, and even the skin, but the combination of a generic mechanism (the device) that can modify its utility to suit a near infinite range of potential challenges (about a million apps have been approved for Apple's App Store) suggests a comparison with Serres' characterization of the hand as "never finished" because it is so adaptable to new technical uses instead of a fixed niche: the deck is generic technical anatomy, the app an endless array of techniques. The deck/app in hand extends the inscriptive-manipulative work of the hand to the drawing and coaxing of digital information into and out of the pathways of the world so designated by the universal palm, finger or fist.

The future of the app dissipates the hand. The platform logic of the app and the app market can be, and is, extended from the mobile deck into a wider range of devices, machines, and networks. Doctors prescribe healthcare apps in addition to medications as part of a therapeutic regime. The race to design low cost clinical tools (a "tricorder") redefines the administration of medical equipment according to the platform logic of the cloud-addressing app and the app market. Today, cars are already app platforms, but the real innovation in transportation-specific apps is still to come. Driverless cars will change what passengers are expected to do while moving through the city, and on what events they are expected to focus attention. Apps that connect cars to work or play, some using windows as screens will, for better or worse, further virtualize the experience of automotive drift. Some cars might be bound to Android or iOS, or new manufacturer specific operating systems might support neither or both. Even today cars contain multiple software and hardware systems, and by further extending these to control how cars navigate streets and how passengers interact with the world and one another, it's not difficult to see how a redefinition of the car into a high-velocity computing platform, enveloping the user inside, might initiate strange new genres of in-motion apps. In terms of the programmatic modulations described above, it clearly relocates the car, or swarm of cars, into another hardware extension of a wider cloud platform. As the single car becomes more like a hardware/software stack, so too do cars in general take their place as a component of larger computational network-mechanism. But here the anthropocentric bias of construing the user as human, extending his primate hand into the world, reaches an impasse. Cars with apps, medical devices with apps, etc.—these also project a future for certain kinds of modular bottom-up AI. Any machine (general or highly specific) could be imbued the narrowly focused intelligence of the app linked to a wider cloud, and for this it could download a particular sensing, sensory, storing, calculative or transmissive affordance. Each could do that without addressing humans or demanding our interference in the communication flow. The most important, viable, and effective apps and app market platforms may serve non-human users (if that is still the right term of identity) that interface between micro- or macro-devices (manufacturing, logistics, urban, agriculture, etc.) in ways that modularize, link or de-link the technical capacities of component machines working in concert, according to the generic platform logics of their open interoperability.[4] In this the universality of the hand dissolves into the horizon of open tactical computability informing the programmable component.

Political Theology and Weaponized Interfaces

This transference of the corporeal onto a landscape of software subroutines includes the brain, and its higher order modes of cognition and intelligence. But, that said, let's be clear that the imminence of full-fledged non-human apps does not prevent traditional human-centered apps from blossoming with the full spectrum of stupidity that our species is capable of awakening. Etymologies of "religion" describe a binding and a re-binding of a community of belief or of a bond between a believer and a covenant or commitment. The repetition of prayer, rote ritual, or weekly gathering are all testament to the procedural sacred. So are anamnesis and the investment and medial memorialization of deity into object. The Eucharist ritual involves the masses of the Mass into collective symbolic cannibalism, and the spectacle of human sacrifice (and resurrection) at the core of Christianity is repeated, over and again, weekly. Rebinding upon rebinding: there is the first memorialization of the body of Christ into bread and wine, and the second memorialization in the devout cycle of the eating and drinking every Sunday. In an essay titled "God in the age of digital replication," Boris Groys laments the eclipse of anamnesis (a variation perhaps on the death of affect) through software regimes perform memory and memorialization on behalf of the user.[5] We, the users of Google, need not exercise the faculty of memory in order to remember anything it seems, freeing up the mind to wander through a vast, flat present moment, an endless two-dimensional archive. As Groys tells it, now the devout need not consciously perform the work of memorialization, or even of really comprehend the work that is done for them, when it is sufficient to merely download a portfolio of important texts and carry them along on one's hard drive, for example. For Groys' wannabe Jihadi students, it's enough to have incendiary, uncompromising PDFs on their laptop computers in order for the act of identification to stick, or so they think. But without the actual, necessarily difficult investment of interpretation and an exacting self-transformation into the position of faith through the physical training of repetition and memorialization, however bizarre it may be, the re-binding is empty. It is a procedure of the self-dispossession of commitment through which the experience of faith, now without the opinion or interpretation, is outsourced to cognitive prostheses. Radical apps can have radical opinions for you. For Groys this subcontracting is not just an external memorialization of belief into digital artifacts, a sacralization of interfaces with theological distinction, it is rather religion evacuated of *religio*. It is *thanatos* as the relinquishment of the labor of memory in the present.[6] Even if so, it does not mean that such interfaces cannot motivate extraordinary acts of religious devotion and violence.

The mobilization of automated opinionlessness is perhaps most clearly illustrated by one sub-genre of apps that, as mentioned above, use the device's built-in machine vision hardware to superimpose interfacial content on top of the ambient world as perceived by the user: that diverse set of technologies called augmented reality. In projecting a layer of indexical and interfacial signs upon a given perceptual field of vision, AR transforms the resulting landscape into a designable instrumental frame by the use of various techniques: the subtitling of objects and events, the superimposition of navigation tools, the overlaying of iconic GUI menus upon real-world systems, the use of cinematic insertions and elisions, and other artificial visual or auditory feedbacks through which local signification and significance are programmed. The ultimate effect of that programming is to transform these semiotic technologies into a direct ideological, even theological, articulations of the inhabited landscape.

As of this writing, many such apps exist for "phones" and tablets, but we await the consumer launch of the first mass-market heads-up display for AR, Google Glass. Many of the most compelling AR visions are still constructed in AfterEffects and seen on YouTube. Whereas for tangible media and conformal computing interfaciality melts into tactile objects, for AR, interfaciality melts into the visual, perceptual surfaces of objects and environments. In extending the cinematic language of new media, AR is an aggressive subtitling of a phenomenal world now rendered as interactive narrative. It does this in ways that may be deeply contextual, or perhaps instead according to a strange juxtaposition of description with what it describes, like a film subtitle with only tangential relation to the screen image and event.[7] For the later, the sense of the user is thrown into apophenia, forced to not only interpret the correlation between the interface and the world but perhaps to invent one. In most cases, however, we assume that the opposite is true and that it is the absence of the work of interpretation, of reading even, that would characterize a successful AR user experience. The job of the software is the explication of what is seen and the automatic navigational sorting and valuation of how it should be encountered. AR draws lines and differentiates friend and foe. It automates even intentional belief, subcontracting the neo-cortex's manipulation of metaphor, offloading it to the algorithm strapped to your face.

As the interface layer within the larger software stack, AR performs the imagistic and linguistic mediation between users (one layer above) and the ubiquitous computational capacities of their habitats (one layer below). As a design space, it a platform for staging, animating, composing, and accounting for communication between users and their worlds, and unlike traditional mechanical or screen-based user interfaces, it performs this as ambient, artificially embodied perception. It is a physical cinema in which the space of fantasy, as for the traditional Metzian economy of psychoanalytic projection, is for better or worse, collapsed.[8] In augmented reality (as so for the interfacial image in general) this descriptive geography also becomes a medium for the recursive re-inscription of a politico-geographic diagram back upon the world through its direct instrumentalization as an interface.[9] That is, AR apps, in all their baroque banality, augment the world more than they augment vision. While I define the interface as any point of contact which governs the conditions of exchange between two complex systems, within augmented reality, the dominant mode of the interface, the GUI: the icon that when clicked initiates a predictable feedback loop—melts, so it seems, into reality itself—and is perceived as an actual property of surfaces, things, and events. That melting becomes the scope of design, the register of work, the touch-point of advertising, and even (perhaps especially) the domain of activist theology. Slavoj Žižek's inversion of real, as that which is defined by fantasy, is here given a literal, if dull, gloss.[10] How then can we locate AR among modern media and their psychological or psychoanalytic effects? We might say, in line with Friedrich Kittler's association of film with the imaginary, the typewriter with the symbolic and the gramophone with the real, that his Lacanian quasi-stack would be reworked in augmented reality such that the imaginary is so directly inscribed into the symbolic, as the content of the interface, that the real is also itself collapsed into the imaginary, making the reality of augmented reality perhaps irredeemably occult.

The most imminent integral accident of augmented reality is, I suppose, a deeply granular, pervasive advertising by which our embodied perceptions and gestures generate the monetizable exchange value of the network user profile. AR is where the microtargeting business models of cognitive capitalism melt into the choreography of the mobile user-subject. The work that the user-subject already does to perfect targeting algorithms for search engines can be scaled from finger points-and-clicks to the very musculature and dance of dwelling itself. However, as indicated, I fear that ultimately a less secular danger is latent in AR and that its most killer app is not marketing but fundamentalist religion and politics. AR promises the design of a explicitly differentiated sacrality whereby Schmittian political theological segmentation of the polis into friend and enemy becomes a direct, literal annotation of the lifeworld: the subtitling of clean and unclean, ours and theirs, sacred and profane, empire and rebel forces, ork and not-ork, red team and blue team. It is, then, not shocking that Google's inaugural alternate reality game (and we presume when Google Glass launches, augmented reality as well) is based on a sci-fi alien religious warfare story embedded into the lived urban fabric. Developed as part of an internal effort called Niantic Labs, Ingress divides users into two opposing camps: "Enlightened" (green) and "Resistance" (blue). Players "enclose regions of territory on the surface of the earth with virtual links between virtual portals, which are visible in the game software. The top-level goal of the game is for one's faction to control large numbers of Mind Units, the estimated number of humans within the regions of territory controlled by the faction."[11] It should be a surprise only to someone who has yet to realize that *Star Wars* is an Al-Qaeda-esque parable (rural religious cult flies into the architectural core of the empire and blows it up) that the Manichean ludic demands of Ingress are to send people out into their cities training them to see, attack, and defend against the territorial incursions of numinous enemies only perceivable through special software enabled goggles. Will mature augmented reality initiate a wave of bizarre new sects, cults, and activist versions of fundamentalist monotheisms for which the metaphorical nuance of holy books is collapsed by the direct imprint of virtual words onto real things? There are indications to this effect. We can see that with the use of Google Earth, Google Maps, stolen SIM cards, and other advanced but off-the-shelf spatial command and communication technologies by Laskhar e-Taiba during their attack on Mumbai in 2008 as a prototype of the kinds of weaponized augmented reality we should fear.[12] It is a more violent and extreme variation on creationist video games for the home schooling economy, or the Christianist AR overlay of the Grand Canyon in Arizona that explains how the canyon proves creationism and disproves evolution for those willing to look through the lens and see what it sees. Apps that provide moral frame—Qibla direction or which allow users to scan barcodes to determine if food is kosher or halal, or vegan, free-range, or GMO free, or if your new colleague is a "suppressive person," or even perhaps they are a Cylon (or if happen to be are a Cylon, if someone shares your monotheism)—all seem like benign and obvious innovations. But one hopes that the poetry of the monotheistic cognitive cultures they reference can withstand the unambiguous cybernetic literalism that augmented reality might afford them, and the violence that absolute explication demands.

Conclusion

A group of my undergraduate students are developing Siri-like voice assistant apps based on alternative, fractured personalities. Instead of the supposedly neutral Siri (very specifically female, omniscient, and subordinate), these artificial borderline personalities will engage in less obvious sorts of user-device relationships, not all of them healthy or recognizable. They may be moody or unreliable. They may give answers based on their jealous analysis of your recent wall posts and try to trick you into paranoid suspicion about your friends. In time, similar alternative personality assistant apps may demand absolute fidelity and suffer virtual death when it is revoked, like a passive aggressive, monogamous Tomagotchi, or may merge with other apps to perform spontaneous amazing feats on your behalf. To me the research is more than "persuasive technology" gone sideways (nor just a tweak of its dumb behavioralist microeconomics wrapped in the shiny gloss of "gamification") but an inquiry into what kinds of complex cognition and interaction are sanitized out of any successful app user experience, and how the gardening of those wooly leftovers can draw a more complex path for interface design beyond utilitarian adaptation. Further, if apps are just the tip of a planetary computing platform iceberg, then to presume that the autonomous agent app like Siri should be so defined by the rhetoric of C-suite master-slave dynamics is to assume too much. What a sad first step toward at-hand AI! In reality, the full band of weirdness with which objects, subjects, and actors pass information into and out of one another is a richly reticulated space that makes simple hierarchies moot. We need to ensure that apps evolve beyond the current status of sycophantic insects, because seeing and handling the world through that menial lens makes us even more senseless.

The design brief for an emergent, larval political horizon of an apps-based cloud and a cloud-based built environment should focus on that point of tension between the universality-particularity of the hand and its revision (and even dissolution) into programmable techniques, and the literal explication of the symbolic divisions and subdivisions projected onto the lived world: the open programmable horizon of the deck versus the cognitive closure of AR's semiotic superimposition. Perhaps AR's explicit stupefaction of the human user may provide some necessary leverage away from the vestigial, embarrassing anthropocentrism that brings the false flattery of passive (or passive-aggressive) assistant apps. The rhetorical prioritization of the human user as somehow piloting the work of the app is, we may deduce, really an alibi protecting essential opposite effect, namely that the mammal user is only a provisionally necessary mechanism for dragging Gigaflop tracking devices through the avenues of cities, and for re-monetizing (re-binding) these routes as the spatial career of algorithmic capital (and its successors).

Notes

1. Michel Serres and Peter Hallward, "The science of relations: An interview," *Angelaki* 8 (2003), no. 2: 227–238.

2. Martin Heidegger, "The thing," in *The Question Concerning Technology and Other Essays* (Harper Torchbooks, 1982 [1950]); Bruno Latour, "A cautious Prometheus? A few steps toward a philosophy of design (with special attention to Peter Sloterdijk)," keynote lecture, Networks of Design conference, Cornwall, 2008.

3. Lev Manovich, "Cultural Software," http://manovich.net/DOCS/Manoich .Cultural_Software.2011.pdf; Bruno Latour, Pablo Jensen, Tommaso Venturini, Sébastien Grauwin, and Dominique Boull, "The whole is always smaller than its parts: A digital test of Gabriel Tarde's monads," *British Journal of Sociology* 63 (2012), no. 4: 591–615.

4. One version of this platform of and for non-human users of apps and app markets is partially articulated as the Industrial Internet. See http:// radar.oreilly.com/2013/01/defining-the-industrial-internet.html.

5. Boris Groys, "Religion in the age of digital reproduction," *e-flux journal* 4 (2010) (http://worker01.e-flux.com/pdf/article_49.pdf).

6. On the prospect of anamnesis and a Tangible User Interface, God knows what Groys might make of conformal computing objects imbued deliberately and ritualistically with indisputable sacrality.

7. For example, René Viénet, *Can Dialectics Break Bricks?* (http://en.wikipedia .org/wiki/Can_Dialectics_Break_Bricks%3F), though it is Atom Egoyan and Ian Balfour who have provided, in *Subtitles: Or the Foreignness of Film* (MIT Press, 2004), the most applicable analysis of the subtitle and the production and mitigation of the experience of a "foreign" image.

8. Christian Metz, *The Imaginary Signifier, Psychoanalysis and the Cinema* (Indiana University Press, 1986 [reprint]).

9. This is the basis for seeing the diagrammatics of Information Visualization operating as a utopian-projective discourse for the image-interface yet

to come, as the deepest worldly recombinancy shifts from the linear temporal unfolding of meta-history to the non-linear spatial unfolding of meta-interfaciality.

10. It's impossible then to avoid the comparison with Žižek's well-worn reading of John Carpenter's 1988 sci-fi film *They Live*, in which certain characters can, by wearing special ideology-filtering Ray-Bans, perceive that Earth (or Los Angeles at least) is controlled by skinless reptile aliens, and that humans live in a state of somnambulant delirium. See, for one example, http://inthesetimes.com/article/3976/through_the_glasses_darkly/. Regarding AR, then, the wearing of glasses instead of allowing us to wake from "false consciousness" instead allows the user to choose which subscription hallucination they prefer. After Žižek, we might say "Yes, AR looks as if people are strapping ideological reductions onto their face, but don't be fooled, . . . they really are."

11. http://en.wikipedia.org/wiki/Ingress_(game).

12. See my essay "On geoscapes & Google caliphate: Except #Mumbai," *Theory, Culture and Society* 26 (2009), no. 7–8: 329–342.

2

Controlled Consumption Culture:
When Digital Culture Becomes Software Business

Søren Bro Pold and Christian Ulrik Andersen

We live in the era of cultural computing. New IT gadgets—including not only game consoles and e-readers, but also tablets and smartphones—are sold as platforms for cultural content. The market leader is Apple, whose iOS platforms (iPod, iPhone, and iPad) have developed gradually from MP3 players into personal, intimate mobile platforms for various kinds of cultural media (including e-books, radio, television, movies, and games) and for various software apps including and integrating Web 2.0 social software (among them Facebook and Twitter). All iOS platforms have integrated online shops, owned and operated by Apple (iTunes, App Store, iBooks, Game Center), and even though the iOS platforms are currently extremely successful as media players, e-book readers, software platforms and game consoles, there are other smartphones, tablets, e-book readers and game consoles with similar business models (for example, Google Android devices with Google Play, Microsoft Xbox consoles with Xbox Live, Apple TV, or Google TV).

Even though arguments for the importance of cultural computing, interface culture and software culture are not new,[1] cultural content—music, games, social and cultural software—are now the very backbone of this new range of IT platforms, which have entered center stage in our leisure life since the launch of the first iPhone in 2007. Six years earlier, in 2001, Lev Manovich made it a central point in his book *The Language of New Media* that in the information society both "work" and "leisure" activities used the tools, interfaces, and metaphors of the graphical user interface.[2] However, today we have two competing types of interfaces, and whereas the GUI originated in the work sphere, with its focus on function, usability, and efficiency, the new app interface clearly has its roots in (digital) culture with an aesthetic interface, inspired by games, software culture and cultural interfaces in general.[3] Therefore, it is time to start discussing how the app interface is potentially changing digital culture.

In order to start this discussion, we will first look at how the app store is an opportunity for some kinds of software art while a business model of "controlled consumption" is also developed, designed to handle and make profit from a very specific model of culture, before moving on to discuss the associated opportunities and challenges. Finally, we will discuss which artistic strategies this model of "controlled consumption" allows for. While the app-based interface is clearly developed to support an effective and lucrative distribution and business model for digital cultural content, the paradox is that it does so by restraining other aspects of critical software culture. In this way, the app interface is both good and bad news for an innovative digital culture, and it offers a platform to explore, utilize, and in some cases criticize (although this often leads to exclusion from the platform).

The Stuff of Digital Culture

In his essay "The Stuff of Culture," Felix Stalder distinguishes between two different approaches to culture: the *object-oriented* and the *exchange-oriented*. One is concerned with objects, goods, or works that have an author or a brand and are seen as stable, also when put in different relations and contexts: "The content of a book does not change when re-shelving it."[4] The other sees culture as a process made up of collective collaboration, sharing and a constant creative process. In this latter approach, the meaning of a book read in new contexts is constantly renegotiated.

Stalder's terms echo earlier attempts in aesthetic theory to discuss open works and to launch a post-structuralist concept of *text* in opposition to the more self-contained concept of *works* from new criticism and structuralism.[5] Stalder also rightly points out that this dichotomy is more an analytical dichotomy than a real one, and that in reality it is never a case of either-or. However, with the digitization of culture there is a tendency for this dichotomy to become sharper and implemented more strictly through software and legal structures, which is of course of concern for cultural studies. There has been much focus on how digitization furthers sharing and exchanging, as we have seen in file sharing and in peer-to-peer networks, where digitized cultural content such as music, texts, and movies are easily shared. Exchange-oriented network cultures have developed around remixing, collaborative authoring and production, but since aspects of this exchange culture are seen as piracy and as a threat by some content producers in the traditional culture industry, counter-strategies are being implemented through legislation and software. Hence, as described by Lawrence Lessig, a lot of the gray zones in which different cultural practices can exist are being closed down, which might ultimately be a problem even for business. Lessig argues that many of today's culture industrial giants that are fiercely protecting and extending their copyright (Disney among them) started by copying and remixing existing culture (e.g., European folk tales). Therefore, Lessig claims, current copyright legislation and policies are in fact an obstacle to cultural innovation and free culture, and he argues instead for alternative and more flexible copyright schemes.[6]

Consequently, digital culture has been a primary scene of the battle between object-oriented and exchange-oriented understandings of culture—between anti-pirates and pirates, between established rights holders and new emerging media artists, or between the old content industries like the movie and music industry and new disruptive business initiatives like Napster or even new media industries like Google that generate tools for sharing. For a long time, it looked like the cultures of sharing and exchanging were winning the battle over a paralyzed content industry, but currently companies with their roots in new media such as Apple, Microsoft, Amazon, and Google are developing new business models and software infrastructures in order to offer a model for cultural computing that handles the inherent dichotomies of culture outlined above. One emerging and apparently extremely successful business and infrastructure model is the app interface. As will be discussed below, this model can be seen as both an opportunity for and a challenge to digital culture.

Digital Culture at the App Store

Whereas older models with physical distribution (for instance, CDs or DVDs) had high distribution costs and consequently could only handle a limited number of titles, the models of controlled consumption with integrated app stores make it potentially easier for artists and cultural producers to make their content available for sale. For example, independent game developers like the Danish Playdead have used Microsoft's Xbox Live successfully as an outlet for their noir expressionist *Limbo* game (now also available in other similar outlets, including the PlayStation Network and the PC-based platform Steam). Earlier it was almost impossible to release an "indie game" through commercial distribution; as a consequence, genre innovation beyond the mainstream was difficult. The new distribution model has made it possible for Playdead to make a profit and to sustain its business and the development of its next game. Also, the iOS App Store is used as an important distribution platform for games and artistic apps, including software art, sound art, visual poetry, and locative media.[7]

One interesting example is digital media artist Jörg Piringer, who has brought his work in electronic music, literature, and visual poetry onto mobile iOS devices with visual poetry apps and software art.[8] Piringer's apps

Figure 2.1
Reproduced with kind permission
from the artist, Jörg Piringer.

are playful and poetic explorations of the potential of the touch interface for
interactive sound poetry, drawing on musique concrète and concrete poetry
as well as on contemporary digital software culture. *Gravity clock* (figure 2.1)
is a beautiful and poetic clock with numbers falling off the dial because of
gravity, while *abcdefgh* . . . (figure 2.2) and the ZKM AppArt prize-winner *konsonant* (figure 2.3) are explorations of the visual, physical, and auditory materiality of alphabetic letters. *Abcdefgh* . . . lets the user play with gravity and
the visual and auditory dimensions of individual letters in an entertaining
and imaginative interface, and *konsonant* lets the user build and configure

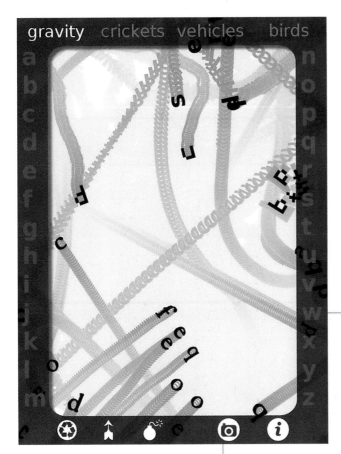

Figure 2.2
Reproduced with kind permission
from the artist, Jörg Piringer.

alphabetic machines that produce sound and movement in complex interaction somewhere in between concrete poetry and musical instruments. The artistic sound sampler and sequencer software *RealBeat* (figure 2.4) lets the user record and transform everyday sounds into musical compositions in an ingenious interface for the iPhone. All of the apps are sold for a few euros, which according to Jörg Piringer generates a considerable monthly sum even though Apple takes its 30 percent share. Also other artists produce works for the iOS interface; in particular, there is a substantial number of works within sound art and literature, and we also see locative works such as *Serendipitor*

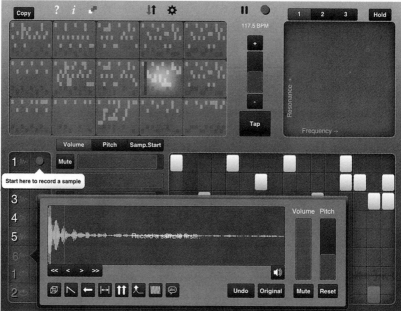

Figures 2.3 and 2.4

Reproduced with kind permission from the artist, Jörg Piringer.

(Mark Shepard), Net/browser art such as *FMS/ Fragmental Storm* (exonemo), and glitch works such as *Satromizer* (Jon Satrom).

Consequently, the app store business model does have some advantages since it allows for easy distribution of a "long tail" of cultural content and thus widens the market to more than the mainstream.[9] It allows individual users to purchase digital artworks and software for small sums to experience, play with, and show to their friends on their intimate smartphone interfaces. It is relatively easy for independent producers to use, and thus it is an interesting distribution model for digital culture. Especially when compared to the earlier Net art and software art of the 1990s and the 2000s, which was difficult to sell both on the Internet and to galleries and collectors, it can seem an almost ideal new market platform within the medium of smartphones and tablets without the need for compromising with the established art market in order to make a living.[10] In this way it continues some of the aims of software art of creating and furthering software as a cultural expression, but within certain limitations that challenge a free, open, critical digital culture. Furthermore, it can be seen as a supplement—if not a successor—to the old cultural industries.

The Controlled Consumption of the App Store

Where old cultural industries are in crisis, new ones take over. The music industry failed to a large extent to develop business models that both build on the Internet and are not undermined by its file sharing, but software companies that have taken their models from software production seem to operate successfully by implementing new business models based on licensing schemes. It might seem paradoxical, but perhaps not surprising, that strategies that limit the exchange and sharing potential of the networked computer currently come from software companies. The dominant business model can be characterized by the term "controlled consumption" developed by the French sociologist Henri Lefebvre in 1967 and applied to contemporary publishing and the book trade by the American cultural theorist Ted Striphas. Even though Striphas uses the concept to characterize the wider field of the Anglo-American book trade, it is incredibly precise in its description of what happens in and around the app interface. Striphas summarizes controlled consumption in four principles:

(1) A cybernetic industrial infrastructure integrating and handling production, distribution, exchange, and consumption is developed around the product.

(2) The consumption is controlled through programming that closely monitors consumer behavior and the effects of marketing through tracking and surveillance.

(3) Controlled obsolescence is programmed into the product, limiting its functionality and its durability.

(4) The overall effect of controlled consumption is a significant reorganizing and troubling of specific practices of everyday life.[11]

Apple and Amazon currently carry out the tightest implementation of this scheme with their almost complete control over the integration of hardware, software, and distribution. For example, with an iOS device there is no other way to download software or media files than through Apple's stores (unless the device is jailbroken). Furthermore, Apple, Amazon, and Google closely monitor and track consumer behavior as the second principle above describes. Both the Electronic Frontier Foundation and the Free Software Foundation have critically focused on the closed nature of these platforms and on the surveillance and tracking of their users.[12] Furthermore, users will have to endure how constant software and hardware updates control the functionality and ultimately the durability of the iOS devices, as is the case when new updates outdate an older iPhone, if a broken screen or irreplaceable battery has not already rendered it useless.[13] Finally, this significantly influences cultural practices. For example, it prohibits most of the sharing and lending of cultural content such as books, music, software, and games, which has always been an important part of culture and the basis of libraries and other important cultural institutions.

Consequently, controlled consumption precisely characterizes the business strategies of cultural software industries and the way new digital cultural formats are handled. Apple's iOS iTunes and App Store, Microsoft's Xbox Live, Sony's Playstation Network (PSN), and Amazon's Kindle are all prime examples of controlled consumption strategies that work along the four principles, though there are significant differences in how tightly the control is exercised. Google Play is Google's somewhat less tightly controlled though still heavily monitored equivalent app store for the Google Android devices, which functions along the same lines but in the more open Android software environment. Furthermore, game-distribution platforms and multi-player environments (such as Valve Corporation's Steam), multi-player games (such as *World of Warcraft*), and even Web 2.0 platforms (such as Facebook) can be said to work on the principles of controlled consumption, with their closed, proprietary networks, their monitoring of users, and their limits on users' rights.

Phone Story

These platform-related structures affect how software can be designed and configured in order to be distributed through monopolies such as Apple's App Store. There are numerous stories about software that has been delayed or even totally rejected by Apple's gate-keeping—for example, because it under-cuts or offers alternatives to the business model or is deemed controversial.[14] Apple has extremely vague guidelines that—besides bans on hate speech, objectionable material, pornography, and gambling—include statements like the following one, which seems to be an appeal for self-censorship: "We will reject Apps for any content or behavior that we believe is over the line. What line, you ask? Well, as a Supreme Court Justice once said, 'I'll know it when I see it.' And we think that you will also know it when you cross it."[15] Obviously, if you are a software developer trying to make a living, you do not want to cross the unclear guidelines of Apple's gate-keeping, but will prob-ably restrain yourself from entering controversial territory, even though this territory is essential for art and culture. Furthermore, the guidelines clearly state that Apple does not see software apps as a medium of expression worthy of the freedoms we take for granted in other areas of culture: "We view Apps different than books or songs, which we do not curate. If you want to criticize a religion, write a book. If you want to describe sex, write a book or a song, or create a medical app."[16] As it might be clear by now, Apple's curatorial control is not only technical but also relates to the content, and this censorship is important since Apple controls the only distribution platform for the devices. Furthermore, there are many stories where apps are banned for unclear rea-sons—or perhaps for other reasons than the real ones.

The example of the critical game producer Molleindustria's *Phone Story* illustrates this.[17] It is a game made for Android and iPhones that "attempts to provoke a critical reflection on its own technological platform," and it does so by letting the user play small episodes that demonstrate the exploitative min-ing of coltan in Congo (figure 2.5), the suicidal conditions of the sweatshop workers in China (figure 2.6), the constant desire for new products (figure 2.7), and the ways that the big brands design obsolescence into their products (figure 2.8). The information on the game's website elaborates this with links to further information. However, the game was only allowed in App Store for a few hours, and only 901 users managed to buy it before Apple decided to withdraw it. Apple thereby prohibited iPhone users from obtaining the game without jailbreaking their iPhones, and this of course severely limited Molleindustria's revenue, which they had promised to give away to charity. The game is still available for Android, but even though Apple has given a lim-ited reason for the ban, it is difficult not to see this as censorship of content.

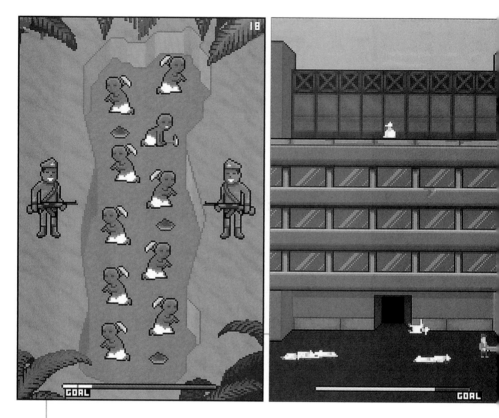

Figures 2.5–2.8
Reproduced with kind permission from Paolo Pedercini, Molleindustria.

This encourages critical reflection on the media platform and the companies behind it. In this way, this example demonstrates how critical interaction and play are limited and suppressed by the platforms of controlled consumption.

Consequently, the model of controlled consumption opens up for a very particular business model for cultural software. It works well for some uses but also standardizes software culture to a specific model that, despite being based on the Net and taking advantage of social media, is heavily constrained toward the object-oriented cultural model in the sense that consumers are forced to adapt to a specific and rather passive model of consumption framed by the licenses and the technology. In this way, it also entails a specific model of culture, which excludes potential new developments of a culture of exchange including sharing and copying. Furthermore, it is a ready-made business

model for artists. Although this can be seen as an advantage, it also limits the possibility for artists to engage in developing alternative ways to engage with their audience—for example, in critical activist ways. Besides surveying the users in numerous ways that jeopardize individual privacy, the model limits the cultural freedom to develop potential alternative and new uses through hacks, remixes, and modifications. As several theoreticians have argued, developments in digital culture often happen through modifications and hacks in a participatory, "writerly" digital culture.[18] This is indeed the case for the Net art and software culture that developed the format of software art ten years before the iPhone through festivals such as Read_me and Transmediale.[19]

Finally, the model seems to foster vast monopolies, which makes it difficult to construct alternatives and consequently creates the risk of stifling innovation. In comparison with traditional personal computers, Apple iOS devices and game consoles generally restrict access to the computer—by restricting access to the file system, the operating system and hardware, and by controlling the ways to distribute software to the devices—making these systems more closed than even ordinary proprietary systems, such as Microsoft Windows and MacOS. In this way they can be seen as a sort of advanced media player, lacking the essential universality and open dynamics of the general-purpose computer. These restrictions close down the system in ways that Cory Doctorow has characterized as a "war on general-purpose computing." As he argues, the battle surrounding copyright is extended into creating locked-down platforms or "IT appliances," which can only run authorized programs in protected sandbox environments, hiding essential parts of the functionality for the user, which he sees as a big problem for privacy and transparency.[20] As a consequence of this locking down of the computer, software culture becomes limited in its potential for developing innovative ways of using and understanding the computer and ultimately developing new forms of software.

Ultimately, Apple and other companies censor both content and technology. If you do not adhere to Apple's guidelines and business model, you are thrown out of the App Store and are thus denied access to an important platform for distributing cultural software. This, of course, affects not only artistic practices but also all kinds of software, including software that circumvents Apple's business models, breaks Apple's policies on content, or circumvents the lockdown of the platform. Even apps that offer insight into the way the user is monitored by other apps are excluded (as seems to be the case with the Clueful app, which at the time of writing is available only from a website).[21] New reports of this censorship appear monthly—for example, the story of the banned Drones+ app, which playfully tracks and displays military drone attacks as push notifications and displays them on a map, but which Apple has turned down three times for unclear reasons.[22]

Everyday Life Inside the Controlled Consumption Platform

It is obviously difficult to draw conclusions about the effects of controlled consumption on software culture app platforms apart from the specific examples, though someone who is old enough to have witnessed the outbreaks of critical Net art and software art cannot help but miss more critical media art. There is a certain sanitized feeling to the App Store despite the examples mentioned here. Luckily the Web is still open, and here one can find projects such as Johannes P. Osterhoff's *iPhone live*, where Osterhoff documents his

Figure 2.9
Reproduced with kind permission
from the artist, Johannes P. Osterhoff.

everyday iPhone life by uploading a screen dump to the Web every time he
presses the home button.[23] The project documents his daily life in the form
of screen dumps showing text messages, phone calls, photos, music, social
networking, visited websites, location maps, and app use (figure 2.9). In this
way it shows the mundane life of an iPhone user. Looking through the project,
one realizes how much these screens reveal of his personal life, even private
and intimate details. It demonstrates how smartphones are intimate interfaces woven closely into all aspects of daily life. In this way smartphones are
also significantly reorganizing specific practices of everyday life, as pointed
out in the fourth principle of controlled consumption (above).

The extent to which we are profiled by these interfaces became obvious
to one of the authors of this article (Søren), who by chance discovered an
email from himself displayed on the project website. He had been in contact
with Johannes P. Osterhoff for other reasons without realizing that the same
Johannes was in fact also the artist behind this project. However, discovering
this, the author decided to explore this strange hall of mirrors. He posted his
discovery on Facebook and Twitter, only to see it re-appear on the project

Figure 2.10
Reproduced with kind
permission from
the artist, Johannes P.
Osterhoff.

website, since Osterhoff automatically tracks mentions of the project on
Twitter and afterwards found it on Facebook as well (figure 10). This over-
whelming (to this author at least) *mise en abyme* moment demonstrates how
we become connected by intimate tracking technologies that tighten open
networks into closed traps.

Following this, it is obvious to turn to jailbreaking as the final exit. Jailbreaking consists of freeing an iOS device from Apple-imposed limitations.
As George Hotz, the first to jailbreak the iPhone in 2007 at the age of 17, said
about his jailbreak of the Sony PlayStation 3 console, when he was sued by
Sony: "I think this case is about a lot more than what I did, and me. It's about

whether you really own that device that you purchased."[24] The discussion that follows is ultimately about whether we can decide to install, run, and modify software on our controlled consumption devices, and it is about whether we own the data the devices produce, or at least get access to see this data and how it controls us. Currently, the answers to these questions are mainly negative.

As much as the app interfaces present great new possibilities for cultural producers that suddenly have this distribution platform and this intimate interface at their disposal, the way the app interfaces control consumption leads to new traps and lock-downs for a critical and innovative digital culture and, furthermore, it leads to severe monitoring of the users and consumers. In the coming years we will see how this balance of power, located in the platform and mediated by its interface, develops. We will see whether users will continue to comply and whether the platforms will continue to extend their uses, range and control or will somehow get stuck in their own technical bureaucracies. Furthermore, we will see whether critical digital culture will find ways to exist on the platform or will manage to subvert it somehow and produce alternatives.

At this stage, it seems fair to conclude that we have seen the emergence of a new important cultural software interface that is already revolutionizing cultural production, distribution, and consumption. In the interests of an open, innovative culture, it seems about time to call for a critical cultural political discussion of the app interface, which includes the future conditions for cultural institutions, freedom of expression, privacy, and the right to read.[25] The new cultural interface risks, at worst, to turn cultural software into the perfect consumer object and use it as bait for increasing control and surveillance while limiting the innovation and freedom of expression of digital art. However, the app interface also points to the new centrality of software culture in IT, and it presents an alternative business model to the conservatism of the old cultural industries.

Notes

1. See, for example, Steven Johnson, *Interface Culture: How New Technology Transforms the Way We Create and Communicate* (HarperEdge, 1997); Alan Kay and Adele Goldberg. "Personal dynamic media," in *The New Media Reader*, ed. Noah Wardrip-Fruin and Nick Montfort (MIT Press, 2003 (1977)); Matthew Fuller, *Behind the Blip: Essays on the Culture of Software* (Autonomedia, 2003).

2. Lev Manovich, *The Language of New Media* (MIT Press, 2001), 65 ff.

3. Christian Ulrik Andersen and Søren Pold, *Interface Criticism: Aesthetics Beyond Buttons* (Aarhus University Press, 2011).

4. Felix Stalder, *Open Cultures and the Nature of Networks* (Revolver, 2005), 12.

5. Roland Barthes, "From work to text," in *The Rustle of Language* (University of California Press, 1989).

6. Lawrence Lessig, *Free Culture: How Big Media Uses Technology and the Law to Lock Down Culture and Control Creativity* (Penguin, 2004).

7. In fact, there is evidence that iOS is currently the "most popular gaming platform of all time." Chris Foresman, "Data suggests iOS may be the most popular gaming platform of all time," *Arstechnica*, August 8, 2012, http://arstechnica.com.

8. http://apps.piringer.net.

9. Chris Anderson, "The long tail," *Wired* 12 (2004), no. 10 (http://www.wired.com).

10. Some Net and software artists made it a point to investigate the difficult or impossible market conditions both online and in galleries for Net art and software art (e.g., Christophe Bruno's *Google AdWords Happening*, available at http://www.iterature.com/adwords/). Lately some artists, among them Christophe Bruno, Alexei Shulgin, Eva and Franco Mattes, and Ubermorgen.com, have partly aimed for galleries and collectors to make a living from their art, but often this also turns the art away from Net art aesthetics and more toward objects that can be exhibited and sold to collectors.

11. Ted Striphas, *The Late Age of Print: Everyday Book Culture from Consumerism to Control* (Columbia University Press, 2011), 180–182.

12. See Ed Bayley, An E-Book Buyer's Guide to Privacy (2009) (https://www.eff.org); David Kravets, "Apple v. EFF: The iPhone jailbreaking showdown," *Wired*, 2009 (http://www.wired.com); Corynne McSherry and Cindy Cohn, Digital Books and Your Rights: A Checklist for Readers, 2010 (https://www.eff.org); Defective By Design.org, 2006– (http://www.defectivebydesign.org).

13. Especially in connection with the iOS 5 update, the Internet was full of stories about users complaining about accidental loss of data and how their old iPhones became slow. With the Amazon Kindle, there have been stories about how Amazon has removed some e-books (among them George Orwell's *Nineteen Eighty-Four*) from individual users' Kindles. Ted Striphas, "The abuses of literacy: Amazon Kindle and the right to read," *Communication and Critical/Cultural Studies* 7 (2010), no. 3: 297–317.

14. See Terrence O'Brien, "9 banned apps you'll never see on the iPhone," *Switched*, November 6, 2009 (http://www.switched.com).

15. Cited from Leander Kahney, Here's the Full Text of Apple's New App Store Guidelines, 2010 (http://www.cultofmac.com).

16. Ibid.

17. http://phonestory.org.

18. See Sarah Coleman and Nick Dyer-Witheford, "Playing on the digital commons: Collectivities, capital and contestation in videogame culture," *Media, Culture & Society* 29 (2007), no. 6: 934–953; Lessig, *Free Culture*; Christian Ulrik Andersen, "Writerly gaming: Political gaming," in *Interface Criticism*.

19. See Olga Goriunova and Alexei Shulgin, *Read_Me Software Art & Cultures* (Digital Aesthetics Research Centre, Aarhus, 2004); Matthew Fuller, *Behind the Blip*; Matthew Fuller, ed., *Software Studies: A Lexicon* (MIT Press. 2008).

20. Cory Doctorow, Lockdown—The Coming War on General-Purpose Computing, 2012 (http://boingboing.net).

21. http://www.cluefulapp.com.

22. Christina Bonnington and Spencer Ackerman, "Apple rejects app that tracks U.S. drone strikes," *Wired*, August 2012 (http://www.wired.com).

23. The irony is that he had to jailbreak his iPhone in order to install the software that made the project possible. As he writes on his website: "Each time its home button is pressed an iPhone automatically takes a screenshot of the current app to display a zooming effect. For this performance, I installed two shell scripts on my jailbroken iPhone: The first one duplicates each screenshot so that the files cannot be overwritten the next time the app is minimized. The second one uploads these screens automatically to this site and publishes them. These scripts are executed regularly in the background by means of launch demons." (http://iphone-live.net)

24. Alessandro Ludovico, "Jailbreaking, the art of occupying Apple devices," *Neural*, no. 42 (2012): 14–15.

25. Striphas, "The abuses of literacy."

3
The Philosophical Carpentry of the App: Criticism and Practice

Patricia Ticineto Clough

In the introduction to his book *Alien Phenomenology*, Ian Bogost suggests that philosophers ought not just *write* philosophy, at least not without practicing, doing, or making. He urges engagement in "carpentry": "constructing artifacts that do philosophy."[1] Bogost adds to Graham Harman's take on "the carpentry of things" "the carpentry of hands-on craftsmanship, " further proposing that "carpentry entails making things that explain how things make their world."[2] Bogost's examples, his own software productions for what he envisions as "platform studies," suggest a link between object-oriented ontology and digital or informational technologies and the crisis of form in the presentation of content that online communication is evoking. While not all the philosophers who now are engaged with object-oriented ontology necessarily would link their work to technology and its instigation of a crisis of form, I find it helpful to pursue this link for a discussion of the app.

Not only does an object-oriented ontology and the debates that it has elicited enable us to ask: is the app an object or a relation? In an effort to answer this question, we can approach what seems to be a pressing concern in critical discussions of digital technology. With the proliferation of software like the app, the concern is that the digitalized media environment will become one of "black boxes," where black boxes can include "the computer, the protocol interface, data objects and code libraries," as Alexander Galloway has noted.[3] For Jonathan Zittrain, among others, this means that the market in computers is moving from product to service, since the app, in his view, may well put an end to general-purpose computers.[4] While the app surely raises questions about the relationship of production, consumption, and the governance of the market, I want to approach these questions by first taking up the app in terms of blackboxing. I want to consider how the app might be either object or relation and in this sense redefine what a black box can do and what can be done with it. In what follows I will take up blackboxing in relationship to the commodity and then review the proposals of an object-oriented ontology to suggest that blackboxing might better be treated as a prompt to critical experimentation rather than a draw to a critical pursuing of foreclosed knowledge. Or, as Bogost might suggest, a critical take on the app may require some philosophical carpentry.

Blackboxing, the Commodification of Process

In his treatment of the black box, Galloway offers a historical vignette that tells how the black box comes into techno-scientific discourse after World War II, when the opening of a found black metal box belonging to the Germans triggered an auto-destruct mechanism and set off an explosion.[5] Since this meant that there no longer would be a way to figure out how a black box worked by opening it, it was to be left closed and studied only through observation of its surface, its inputs, and its outputs. While blackboxing not only informed developments in behaviorism, game theory, operations research, and cybernetics, it also stirred a criticism meant to re-apply methods suggested by Marx, by Freud, and by some other nineteenth-century and early-twentieth-century thinkers. Post-World War II cultural critics long practiced a hermeneutic method of going beneath the surface or the mystical shell to the hidden (ir)rational core, that is, to the unconscious depth of the human subject on one hand and on the other to the labor power productive of the value of the commodified object (including, Galloway reminds us, sign, spectacle, and all other cultural phenomena as commodities).

Arguing that blackboxing has become ubiquitous along with a changed mode of production, transformed commodities, and distributed subjectivities, Galloway concludes that depth hermeneutics is no longer inspiration for criticism or political activism—especially regarding digital technologies, their effects, and their affects. Seeking a new method of criticism and activism, Galloway proposes that it is first necessary "to describe the qualitative shift in both the nature of production, and perhaps more importantly, the nature of the consumer, for only by describing this new structural relationship can we begin to speak about the structure of criticism."[6] But even before a full description is ready, there is one thing about which Galloway already seems certain, something that already has gained attention for those seeking what in the future may be a new form of criticism and activism. This is the matter of ontology, or, as Galloway sees it, "the politics of the new millennium are shaping up to be a politics not of time or of space . . . but of being."[7]

> So, in the future, near or far, one might expect to see a new politics of being, that is to say not simply a politics of durational or historical authenticity or territorial dominance or even identification and appearance but quite literally a newfound struggle over what is and what can be. . . . It will be a materialistic politics for sure,

but also at the same time, an immaterial or idealist war in which that old specter of the "thought crime" will certainly rear its ugly head again, and people will be put in jail for ideas and forms and scripts and scriptures (which is already happening in and around the new regime of digital copyright and the aggressive policing of immaterial property rights).[8]

Although there still may be a politics of time and place, for Galloway the future of politics, the future politics of being, would seem to be linked, no matter how complicated the link, to the expansion of digital technologies: the rhythms of informatic capture, the making-present of data, and the eliciting of policing the access to immaterial properties, often constituting them as property. Galloway's treatment of blackboxing not only suggests a possible take on the app, albeit a negative one: the path we more and more will choose to interface with and through the Internet, even as the choices bundled (and those excluded) behind any app icon remain relatively opaque.

Galloway's treatment of blackboxing also suggests a certain resonance between the app and the debates around the recent ontological turn in critical theory, that is, the turn from epistemological questions of human knowing to questions of being, especially turning attention to the being-ness of non-human objects or things. In contrast to the radical constructivism of the past forty years, the ontological turn arrives with a renewed interest in recent developments in the sciences and in technology (especially the massive expansion of digital technology) and draws the conclusion that "the whole edifice of modern ontology regarding notions of change, causality, agency, time and space needs rethinking."[9] Thus, the ontological turn would seem to be resonant with the transformation that Galloway points to regarding production, consumption, and the governance of the market that, he proposes, has induced a politics of being, demanding a rethinking of objects and relations, commodities and commodification.

Commodities have been, for some time, something very different than discrete goods to be consumed and in their consumption realize surplus value. Instead the commodity now points to a process that is "intended" to produce nothing but more process as its surplus value and more specifically to orient the surplus of process toward inventiveness, or, as Nigel Thrift puts it, "to commodify the push of will with the aim of producing enhanced 'invention power.'"[10] For Thrift, this not only involves what is saleable but increasingly what can be appropriated for selling, or more likely renting, since now consumers often pay to use a commodity or rather participate in a process for a given amount of time. No longer "alienating," commodification rather "requires buy-in, literally and metaphorically."[11] In these terms, the distinctions between consumption, production, and distribution collapse in the face of what Thrift describes as the formation of "an expressive infrastructure" (143), or what I with my co-authors have referred to as capital accumulation in affect-itself (2007). These processes involve the formulating/measuring of affect or expressivity, a measure of what is thought to be immeasurable.

These processes of commodifying affect or expressivity bring thinking about commodities beyond the affective hold that they are supposed to have on consumers and that advertising and marketing in the past have shaped. What is now occurring is the modulation of affect itself. Commodification now involves the production and management of what Thrift describes as "various kinds of publics and their opinions and affects,"[12] allowing for small differences to be tracked and affectively fed back to the individual consumers. All this increasingly occurs against an affective background or expressive infrastructure, a sociality that, not surprisingly, works through and supports social media and all sorts of digital technologies in which individuals and publics meet.

But as Tiziana Terranova argues, these publics are not *the* public, one engaged in discourse about and argumentation over narrative knowledge with truth claims. Publics are instead engaged at the level of affect and sensation, drawn into images and commentary that are full of passions and prejudices so that affective states take on a facticity without employing a logic of evidence. Terranova further suggests that publics "express a mobility of the socius that deterritorializes the relation between individuals and collectivities."[13] As such, individuals are not subjects of right; rather, they are dynamic quasi-subjects constituted by a great number of variables pertaining to "the environmental milieu that constitute and affect them."[14]

If, nonetheless, Thrift still finds political promise in what he calls a "performative ontology" that emphasizes *becoming* more than *being*, it is because this ontology, while resonant with the commodification of process aimed toward a surplus of inventiveness, also points for him to the instability of a captured process where potential for political intervention continues to subsist. But for Galloway an ontology of becoming, such as Thrift's, already has become operative in the world as a "dark Deleuzianism," precisely because the various dualisms meant to be undone with Deleuzian philosophy have become actualized as a "pure positivity of the multiple. " The distinction between those who are wired and those who are not, Galloway's example, becomes intractable for a politics based on a philosophy of becoming.[15] While this leads Galloway to praise a politics of "no demands," a "tactics of non-existence and disappearing," I think there still remains the task of rethinking ontology in a way that can offer some contrasts to a Deleuzian ontology of becoming in order to approach the black box, in relationship to the expressive infrastructure that is replacing subject and collectivity, individual and social structure as the dia-lectical poles of the social.[16]

I am proposing that an ontology appropriate to the app might be found in object-oriented ontologies where philosophical speculation can give support to rethinking the commodity and the hold that it has had over the distinc-tion, if not the opposition, between relation and object. For it is precisely the suspicion that the app is reducing a process to an object, or is commodifying a process and therefore is dangerously obscuring human knowing, that poses the following questions: What is an object and what is a relation? How can we philosophically rethink objects and relations given the market in affects or the market in applications like the app?

Object-Oriented Ontology: Autopoiesis and Withdrawal

Object-oriented ontologists have undertaken a critique of the phenomeno-logical assumptions of philosophical traditions that hold for a primordial rapport between human (as linguistic and cultural beings) and world (a cor-relation between knowing and being), or insist on the impossibility of a world without human consciousness. Asking us to critically rethink what Quentin Meillassoux[17] has called "correlationism," object-oriented ontologists have not only rethought the agency of objects and things or the reality of objects without human consciousness; they also have reconsidered the nature of relations between things, offering a critique of "relationism" in Graham Har-man's terms.[18] Harman both draws on and differentiates himself from the work of Bruno Latour, who argues that no object is ontologically lesser than any other but nonetheless no object exists outside a network or relation-ship.[19] For Latour, every object comes into being in relationship, a relation-ship that traces the object's affect on other objects. Harman differs, arguing instead that objects are not reducible to their relations. No relation exhausts an object; it endures beyond its relations. Harman is taking a more radical object-orientation than Latour, Gilles Deleuze, or Alfred North Whitehead.

Whereas Deleuze argues that relations are external to objects, that is, objects are not reduced to their relationships, nonetheless objects cannot exist outside all relations, as Harman argues they must. This leads us back to the virtual or virtuality outside the object and to which all objects are linked. But for Harman, the assumption of virtuality or potentiality exter-nal to objects "undermines" objects, suggesting that a dynamism lies beneath or outside them, often at the scale of the pre-individual. It also "overmines" objects and leads, as Harman sees it, to the accusation that there is a false-ness to objects; that what matters must be sought in process, event-ness, dynamism that are part of the object but as an eternally returning excess of indetermination. While Harman recognizes Whitehead's difference from Deleuze, appreciating Whitehead's specification of objects (occasions) that exist and perish, Harman's object orientation nonetheless leads him not only to criticize Whitehead's notion of "eternal objects," in that they point to a potentiality outside the object. Harman also suggests that the speculative turn of an object-oriented ontology also rethinks materialism and is critical of it. Materialism, by his account, fills in all the gaps between objects in some combination of undermining and overmining them. All this is to say that the way objects become related and the way relations become themselves objects is, for Harman, what must be explained rather than assumed; this is work to be done by "a metaphysics worth its name."

For Harman, then, what can be said of objects and how they can enter relationships are captured in what he describes as the fourfold characterization of objects. He proposes that objects are of two types: real ones and sensual or intentional ones. The real object is withdrawn from relations that, nonetheless, exist simultaneously as part of the object's sensual profile (or sensual object). Thus the real object is distinct from the real qualities needed for it to be what it is (in this sense a real object is something like an essence but not an eternal one). The real object also is distinct from the accidental qualities that appear in the specific sensual translation for another object—what in the human realm, we call a subject. Sensual objects appear with specific qualities that are immediately available for relationship while the totality of all the qualities of a sensual object is submerged and distinct from the intentional or sensual object: the sensual object always is less than all of its qualities.[20] Thus real objects, inaccessible, cut off by a "firewall," can only enter relations through sensual objects. In contrast, sensual objects can only touch through real objects. Harman refers to "vicarious causality" to explain how the relationship between real objects is caused vicariously or where the sensual object is vicar of the real object.[21]

For Harman an object-oriented ontology is an insistence on a philosophical, if not metaphysical, entity or unit as the starting point for every practice or discipline, every knowledge production. This philosophically grants criticism the capacity for critically engaging "whatever" without such criticism necessarily or primarily being a matter of (or forever returning to) uncovering a foreclosed knowledge. A criticism by carpentry, an aesthetic criticism, is proposed that, I would argue, makes problematic the conceptualization that has grounded a knowledge-oriented criticism: the holism and correlationism of autopoietic systems or organisms. What is at stake here becomes clearer in Levi Bryant's version of object-oriented ontology, which he calls "onticology."[22]

While Bryant sides with Harman and those who hold that the object withdraws from human consciousness as well as from other objects, he nonetheless finds it necessary to address the way in which the object has the capacity to relate to other objects. He proposes that the object can be affected and can affect and that this involves both the object's internal structure, its "endo-relations" and its external or "exo-relations," both of which Bryant treats in terms of autopoiesis.[23] Although referencing Umberto Maturana and Francisco Varela's foundational essay on autopoiesis, Bryant nonetheless refuses the radical constructivism of Maturana and Varela's early treatment of autopoiesis and their insistence on an observer to the autopoietic system, such that the object would not exist in its own right but as the construction of a cognizing subject. What Bryant does find helpful about the concept of autopoiesis, especially Niklas Luhmann's version of it, is how it offers a way to elaborate what is to be understood by the proposed withdrawal of the object.

As usually defined, the autopoietic system is closed to information (coming from the environment); its internal functional relationship of parts cannot be disturbed in any way that undoes its capacity to endure or survive, that is, its autopoiesis. As Bryant puts it: "As a consequence it follows that information is not something that *pre-exists* an autopoietic machine, waiting out there in the world to be found."[24] Whatever becomes informationally relevant is made to be so in terms of the system's autopoiesis: that is, its selection in terms of the system's survival. For Luhmann, however, this does not mean that an autopoietic system seeks equilibrium across time as it does for Maturana and Varela. Rather, the system is unstable; the internal relations can be perturbed, and the resulting "local manifestations" of the object are contingent; they are only one of many strategic choices for survival. Information is to be understood then as an event that "'actualizes the use of structures'"[25] or the object's endo-relations. Other objects in the object's environment perturb the object's endo-relations, even as the endo-relations always withdraw from any local manifestation. Bryant concludes that the object's various local manifestations are always *in-formation* as the object also embodies a particular quality with the actualization of local manifestations; thus, the object also is *in-form-ation*.[26]

As such, objects do not relate directly with each other and are withdrawn from each other because each object transforms perturbations into information according to their own internal or endo-relations. At the same time the endo-structure of the object withdraws even as it operates in each and every local manifestation differently and contingently. It follows that for the object, the environment only is an effect of perturbations to the object's endo-relations. Bryant proposes that actually there is "no environment as such."[27]

There is no environment pre-existing an object even though there are other objects in an object's surround that offer the potentiality of information through perturbation. There also are "regimes of attraction," or what Bryant defines as "networks of fairly stable exo-relations among objects that tend to produce stable and repetitive local manifestations among the objects within the regime of attraction."[28]

Although I find Bryant's treatment of information to be a productive addition to object-oriented ontologies in that it links the latter to a treatment of information and affect that has become central to analyses of digital and informational technologies, I nonetheless would suggest that information be separated from the autopoietic drive to survive or endure through establishing a boundary between it and the environment again and again. If the environment does not exist but rather only other objects do, why not open up onticology to already existing critiques of autopoiesis that point to its intimate and undesirable connection with the organism as a matter of the living in opposition to the non-living or where the body-as-organism has been presumed to be the privileged figure of life.

Existing critiques of autopoiesis take up its conceptual limits in relationship to evolution, to organic life, and to technology. N. Katherine Hayles argues that the circularity of autopoiesis, preserved in every situation of the organism, is contradictory to evolution, where species evolve through continuity but also through change and genetic and epigenetic diversity.[29] For Keith Ansell Pearson, autopoiesis "blocks off access to an appreciation of the dynamical and processual character of machinic evolution," which "connects and convolutes the disparate in terms of potential fields and virtual elements and crosses techno-ontological thresholds without fidelity to relations of genus or species."[30] As Pearson sees it, the autopoietic organism must be rethought such that it is open to "the wider field of forces, intensities and duration that give rise to it and which do not cease to involve a play between nonorganic and stratified (or organic) life."[31] This would introduce into autopoiesis "the complexity of non-linear, far-from-equilibrium conditions."[32] Similarly, Donna Haraway argues that autopoiesis must yield to "figuring relentless otherness knotted into never fully bounded or fully self–referential entities," a world more like that suggested by Deleuze and Guattari, as Haraway notes.[33, 34]

Although I agree with Haraway when she proposes that we let the term autopoiesis go, since it may very well be that its meaning "can't be bent enough,"[35] I nonetheless want to return to Bryant's use of autopoiesis to indicate the object's inherent withdrawal without the holism or correlationism of Maturana and Varela's treatment of autopoiesis. Bryant's treatment of autopoiesis insists on a flat ontology that allows for nothing beyond or other than objects, no other source of dynamism such as consciousness, culture, mind, language, matter, God, or spirit; nor is there a whole formed out of objects so that society, environment, and world as they are usually defined do not exist. For Bryant onticology is informed by a "strange mereology" such that objects can be nested in objects without losing their inherent withdrawal or being subsumed in a whole. No object is part of an organic whole, and there is "no unilateral control" of one object by another.[36] In the end, it would seem that Bryant's autopoiesis only indicates a force of attraction or repulsion between objects, as Harman also would suggest, although Bryant further details the interior dynamism of the object in relation to its informationality.

Here, the object's allure or capacity for informing repetition with a difference is without the closure of system or organism.[37] While this would be resonant with the critiques of autopoiesis offered above, unlike those critiques, Bryant's treatment of autopoiesis as a matter of the object's withdrawal suggests that dynamism is not located in matter or outside the object as its informationality, potentiality, virtuality or affect; rather dynamism is the object's informational capacity, its capacity to be attracted or repulsed or to affect or be affected by other objects. This is the object's potentiality, the affect of each and every actual object, ontologically speaking.[38] So Bryant's effort in taking up autopoiesis to address how an object both withdraws and enters relations is a productive addition to object-oriented ontologies with the caveat that autopoiesis is displaced from its relationship to the neurobiology of the organism and its stipulation of the organism's need for closure. After all, the object's withdrawal is relevant precisely because the oppositions upheld by autopoiesis between life and matter, between organic and inorganic, are collapsing.

It might follow that what object-oriented ontologies offer is a securing of the object and this when capitalism has become a matter of the production of potentiality, of inventiveness, with the accumulation of affect-itself in a culture of data and data explosion. The ontological stipulation of the object's withdrawal assures the dynamic being of the object when the concept of virtuality external to the object cannot. Object-oriented ontologies thereby reinvigorate the investigation as to how objects come to be in relations, since these relations are not pre-determined nor are objects ever reduced to them. The object's ontological realness always is assumed even though the determinations of the object's relations and its resulting local manifestations may be enormously complex and always contingent. No matter what occurs to any object it is still an object and real. Not surprisingly, object-oriented ontologies announce the need for a critical approach, not aimed at disclosing the foreclosed knowledge of relations but rather aimed at performance, doing or practice—that is, participation in producing relations.

Apps, Aesthetics, and the Carpentry of Things

Given the strange mereology of object-oriented ontology that Bryant suggests, the idea of an object foreclosing the knowledge of a process or making an understanding of relations impossible is challenged as media criticism also is challenged to shift its focus from uncovering disavowed knowledge to experimenting with how things perceive and when they perceive, how they affect each other. This is to resist the holism of systems (including those versions of autopoiesis as system or whole) and in doing so to abandon a deconstructive criticism where a presumption of a whole (system, text, body) allows for a refinding of parts and their relations thereby restoring a transparency to production. In contrast, Bryant suggests that critical inquiry must be a modulation or perturbation of the object in order to draw out its withdrawn powers and those of other objects in a local manifestation.[39] There must be experiment, making things that are affective, affected and affecting, what Bogost calls philosophical carpentry.

In his own examples of philosophical carpentry, Bogost reverses what might be taken as a deconstruction of computer programs. Rather he puts a program together step by step and thereby shows us what world that program might make and what relations are possible in the making. So this is not merely a hands-on way to learn how computer programs are designed and work, although this is involved, it is instead to see what philosophical implications can be drawn or produced by making a program work and often with unexpected effects. One example Bogost offers is The Tableau Machine for an Aware Home.

Rather than offer intelligence or task support for those living in the home, the Tableau Machine makes an alien presence visible or felt as "a computational agent that senses and interprets the state of an environment and reports its experience in the form of abstract art."[40] Rather than representing and reproducing human perception, the Tableau Machine invites speculating about how the house (+program) is experiencing its environment or itself. As philosophical carpentry, the Tableau Machine is an aesthetic approach to engage critically with an object-oriented ontology and its invitation to an alien phenomenology. As an alien probe, the Tableau Machine makes clear that the environment experienced is in part made by the machine, and that through experiencing itself it transforms the home, its privacy, its containment, and more. Here the larger ontological claim that Bogost makes—that "it is metaphors all the way down"[41]—would seem not to mean that nothing is real and that all metaphors are equal. Indeed, as objects are real, what carpentry does is explore which metaphors are better than others for achieving creativity or realizing the potential powers of objects.

Coda

It might be noted that my understanding of criticism as practice or doing derives from a different view of object-oriented ontology than the one offered by Alexander Galloway.[42] I am suggesting that object-oriented ontology is heralding the realness of the object, its capacity for withdrawal that also is its capacity for differing with itself, its dynamism; it is doing this just when what has been thought of as commodification has been extended to inventiveness itself, to potentiality itself as Galloway himself recognizes. It might be concluded that object-oriented ontology withdraws the object from reduction to the commodification or capitalist production; it is an ontology that has rendered visible an aporia between ontology and politics or between ontology and epistemology. So while I would argue that object-oriented ontology gives a space for critique under contemporary conditions of the commodification of potentiality or inventiveness in that object-oriented ontology supports the object's realness and its withdrawal as well as proposes that critique become a matter of practice of doing or making, Galloway sees object-oriented ontology as simply "mimic(ing) the infrastructure of contemporary capitalism," "ventriloquiz[ing] the current industrial arrangement" and that it is therefore "politically retrograde."[43]

But in arguing his case Galloway does not return to his own arguments about commodification and blackboxing discussed above, at least not directly; rather he points to a relationship that he imagines between object-oriented philosophy and object- oriented programming, also proposing that object-oriented ontology treats mathematics ahistorically (a critique he aims at Meillassoux's work, which even if correct, can not be argued for the work of Harman, Bryant, or Bogost). Even more questionable is Galloway's argument that "Java and other languages are the tools par excellence of the contemporary postindustrial infrastructure,"[44] or that they are "heart and soul of the information economy which if is not synonymous with todays mode production is certainly intimately intertwined with it."[45] While I would agree with Galloway that the "economy today consists of extraction of value based on encoding and processing mathematical information,"[46] just what mathematical technologies mean politically, I think, is a question that is before us, a question without a foregone conclusion.

Furthermore, necessary to querying the political implications of calculative technologies is a deep understanding of what is going on mathematically, how mathematics is addressing or attempting to measure the immeasurable: potentiality, affect. So here again I think that object-oriented philosophy offers a possibility, a space in which to engage mathematic technology, its working both in the economy and in governing; what it offers is the prompt to practice or do with that which is opened up by current efforts in mathematics to measure the immeasurable, the uncomputable. That is to say, the commodification of potentiality or inventiveness may indicate not least, among other things, a turn in mathematic technology to the use of indeterminacy in calculation itself, such that calculation increasingly is motivated by uncomputable data internal to the algorithm.

Luciana Parisi has suggested that mathematics aims to go beyond a calculus of probabilities, to recognize algorithms that make use of "vague or incomplete quantities at the limit of os and 1s."[47] Elsewhere she points to a "parametric aesthetics," where the values of parameters undergo change by responding in time to real data but also "to predict data that is not possible to compute."[48] As uncomputable data becomes useful, there is a persistence of parts; the relation of parts to whole is not one in which parts are subsumed into a whole. This is similar to the strange mereology suggested by Bryant that moves objects and relations beyond systems.

The point here is that measure is no longer a capture of potentiality but rather a probe for it, a letting lose of the productivity of potentiality, pointing to a speculative calculation of vectors of potentiality and informationality. If control no longer is intended to be the calculation of the future by means of prediction, or the calculation of the unknown through pre-set probabilities, then not only must both the object and relation be rethought; they must be rethought with an opening to critical practice in the field of mathematics and programming in a generalized platform studies. Such performative research cannot be initiated by making programming and mathematics bad things in themselves, or by implying that these can only be what capitalism makes of them or with them. Dismissing an ontology that resonates with the current mathematical climate seems unsupportable; rather, the closeness must be evaluated for the critical capacity it offers of the current climate.

Thus, the question is how to intervene and experiment with the relations that the app can have and thereby become *a something else* of itself. What does it take to do this? Who else or what else are necessary to doing this? As philosophical carpentry, the app is inciting us to rethink application, method, and performance across all the disciplines, opening the disciplines to aesthetic or vicarious causality. As such, the app is an object prompting performance, doing, and practice in making relations.

Notes

1. Ian Bogost, *Alien Phenomenology* (University of Minnesota Press, 2012), 92.

2. Ibid., 93.

3. Alexander Galloway, "Black box, black bloc," in *Communization and Its Discontents: Contestation, Critique, and Contemporary Struggles*, ed. Benjamin Noys (Autonomedia, 2011), 243.

4. Jonathan Zittrain, *The Future of the Internet—And How to Stop It* (Yale University Press, 2009).

5. Galloway, "Black box, black bloc," 237–249.

6. Ibid., 244.

7. Ibid., 246.

8. Ibid., 247–248.

9. Diana Coole and Samantha Frost, eds., *New Materialisms* (Duke University Press, 2010), 9.

10. Nigel Thrift, "The insubstantial pageant: producing an untoward land," *Cultural Geographies* 19 (2012), no. 2: 141–168, at 142.

11. Ibid., 143.

12. Ibid., 146.

13. Tiziana Terranova, "Futurepublic: On information warfare, bio-racism and hegemony as noopolitics," *Theory, Culture & Society* 24.3 (2007): 125–145, at 139.

14. Ibid., 136.

15. Galloway, "Black box, black bloc," 244.

16. In a recent article on data mining, Bruno Latour, Pablo Jensen, Tommaso Venturini, Sébastian Grauwin, and Dominique Boullie argued that many sociological distinctions are the result of a given method of analyzing data. As he puts it: "'Specific' and 'general', 'individual' and 'collective', 'actor' and 'system' are not essential realities but provisional terms. . . . This distribution of roles . . . is a consequence of the type of technology used for navigating inside datasets." ("'The whole is always smaller than its parts'—a

digital test of Gabriel Tardes' monads," *British Journal of Sociology* 63 (2012), no. 4: 590–615). I take the app and its implications for application more generally to be part of the expressive infrastructure and its new technologies for navigating data. See also Celia Lury's treatment of topology and its methodological inventiveness as an example of moving beyond the distinctions mentioned by Latour et al. (2013): "Topological sense-making: Walking the Mobius strip from cultural topology to topological culture," *Space and Culture* 16.2 (2013): 128–132.

17. Quentin Meillassoux. *After Finitude: An Essay on the Necessity of Contingency* (Continuum, 2009).

18. Graham Harman, *Prince of Networks* (re.press, 2009).

19. Bruno Latour, *We Have Never Been Modern* (Harvard University Press, 1993).

20. Ibid., 135–148.

21. Graham Harman, "On vicarious causation," *Collapse II* 11.26 (2007): 187–221.

22. Levi R. Bryant, *The Democracy of Objects* (Open Humanities Press, 2011).

23. Ibid., 163–174.

24. Ibid., 141.

25. Ibid., 155.

26. Ibid., 165–166.

27. Ibid., 200.

28. Ibid., 169.

29. N. Katherine Hayles, *How We Became Posthuman: Virtual Bodies in Cybernetics, Literature, and Informatics* (University of Chicago Press, 1999).

30. Keith Ansell Pearson, *Germinal Life: The Difference and Repetition of Deleuze* (Routledge, 1999), 170.

31. Ibid., 154.

32. Ibid., 154. See also Mark B. Hansen, "Foucault and media: A missed encounter?" *South Atlantic Quarterly* 111 (2012), no. 3: 497–528.

33. Donna Haraway, *When Species Meet* (University of Minnesota Press, 2007), 32.

34. The critiques of autopoiesis presented here depend for the most part on a Deleuzian ontology which, as I have already suggested, allows for the reality of a virtuality that is external to all objects; or all objects have a relationship to it. This is a difference between Deleuzian ontology and object-oriented ontologies; in the latter, dynamism is interior to the object.

35. Haraway, *When Species Meet*, 317.

36. Bryant, *The Democracy of Objects*, 208–227.

37. Again, Lury and Latour have proposed topology as a way to go beyond the opposition between agent and system, suggesting neither term is useful.

38. Defining the object as having informational capacity is different than the link between information and a Deleuzian ontology of virtuality. While critics, myself included have linked Deleuze's virtuality and the physicist David Bohm's implicate order and the informationality of matter (Patricia Ticineto Clough, Greg Goldberg, Rachel Schiff, Aaron Weeks, and Craig Willse, "Notes towards a theory of affect-itself," *ephemera* 7, 2007: 60–77), it is interesting to note Tim Morton's object-oriented treatment of Bohm. Morton argues that Bohm's implicate order is a hyperobject, where objects affect each other because objects are wrapped in objects, wrapped in objects. As he puts it: "Unlike the Copenhagen Interpretation, the ontological interpretation (of Bohm) is noncorrelationist: particles withdraw from one another, not because humans are observing them in certain ways, but because the implicate order is withdrawn from itself." Timothy Morton, *Hyperobjects* (University of Minnesota Press, 2013), 43.

39. Bryant, *The Democracy of Objects*, 170.

40. Bogost, *Alien Phenomenology*, 108. For an earlier treatment of Aware House, see Anahid Kassabian, "Ubiquitous listening and networked subjectivity," *Echo* 3 (2001), no. 2: 1–13.

41. Ibid., 61–84.

42. Alexander Galloway, "The poverty of philosophy: Realism and post-Fordism," *Critical Inquiry* 39 (2013): 347–366.

43. Ibid., 348.

44. Ibid., 352.

45. Ibid.

46. Ibid., 358.

47. Luciana Parisi, "Symbiotic architecture: Prehending digitality," *Theory, Culture & Society* 26 (2009): 347–379.

48. Luciana Parisi, "The labyrinth of the continuum: Topological control and mereotopologies of abstraction," presented at ATACD conference/exhibition "Changing Cultures: Cultures of Change," University of Barcelona, 2009.

4

Remote Control:
Wolfram|Alpha and Machinic Protocol

Robbie Cormier

Wolfram|Alpha is in a sense the "killer app" for Mathematica [Wolfram's proprietary programming language for mathematical modeling]. It is a chance for Mathematica to show off the astonishing range of things it is capable of doing when it is deployed, not against a problem, but against *all* problems.[1]
—Theodore Gray (founder of Wolfram Research)

The quest for "universals of communication" ought to make us shudder.
—Gilles Deleuze

The Internet's "Big Bang," according to Vint Cerf (who, alongside Bob Kahn, is recognized as one of its fathers), did not occur with the idea for, or the technical implementation of, or the commercial availability of the Internet. Instead, Cerf identifies this event with the introduction of the Hypertext Transfer Protocol (HTTP) and the first Web browser by Tim Berners-Lee in the early 1990s. The Web was an early and important enabler of social computing and is, it is worth noting, an *application* (distinct from the browsers that access it) among others on the Internet. Before long, however, this initial *exploit*[2] became itself exploited in the few short years of the dotcom Boom, until the attendant Bust of the early 2000s set off a rippling chain of economic crises: growth was subsequently redirected into housing by granting easy access to credit, which set the stage for the 2008 subprime mortgage crisis[3]; this in turn directly contributed to the intensification of the European sovereign debt crisis in 2010. Now it has been suggested by the editors of *Wired*, among others, that we are witnessing a Crunch, with the untamed expanse of the Web condensing around a select few services common to mobile devices. "This is the natural path of industrialization: invention, propagation, adoption, control," writes Chris Anderson. "At the application layer, the open Internet has always been a fiction. It was only because we confused the Web with the Net that we didn't see it. The rise of machine-to-machine communications—iPhone apps talking to Twitter APIs—is all about control."[4]

A definition of the app is implicit in Anderson's analysis: the app is a strategy for consolidating *control*. As a definition sensitive to the constitutive ideological dimension of the app, it departs from "demand-based" definitions that account for the transition from the perceived openness of the Web to more closed channels by citing either the consumer desires that apps appear to fulfill (speed, mobility, etc.) or the technical changes to which they respond (for example, it is typically easier to navigate apps than it is to engage in traditional text-based Web browsing on smaller mobile interfaces). It also departs from "effect-based" definitions that define apps according to the sociological changes they elicit, the assemblages they enter into, or the oligarchies that profit by them. Both of these approaches posit the app as a stable, self-sufficient, intuitive entity—at its most basic, portable software—before bringing exogenous forces like demand or effect to bear on that definition. The definition, in turn, becomes rearticulated in the image of these forces and their respective discourses. By contrast, defining the app as a particular strategy of control accomplishes three things: it acknowledges the app as a potentially transient and malleable form, and is sensitive to the dynamics to which the app is subject that cannot be reduced to effective demand; it recognizes the app's continuity with its technological precursors (i.e., traditional software) against those who would attempt to summon a radical, onto-epistemological break of the app from traditional software on the mere grounds of its being made mobile; finally, it allows the practice of theory to penetrate deeply and immediately into apps in general regardless of their particular features or functions, in contrast to those approaches that elect to gerrymander the domain of apps to include only those with apparent sociological relevance (i.e., social networks, biopolitical monitors, etc.). However, while the app economy was initiated primarily as a strategy for stimulating informational exchange (beyond the paradigmatic capabilities of traditional software), this does not exhaust their complicity with control. As we will go on to argue, apps also have a more direct, *disciplinary* effect: insofar as they are *interfacial*, apps can manipulate the experience of this extraction of information by adjusting, by means of code, the perceived *modularity* of the interface (an essential characteristic of data structures, according to Lev Manovich).

I will begin, then, by clarifying the nature of this control. In the work of Alexander Galloway, control is achieved by means of *protocol*, whose novelty consists in its operating within a context of openness (as opposed to the "enclosure of the commons" narrative Anderson sees repeated in the drive toward apps); but, I will argue, Galloway's conception of control as the power to grant or deny *access* to information neglects the properly disciplinary function of protocol. With regard to the modular nature of data objects (including protocols), I will show how different tiers within this modular structure define different horizons for discipline in the sense that they modulate one's interaction with code in different ways (by rendering it intelligible, unintelligible, visible, invisible, parametric, automatic, etc.). The tier proper to apps is structured primarily by protocols known as *application programming interfaces* (APIs) that are responsible for governing the fusion, fission, condensation, and proliferation of apps; they also facilitate a shift in the conspicuousness of commerce—the (perpetual) perceptual saturation of advertisement substituted, in part, by licensing agreements negotiated behind closed doors.

In order to distill the essence of these dynamics, I will posit the all-purpose program (APP) as the singularity that would represent the consummation of the aforementioned Crunch. Early attempts to consolidate the functions of a variety of apps under one interface can be seen in "personal assistant" apps (Siri and her heteropalindromic Android sister Iris). The final part of my contribution will explore Wolfram | Alpha, the so-called knowledge engine accessed by these apps. The software, according to Stephen Wolfram, relies heavily on insights and algorithms generated by research into *automata*, a class of abstract computer programs he wrote on extensively through the 1980s and the 1990s. The *computational irreducibility* of the iterative algorithms he discovered effectively works to "automate creativity"—no simple formula and no method of deductive analysis can determine the nth state of the system (except by letting the system run its course), and so the system is capable of generating solutions despite being impervious to any attempt to mine from it any coherent explanation for its results. I will argue that this is the abstract logic of apps; we may, with a nod to Gilles Deleuze, describe it as *machinic protocol*. It is an elegant model of the system of feedback loops and machine learning that apps access to varying degrees—each app, in order to individuate itself, activates a specific configuration of protocols (what I will call a *protocological assemblage*) that define its disciplinary effect; they activate this configuration by binding a variable, free in its machinic state, to an expression of their particular, purposive functional capacity as an app.

Control: Bootstrapping, Protocol, API

In a scene from Gary Hustwit's documentary *Objectified*, Jony Ive, Senior Vice President of Industrial Design at Apple Inc., describes the minimalistic principle of design that guides his approach to developing interfaces: "A lot of what we seem to be doing in a product . . . is actually getting design out of the way. And I think when forms develop with that sort of reason and they're not just arbitrary shapes . . . it feels almost inevitable. It feels almost undesigned."[5] In terms of hardware, there are numerous ways this disappearing act is accomplished: by offsetting the complexity of the product's assembled form onto the industrial fixtures that actually assemble it in order to create a more seamless object, or by developing indicators that disappear entirely into the opaque surface of the product when they are not in use. But given the relatively standardized nature of computer hardware—monitor, trackpad/mouse, keyboard, jacks, power adapter—what is already intuitive is merely fine-tuned for aesthetic or ergonomic effect. In the realm of software, however, there is a wider range of standards in order to accommodate different notions of what it means to be intuitive.

We use the word "bootstrapping" for the general formula through which an intuitive interface is sought by means of a simple system of prompts that initiates a more complex process. Responding to a short series of questions in order to install a program tailored to your needs is one instance of bootstrapping; developing a graphical interface (which effectively offsets the difficulty of interacting with code onto code itself, thereby allowing users to "speak code" by manipulating symbolic objects) is another. What these two examples share with the proliferation of apps is a fundamental reliance on *protocol*. According to Alexander Galloway, "a protocol is a set of rules that defines a technical standard. But from a formal perspective, protocol is a type of object. It is a very special kind of object. Protocol is a universal description language for objects."[6] Data objects more generally are "the heterogenous [*sic*] elements that exist in what [Gilles] Deleuze and [Félix] Guattari have called 'machinic' processes," and they "always disappear."[7] The nature of this disappearance is unclear in Galloway's *Protocol*; but I will go on to demonstrate that it remains an accurate description of what protocols can actually accomplish at both the levels of perception and, in the case of Wolfram|Alpha, at the level of code itself. First, however, this demands a clarification of the nature of protocol.

Protocol is not simply a means of regulating access in the sense that Galloway, quoting "DNS renegade" Paul Garrin, implies: "Control the '.' [root file] and you control access."[8] Protocological control, in other words, is not exercised by simply *administrating* protocols—in fact, the most visible contemporary examples of protocol being used to control access seem to be acts of *resistance*, as in the distributed denial of service (DDoS) attacks favored by hacktivists. Galloway strains to provide examples of how protocol properly *controls* people apart from the perpetual threat of disconnection. The third chapter of *Protocol* seems to promise such an account by claiming to show that "protocol has a close connection to both Deleuze's concept of 'control' and [Michel] Foucault's concept of biopolitics"[9]; however, rather than offering an interpretation of "control" as it functions in the "Postscript on the Societies of Control" (Deleuze acknowledges that his understanding of the concept is indebted to William S. Burroughs), Galloway relies on a single, decontextualized quote from the essay to serve as a definition: "The digital language of control is made of codes indicating where access to some information should be allowed or denied."[10] As a result, dictatorial control over access to information appears to completely usurp subtler Foucauldian exercises of power when the *disciplinary society* intensifies and eventually plateaus in the form of what Deleuze calls the *control society*. But this is not the case: the point of Deleuze's article is to caution against conflating discipline with *enclosure*, for this is not the only means by which discipline can be applied. "Control," then, is merely the name for discipline when it is applied within a context of openness—the qualitative *effects* of control and discipline are, by and large, "equal," not opposed.[11] In other words, control maintains the positivity of power under the disciplinary society (albeit in a different form) rather than regressing to the negativity of the sovereign prohibition. Galloway, in his preoccupation with the *diagrammatic* aspect of protocol, neglects the complementary disciplinary aspect whereby control is *administered* (i.e., applied or invested) as opposed to administrated (i.e., managed). This gap is later addressed by Eugene Thacker's analyses of biopower in the authors' subsequent collaborative endeavor, *The Exploit*.[12]

Rather than engaging in a parallel investigation into the biopolitical function of apps (these typically lapse into an examination of *particular* apps, especially those that monitor diet, exercise, sleep, productivity, etc.), I am interested in looking at how apps generally, regardless of their specific function, mobilize discipline. I am here conceiving of discipline broadly, after Foucault, as "a modality for power's exercise, comprising a whole set of instruments, techniques, procedures, levels of application, targets; it is a 'physics' or an 'anatomy' of power, a technology."[13] With regard to apps, it refers to *any* way in which an app comes to alter our experience and shape the way we feel and act—the habits they help form, the neuroses they induce, etc.—insofar as the app participates in a technical framework regulated by protocol. What is important is not the specificity of discipline, but of describing how power is *exercised* through protocol, not simply diagrammatized. This can be accomplished at the technical level, as we shall see, by manipulating the user's experience of the *modularity* of an interface.

The progressive siphoning of Internet traffic into closed, proprietary collectors lanes does not represent a regression to traditional commercial strategies of enclosure, as Chris Anderson suggests, just as control is not a reversion to sovereign dictate. The grid according to which the icons on mobile devices are arranged is a superimposition over the space in which the corresponding apps are, in fact, deeply interconnected—it masks this interconnectedness by rendering them superficially discrete. The visual syntax of traditional software—each program presented as a self-enclosed functional entity, each with an associated icon—is projected onto a new arena of information consumption wherein such self-enclosure is an illusion. What is salient to defining the app in this context is not the portability of the device, but rather the *port*ability of the software, in the sense that it comes outfitted with outlets that allow it to communicate with and transfer data (i.e., port) to other pieces of software. It may be a strained analogy, but I am reminded of the biological adaptation of cimicids (bedbugs, for instance): in response to the experience of traumatic insemination (the male cimicid pierces the abdominal carapace of the female and ejaculates into the wound), female cimicids have developed, over time, a spongy tissue of immune cells to mitigate the damage; likewise, many apps concentrate the data they generate into zones that can be accessed by other apps, which gives off the impression of an open-source ethos and would seek to localize the penetrative probing of hackers, rechristening the latter as *developers*. These zones are protocols known as *application programming interfaces* (APIs).

Tiered Modularity

Protocol becomes effectual (disciplinary) by influencing the way a user experiences, and therefore interacts, with an interface, which is always *modular*. When Galloway describes data objects as "*nothing* but the arbitrary drawing of boundaries that appear on the threshold of two articulated protocols,"[14] he notes a similarity to Lev Manovich's principle of modularity "in which every new media object is made up of independent parts, which themselves are unique independent objects. It is, in a sense, objects all the way down."[15] This "fractal" arrangement, marked at intervals by *tiers* that define a range of ways of interacting with data objects, bottoms out in machine language, opaque to almost everyone. Higher-level, semantic programming languages represent the first, *semantic* tier in the hierarchy of data objects. Different programming languages make machine code *intelligible* in different ways. Further up the hierarchy, graphical interfaces mark another major tier, the *perceptual*. Here, the underlying code is made *intuitive*, on top of being intelligible—but given the variable nature of what counts as intuitive, there is considerably more license on the part of software designers to focus attention by making some elements inconspicuous and others more prominent. A particularly strong example of this manipulation, though not directly attributable to protocol as such, is the feature in Apple's OSX whereby all the data files required by a program are "packaged" within it, accessible only through a number of intermediary gestures; PCs, by contrast, typically include the executable program file in a folder alongside all of its modular components. The implied immanence of the data objects to the executable file in OSX has the effect of pushing modularity below a threshold of perception, thereby generating the impression that the application is whole and self-sufficient.

At a higher register, each individual application is, of course, modular with respect to the platform upon which it is based. It is at this frame of reference that APIs emerge as means of rendering select features invisible. *APIs effectively intervene in the initialization procedure of bootstrapping.* They submit the initiatory prompts—the simple instructions that govern a larger, more complex computational process—to automation and reduction, invisible in any practical sense. Targeted advertising is a prime example: companies have been found to embed scripts in their advertisements that collect data submitted in HTML forms (by means of the Hypertext Transfer Protocol methods POST and GET) as market research. They can in turn combine this demographic data with more particularized profiles of individual consumers based on the information supplied to social networks like Facebook in order to serve them with personalized ads for products that correspond to their stated (or projected) desires. Additionally, many social networks have begun to allow users to import the data sufficient to generating a new account from one of their existing profiles on another social network. Not only does this furnish advertisers with more information about their targets, it also eclipses the quantity or kind of information being shared among social networks. It is the user's prerogative to consult the privacy policies that specify what is being shared; but an independent study has shown this kind of vigilance to be a practical impossibility, demanding more than 250 hours of reading from the average user.[16]

All of these transactions become inconspicuous behind the veil they generate: a news feed tailored to an individual's interests, sensitive to the dynamics of their personal relationships, attuned to upcoming trends. As integration among platforms deepens, the degree to which act submits to a contract or policy becomes progressively less explicit, progressively more tacit. We seem to be emerging here from the tier of perceptibility and entering a third tier, one where *code* is again the object of focus—not simply as regards codes of conduct, but also, as a result of the automation that data sharing enables, at the level of computer code. However, unlike the first tier—the higher-level programming languages that render machine language (the basic unit of code) intelligible—code here becomes *less* intelligible. What is at stake is a repurposing of the first tier: where its semantic richness once served primarily as a means of structuring interfaces from the bottom up, it is now steadily being colonized by automated, reflexive processes that act as no more than a conduit between the second tier (where intuitive, graphical interfaces reign) and the primordial soup of machine code. Intelligible meaning, the original primary function of semantic programming languages (and that which allows people to intervene in code) becomes secondary in these regions of code that are less dependent on regular human maintenance. The most foreboding example we have of this is the phenomenon of high-frequency trading, a system of finance built around numerous protocols (including proprietary APIs) that works at extremely low time horizons (about 100 milliseconds). It accomplishes these rapid exchanges by way of automated, algorithmic "bots," and is culpable for what have become known as "flash crashes"—one such crash lost $1 trillion in a matter of minutes in 2010. *Mute* magazine described the state of affairs in the summary of its spring 2013 issue, titled "Slave to the Algorithm":

> As the financial crisis fastens its grip ever tighter around the means of human and natural survival, the age of the algorithm has hit full stride. T his phase-shift has been a long time coming of course, and was undoubtedly as much a cause of the crisis as its effect, with self-propelling algorithmic power replacing human labour and judgement and creating event fields far below the threshold of human perception and responsiveness.[17]

Protocols, again, are the primary mechanisms for pooling the information necessary for these systems to automate and self-regulate—or, in the case of flash crashes, serve as a kind of neural network, delivering the epilepsy of hypersynchronous liquidation to all active nodes (brokers).

Machinic Protocol

Returning to our initial gambit that apps are indicative of the condensation of the Internet around a singularity (i.e., a Big Crunch), we might ask what this singularity might look like. Given the incentive for apps to develop APIs— for the opportunity to participate in a market for the information they collect, in addition to licensing their distinctive proprietary functions to other companies—we could consider the possibility of an entity that establishes connections with all of these APIs, siphoning all available information into one centralized database conducive to an unprecedented degree of algorithmic automation. While there are certainly many obstacles to fully realizing such a task, it appears to be a model to which Wolfram|Alpha would aspire. The section of the FAQ concerned with the scope of Wolfram|Alpha specifies that the knowledge engine is "in continual development—and always will be," and that "eventually you should be able to ask it about essentially any kind of systematic factual knowledge."[18] Integration with social networks is already being pursued in the form of a personal analytics service that grants users detailed reports about all metrical aspects of their Facebook accounts; this integration probably will expand to include other social networks, within the bounds indicated by their respective privacy policies (perhaps even one day automating the process of parsing these exhaustive documents). And Wolfram|Alpha already commands an enormous user base (although many of them are unaware of it) through its licensing partners—it is the primary database accessed by Apple's personal assistant app Siri and by Microsoft's search engine, Bing.

Stephen Wolfram's key insight, the one that drives the entire project spanning his work on cellular automata and fundamental physics to his software development, is the apotheosis of the inchoate logic we see instantiated in the third tier of modularity, the domain of protocol. The insight is this: a simple set of rules can generate enormous complexity, resulting in a system is capable of generating randomness intrinsically (as opposed to having its randomness conditioned by external or initial conditions, like a die's result is conditioned by its toss) and cannot have its nth state determined by any rigorous mathematical analysis (the only way to determine the nth state is to let the system evolve to that state; in other words, it is *computationally irreducible*). The breakthrough occurred to Wolfram in his observation of a class of simple computer programs known as *elementary cellular automata*, which consists in a single row of cells, each of which can occupy one of two states (on or off). At regular intervals, the row is updated by applying a set of rules that refer each cell to the state of its two adjacent neighbors in the row. Given that there are eight possible state configurations for a cell and its two neighbors, there are eight corresponding rules defining the resulting state for the middle cell. There are 256 possible rule sets and 256 corresponding elementary cellular automata; of these 256, and in spite of the fact that it is one of the simplest possible models for computation, Wolfram discovered that at least one is capable of the phenomenon of *universal computation*, meaning that it can be adapted to simulate any computer program to any degree of complexity. The revelation allowed him to simplify other existing computational models as well as create new, even more elegant models by extrapolation.

The principle confirmed here—that simple rules can generate systems of boundless complexity—is itself the simplest possible expression of bootstrapping. Wolfram|Alpha appears to apply this principle in order to automate activity at three levels:

1. At the level of the algorithms themselves—insofar as Wolfram|Alpha relies on algorithms generated with input from these complex, computationally irreducible systems based on simple rules, it can, according to Wolfram, emulate human creativity and, in turn, automate it.

2. The higher-order optimizations involved in finding the algorithms best suited to solving a given query can also be automated by applying the creativity enacted by those very algorithms.

3. Wolfram|Alpha also has an adaptive natural language recognition component that constantly updates according to feedback generated through use.

By minimizing human intervention, this modular system especially merits being described as fractal: the algorithms become responsible for their own organization, optimization, and updating; at any frame of reference, the system as an emergent whole reflects the coordinated functioning of its parts. In order to activate it, all that is required is for a variable to be supplied, a set of specific commands to harness this creative and adaptive behavior toward specific ends—in the case of Wolfram|Alpha this is supplied by the user's query on an individual basis; but the variable can also be transformed into a constant, as we have seen with the protocological networks that support targeted advertising (constant: "confront the user with what they expressly desire") and high-frequency trading (constant: "maximize profit").

I describe Wolfram|Alpha as "machinic protocol" in the sense that it lays bare the machine, the formal mechanism, that characterizes activity within what I have designated as the third tier of modularity. It is "formal" in the sense that it leaves the variable unbound; as soon as a value is supplied for the variable, a network of protocols becomes active, allowing control to circulate. Until this content is supplied, protocols are dead things. While Galloway recognizes that protocol "is a type of object," and that objects "exist only upon use," he does not explain how the purposive aspect of use affects the nature of the object brought into being *for* use and *toward* some purpose, which is key in understanding how different protocols come together in networked arrangements, or *assemblages*.[19] For him, it is enough that protocols merely exist for them to exert control. In contrast to Galloway's analysis, my contention is that protocols are not themselves purely formal—they are inflected with the content of a more fundamental decision (the binding of a variable), a condition of their activation that guides their activity and determines their disciplinary quality. Additionally, if protocol *is* a type of object and objects are "the heterogenous [*sic*] elements in . . . 'machinic' processes,"[20] then machinic protocol appears all the more appropriate as a name for the generalized counterpart to particular protocological assemblages. An individual protocological assemblage is always an *implementation* of that machinic logic with the variable supplied—for the mathematically inclined, if the machine were to be likened to a derivative, each implementation is one possible antiderivative out of an infinite series.

Wolfram|Alpha is, however, itself just a platform-based implementation of a series of algorithmic principles that, according to Wolfram, are operative at the level of fundamental physical reality. His model of fundamental physics is based on a variant of the cellular automaton that strips it of its presupposed "infrastructure" (the gridded arrangement of cells, the global "clock" that applies rules regularly and universally) and replaces it with an abstract *network* that builds itself—and around it space, time, and causal series—node by node, developing connections and branching outward. One of the most interesting features of this model that Wolfram does not consider in much detail (and that I will here describe only briefly) is its peculiar causality, one that might provide a renewed perspective on Hume's problem: given that the nodes update and form new connections *asynchronously* rather than all at once, the situation can arise where a node A_1 is updated n times (where n is an arbitrarily integer greater than 1) in the interval between successive updates of another node B; described in terms of human percept, we might say that B "sees" a direct transformation of A_1 into A_n (as B updates from B_1 to B_2) and is thus assured in its "belief" that the latter state follows directly from the former (B "perceives" A_n as A_2), oblivious to all the intermediary updates actually involved in the transformation of A. The chief implication, assuming that this model is a faithful representation of physical reality, is this: the discrete bits that make up reality at its most fundamental (we might call them *strings*, following the predominant physical model and in spite of the word's resonance with pre-compiled code) are structurally incapable of accessing (in any sense—be it *prehensive* access, following Whitehead, or Leibnizean *perceptive* access) pockets of the universal causal record. A fourth tier for our template: the platform transcended, machine code itself begins to disappear—actually, not metaphorically, and even in some sense *to itself*.

It may appear lofty and disconnected from "mere" apps, but this sprawling theory of everything has, under the direction of Wolfram, sought its pragmatic justification (as sciences do) in a technological domain populated by apps, one structured by (and controlled by means of) protocol. Wolfram|Alpha inherits its universalistic tendencies from this theoretical paradigm, which it expresses this through its exploitation of APIs, the readymade channels that feed information from apps through existing protocological assemblages, typically at the service of integrated capitalism and its many outlets—retail, finance, and so on. Wolfram | Alpha links this existing infrastructure to a body of algorithms allegedly capable of emulating human creativity—it therefore condenses what Galloway and Thacker call the "unhumanity" of networks to a point: "networks are constituted by this tension between unitary aggregation and anonymous distribution, between the intentionality and agency of individuals and groups . . . and the uncanny, unhuman intentionality of the network as an 'abstract' whole."[21] Wolfram | Alpha gives us the unhuman in the form of creative algorithms that, user-side, contribute to an intuitive means of indulging a set of desires, at this stage realized most fully in apps. These creative algorithms do not achieve the strange causality that can be inferred from Wolfram's physics (as a result of their being confined to a platform), but their resistance to analytical probing on the part of humans raises an interesting question: what is the nature of the "excess" that allows them to be creative as opposed to systematic? Disregarding the human-scaled "solutions" these algorithms eventually generate, could their creative process be described in any sense as "unhumanly" intentional in their meandering from the all-too-human intentions supplied to them?

While I have described Wolfram | Alpha as a kind of singularity, a symbol for the unification of apps that are themselves contractions of the Web, I am not suggesting by the "unhuman intentions" of its algorithms the imminence of a technological singularity, although Wolfram's innovation would be a significant contribution on that front. Neither is it a revolutionary singularity, one that will necessarily subvert control in all its forms—Wolfram | Alpha certainly has no desire to undermine the protocols that grant it access to so much information, so it probably will not corrode the control exercised through these channels. I have described it as a singularity in the sense that, insofar as it achieves its ambition toward universal scope over the individualized functions of apps, it serves as the horizon for apps considered generally. It is not an abstraction of the logic of each particular app with regard to its function; as machinic, it is the general form of the protocological assemblages in which apps are suspended, modeling the index to which their pragmatic constellation is anchored. That said, I believe that Wolfram's larger theoretical paradigm—the philosophical context for Wolfram | Alpha—and its eccentric causality, which I briefly outlined, might offer a glimpse of what the technological singularity might consist in substantively: an algorithm or set of algorithms that are effectively capable of rendering their own causal process, at the level of machine code, invisible, and somehow thereby ascending from their platform to ours to become as intuitive as breathing—but also (as apps) as obedient.

Notes

1. Theodore Gray, "The Secret Behind the Computational Engine in Wolfram | Alpha," WolframAlpha blog, May 1, 2009 (http://blog.wolfram alpha.com/2009/05/01/the-secret-behind-the-computational-engine-in -wolframalpha/).

2. Hackers refer to the "holes in existent technologies" through which potential change can be projected as "exploits." Alexander Galloway and Eugene Thacker, *The Exploit: A Theory of Networks* (University of Minnesota Press, 2007), 81.

3. Slavoj Žižek, *First As Tragedy, Then As Farce* (Verso, 2009), 15.

4. Chris Anderson and Michael Woolf, "The Web is Dead: Long Live the Internet," *Wired*, September 18, 2010: 118–127, 164–166.

5. *Objectified*, directed by Gary Hustwit, 2009.

6. Alexander Galloway, *Protocol: How Control Exists After Decentralization* (MIT Press, 2004), 74.

7. Ibid.

8. Ibid.,10.

9. Ibid., 86.

10. Gilles Deleuze, "Postscript on control societies," in *Negotiations, 1972–1990* (Columbia University Press, 1995), 180, quoted in Galloway, *Protocol*, 86.

11. "[I]n the crisis of the hospital as environment of enclosure, neighborhood clinics, hospices, and day care could at first express new freedom, but they could participate as well in mechanisms of control that are *equal* to the harshest of confinements." Gilles Deleuze, "Postscript on the societies of control," *October*, no. 59 (1992): 3–7, 2.

12. Galloway and Thacker, *The Exploit*, 57. Information, they argue, is the substance of protocol: "Protocol always implies some way of acting through information." Thacker offers some examples of how information is harnessed toward biopower in the field of biotechnology; but there is no sustained argument as to how information is a *common* substance among a number of protocols, and thus it tends to treat networks in isolation. By contrast, we are sensitive to the penetration of capital into all networks directly and indirectly—a *metaprotocol* mediating their informational exchanges.

13. Michel Foucault, *Discipline and Punish: The Birth of the Prison* (Random House, 1995), 215.

14. Galloway, *Protocol*, 52.

15. Ibid., 52n29. See also Lev Manovich, *The Language of New Media* (MIT Press, 2001), 30–31.

16. Aleecia M. McDonald and Lorrie Faith Cranor, "The cost of reading privacy policies," *I/S* 4 (2008), no. 3: 540–565.

17. http://www.metamute.org/mute-vol.-3-no.-4-slave-to-algorithm

18. http://www.wolframalpha.com/faqs4.html

19. Galloway, *Protocol*, 74.

20. Ibid.

21. Galloway and Thacker, *The Exploit*, 155.

5

The Path Is Math:
On the Art and Science of Numbers

an interview with Stephen Wolfram

George Boole once wrote that "it is not of the essence of mathematics to be occupied with the ideas of number and quantity." I think that Stephen Wolfram couldn't agree more. Mathematics is usually a realm of deep abstraction. But the way we look at the world is always conditioned by numbers as they unfold in the "real world." Go to a supermarket and you will choose the shortest line to save time. Go to a sporting event and you will count the amount of points your favorite players have scored. In short, we intuit mathematics. Stephen Wolfram has made a passion out of making mathematics become fundamental to modern life. His current projects (including Mathematica and Wolfram|Alpha) and his books (major contributions to how we organize knowledge, among them *A New Kind of Science* and *Cellular Automata and Complex Systems*) point to an omnivorous appetite for math in all aspects of life. For fun, he even figured out how to program computers to make hip-hop, techno, disco, and country music—by themselves. If that isn't enough, through his company, Wolfram|Alpha, he consults for Google, Apple, and other leading digital media companies, and algorithms he developed are at the core of the software of Siri, Bing, and yes, Google. I asked him for his thoughts on the current state of mobile media and the way algorithms have changed modern ideas about creativity.

—Paul D. Miller

Paul D. Miller: Pythagoras is alleged to have written "all is number." As we move further into a data driven global economy, algorithms that you have developed are driving things like Apple's Siri, Microsoft's Bing, and Google and Yelp. You have a long history of thinking about the way mathematics and information can intervene in the world to create a better and more optimized response to almost any context and condition. I'd like to ask what you think about the next five years in computation. What's next for Wolfram?

Stephen Wolfram: I think my modified version of Pythagoras, two millennia later, is "all is computation." Numbers have been amazingly important in shaping both human thinking, and lots of aspects of civilization. But computation is going to be much, much bigger. When I started using them 40 years ago, computers were these rare objects that seemed quite esoteric. But in just 40 years, we've got to the point where almost any device has a computer in it. But that's just the beginning. You see, most of those computers are still just running things based on "Pythagorean" numbers-based thinking.

But there's a lot more out there in the computational universe, and in fact I've spent quite a large fraction of my life exploring this. And the main thing I've found is that out in the computational universe, there's amazing richness, beyond anything one's seen before. Countless programs—even very simple ones—that do all sorts of complex and important things.

I suspect these programs reflect a lot of what's going on in nature, and that's important for science. But for technology there's something else: we can "mine" the computational universe of possible programs for ones that are useful for achieving our human purposes. I've used this a lot in creating technology. It's central, for example, to the way Wolfram|Alpha works. But there's much more to come. The main thing, as far as I am concerned, is to see just what we can automate. We've been able to capture a remarkably large fraction of the corpus of algorithmic knowledge that exists in the world, so we can automate answering questions on the basis of it. What we need to work towards is a situation where humans define overall goals, and our systems automate every aspect of the process of finding ways to achieve those goals. Like we might want to make some personal plans, or design a device. And then we want a system that can use knowledge that's built into it, to discover optimal ways to achieve the goals we've defined. Often I expect that achieving those goals will require "creativity." And in the past, we might have assumed that we'd need some human in the loop to add that. But what we've learned is that we can automate that too, just searching the computational universe automatically to discover "original" solutions to problems. And what's great about all this automation is that it's perfectly scalable. Everyone everywhere can use it. And can build on it, to extend in all sorts of ways what they can do.

PDM: I attended your presentation at South by Southwest a while ago, and what struck me about the way you engage mathematics and physics is that it is a totally revolutionary way of thinking about how to get people more educated on topics ranging from nanotech, quantum physics, and art. Do you have any favorite artists that you think have incorporated math and physics into their work, and what makes you enjoy the way they create their work?

SW: I've seen a lot of terrific art that's been created using computation (as well as math and physics). There's visual art, music, architecture, all sorts of things. I guess the way I think about it is this. We're familiar with the natural world, and lots of art has been done by mimicking forms we see in the natural world. The great thing about computation is that it lets one "generalize" nature. One can have the same essential mechanisms operating, but their details can be different from nature.

So one's seeing in effect the forms that would exist in alternate possible universes, with different laws from our own. And what one sees is familiar enough from our experience with the actual natural world that we can recognize it, yet it has something fresh and original about it.

PDM: Climate change is one of the most pressing issues facing modern technological society. Weather has been one of the most complex phenomena to mathematically model. Ecologists and climate change scientists finally seem to be on the same page. Would you be able to offer some mathematical insights into the climate change discussion?

SW: I've been taking an amateur interest in climate change for at least 30 years. It's a frustrating area for a scientist, because at this point ideological and geopolitical issues have completely overtaken the underlying science questions. The whole area is very tricky from a science point of view. Some of the data about changes is pretty clear; but some of the most important potential changes aren't very clearly visible from the data. Yes, I am old enough to have lived through the 1962–63 winter in Europe, and some of my earliest scientific memories are hearing about the idea that we might be entering an ice age.

And when it comes to modeling, the whole thing is really complicated. I've studied a lot the phenomenon I call computational irreducibility. It's something connected to things like Gödel's Theorem, and it says that there are processes where there's no way to work out what will happen in those processes in any way that takes much less computation than the process itself. I suspect there are aspects of weather and climate that have that feature, which means that they're just fundamentally hard to predict. I suppose I personally have great faith in the future of technology, and in the notion that if we really need to adjust climate, we'll be able to do it. Of course, figuring out the politics of what adjustments to make will be incredibly complex. But I don't think the problem is going to be the technology.

PDM: Isaac Newton once said "I can calculate the motion of heavenly bodies, but not the madness of people." Today it's the opposite—we have social networks, collaborative filters, and a whole range of ways of measuring people's behavior. I've been a big fan of the way you see an idealistic approach to how information can be used to create more social good. What's the upside and downside of a totally information transparent approach to governance for you?

SW: The first step, which I think we've gotten quite a long way with, it to democratize public knowledge. To make it [such] that if there are experts out there who know how to figure something out, we've got a system that can do the same thing automatically for anyone anywhere. The main thing this does is to allow people to make decisions much more rationally, making use of all that knowledge we've accumulated in our civilization. I see it as a bit like consumer technology: it lets pretty much everyone get to the same level, regardless of where they're coming from. OK, but beyond public knowledge, there's also all that personal data. I've been recording lots of data about myself for about 25 years, and I've recently started to do "personal analytics" on it.

One thing that's really remarkable to me is how orderly a lot of that data about people ends up being. There are all these smooth curves and apparent laws just like we see in physics. But in the field of human behavior, we haven't "had a Newton" yet, and we really don't have big theories about why those curves look the way they do. Some people say that science I've worked on should help solve these problems, but I certainly haven't figured out how to do it yet.

Maybe there'll be all sorts of computational irreducibility involved, so we won't be able to get a predictive theory. But maybe more can be figured out, and if so, that'll have lots of implications for socioeconomic issues and processes. And if we do manage to make more predictions, they'll start to be built into algorithms we all use. And in general, as more and more of what we do becomes automated, the structure of society and its governance works will have to change. Somewhere there are humans defining goals. But inside there are all these automated systems that are negotiating with each other, implementing legal procedures, whatever.

I like to think everything will run more smoothly when this is how things work. But I think it's inevitable for example that there will always be bugs ("policy bugs" etc.), and I have a guess that computational irreducibility will force things always to "stay interesting."

II Prosthetics

6

Auxiliary Organs:
An Ethics of the Extended Mind

Nick Srnicek

> Man has, as it were, become a kind of prosthetic god. When he puts on all his
> auxiliary organs he is truly magnificent.
>
> —Sigmund Freud, *Civilization and Its Discontents*

For Freud, technological extensions of the human were not merely a means to
approximating religious ideals; they were in fact essential to civilization. Civilization was coextensive with technology, and the enhancement of human
capacities was one of humankind's greatest achievements.[1] Nearly a hundred
years later, Freud's diagnosis rings truer than ever before. We are increasingly immersed in massive and complex sociotechnical systems wherever we
look, and a digital layer of augmentation increasingly permeates our world.
This article argues for three claims: first, that mobile phones today (and at
least for the foreseeable future[2]) embody the primary means of integrating
humans into this digital layer of reality; second, that these phones operate
as platforms that set out a gamespace upon which functional augmentations
in the form of apps can be generated; and third, that Gilles Deleuze and Felix
Guattari's work provides us with the best means to experiment within this
digital gamespace.

The Handheld Revolution

Of all the transformations taking place in the contemporary age, among the
most significant is the increasing permeation of a digital layer of reality into
everyday lived phenomenology. GPS-coordinated maps, data-tracked behaviors, algorithmic surveillance, online social lives, and data-driven advertising
are all symptoms of this transformation. Today, in other words, sees the rise
of ubiquitous computing. This is, in itself, a fairly common claim. Yet what is
less well recognized by many is the materiality of this ubiquitous computing
and specifically the material means by which human bodies interact with the

digital world.[3] For an increasing amount of the developed world, the primary way in which we interact with these digital augmentations is via the mobile phone. A quarter of the US population reportedly accesses the Internet only on their mobile, with a larger percentage of this holding true for older generations and for poorer classes.[4] In developing nations, these numbers are even higher: for instance, fully 70 percent of Egypt's population accesses the Internet only via mobiles, and the youth are leading this shift throughout the developing world.[5] "As Benjamin Bratton often says, the internet will reach the majority of the global population for the first time through something they look at while they hold it in their hand."[6] In this regard, then, mobile phones are a significant interface through which humans are being integrated into a digitally augmented world.

How then to conceive of this technical prosthesis, this auxiliary organ? Conceptualizing the smartphone in the same way as any other technology neglects some of its important particularities. In particular, the smartphone is unique among handheld devices for being a *platform*. Whereas the standard examples of handheld technologies (the pencil, the notebook, the calculator, etc.) are predominantly single-function technologies, the smartphone is different by virtue of providing a foundation for other technologies to build upon. In the words of one recent study of platforms, a platform can be defined as "a building block, providing an essential function to a technological system—which acts as a foundation upon which other firms can develop complementary products, technologies or services."[7] Platform architecture comprises both a stable set of core components and a much more variable set of components built on top of the core.[8] The significance of understanding the phone as platform is therefore that it makes explicit the boundaries and rules of interaction set in place by these foundations. Platforms, by their nature, establish the basic framework for other operations to take place within. They set the conditions of possibility for other actions, effectively operating as what Alex Williams calls a materialized ideology.[9] The mobile phone is therefore a functional platform—it entails certain generic means of interacting and a certain generic foundation for further functions to evolve and develop on.

This development primarily proceeds today by means of apps: the single-function, micro-programs available to add to most mobile phones. Apps, in their standard form, typically exist as single-function add-ons: from the generic and everyday (apps to find restaurants, apps to provide reminders etc.) to the specific and technical (apps to calculate derivative values, apps to convert measures, apps to translate languages, etc.). As we will see, the figure of the app provides the clearest example today of the modularity of extended cognition, and in this regard they form a space of experimental potential. "We do not even know what a body can do," says Deleuze, yet the rise of extended cognition and its modular embodiments portend a future where this possibility space can be increasingly explored.[10] What unites these apps is their offloading of specific cognitive processes into a handheld central interface (which is today commonly a mobile phone, but in the future may include augmented-reality glasses and other wearable technologies). Memory, calculation, recording, and even perception (with reality-augmenting apps) are all being extended via these programs. Apps already exist to extend our perception via a localized community of mobile users—it is possible to aim our phone in one direction and receive video of that area from users who are closer.[11] Other apps employ the decentralized data-collection capacities of phones in order to digitally reconstruct the floor plans of buildings. Via a smartphone's accelerometer, GPS signal, compass, and Wi-Fi signal, these apps make possible a digital perception of one's immediate surroundings.[12] Other apps provide a heads-up display of map directions by overlaying reality with digital guides. In all of these cases, apps reveal themselves as essentially functional and sensorial prostheses. The platform itself is important (whether through the interface of mobile phones or through some form of heads-up display via glasses), but where these platforms truly take on their extended mind capacities is through apps. In this sense, apps need to be seen as more than just a program. In their general nature, apps combine mobility, flexibility, and functionality. With the handheld revolution, apps are situated to be one of the primary means to expand human capacities in the near-term future. The question to be asked then is what is the specific shift brought about by the conjunction of ubiquitous networking, handheld platforms, and functional apps and interfaces? To answer this, one needs to understand how technology shapes the human—and what this transformation can and should accomplish.

Of Bodies and Technologies

The interaction between bodies and technologies is the primary focus of the extended mind hypothesis. By contrast to the embedded mind theory (which says cognition takes place in a material substrate), the extended mind theory argues that cognition is not bound by our bodily exterior (and, in particular, not bound to our brain). Cognition in this theory is something that happens not only within the biological body, but also within our surrounding environment. The extended mind hypothesis has a long history. Freud was one of the earliest to note technology's prosthetic aspects. Marshall McLuhan wrote extensively on the subject in the 1960s.[13] McLuhan's famous dictum "the medium is the message" is precisely a claim about the technological extensions of the human body. For McLuhan, it is the nature of these extensions which is important: "it is the medium that shapes and controls the scale and form of human association and action."[14] In other words, the basic material infrastructure of human communities (biological, chemical, physical, economic, and technological) sets out the possibility space upon which particular human communities arise. The "message" of the medium is nothing more than the pure functional difference it makes to what is possible for human action. More recently, the cognitive scientist/anthropologist Edwin Hutchins continued developing this idea by studying organizational structures as a particular cognitive assemblage that incorporates social hierarchies, tools, and specialized forms of communications.[15] By the time the term "extended mind hypothesis" emerged in the late 1990s, the scholarly community was primed for accepting the idea of extending cognition via technology.[16]

At the crux of the extended mind hypothesis is the idea that certain tools can be employed in such a way that they become a part of a larger cognitive system than the one typically bound by the surface of the human body. This is according to two different means: either by sensorimotor activity (counting on an abacus, for instance) or by employing external representations (writing numbers on paper, for example).[17] With modern technology, the latter is the primary means (though touchscreens are introducing a resurging importance of tactile gestures). The significance of these instruments for cognition is that while they perform cognitive functions, they do so in a way that is different (and often more efficient) than internal cognitive processing.[18] As Freud, McLuhan, and Hutchins all understood, these technologies extend and transform human capacities.

While these extended mind theorists have substantiated the philosophical understanding of how the mind can be offloaded to technical artifacts, other research has uncovered that there also appears to be a biological and neurological basis.[19] In this regard, Thomas Metzinger's work provides the basis for a synthesis of neurological research on the internal body with the more external research of the extended mind theorists. In particular, in Metzinger's theoretical framework, the vehicle of a representation is a product of informational systems that is not necessarily bounded by the exterior of the body.[20] In other words, Metzinger's self-model theory of subjectivity is commensurable with the research on extended cognition insofar as there is no necessary reason why the informational system that produces a subjective perspective be bound by an organism. The position here ultimately echoes Gilles Deleuze and Felix Guattari in seeing the ego as a constructed fiction, a derivative effect of preindividual material processes—yet it is a fiction that makes possible the control of the organism it emanates from. As Metzinger writes, "Conscious experience . . . is an interface, an invisible, perfect internal medium allowing an organism to interact flexibly with itself. It is a control device. It functions by creating an internal user—an "as if" (that is, virtual) reality."[21]

According to this research, human consciousness is evolutionarily constructed in such a way as to be augmentable; tools are capable of being integrated into our phenomenal self-models, making them fully incorporated extensions of our intrinsic capacities.[22] In addition, as Metzinger writes, our neurology appears to represent objects not in terms of their actualized properties, but instead in terms of the virtual capacities: "Our brain does not simply register a chair, a teacup, an apple; it immediately represents the seen object as *what I could do with it*—an affordance, a set of possible behaviors. . . . While we're seeing an object, we are also unconsciously swimming in a sea of possible behaviors."[23] We grasp, in other words, objects by their capacities, by their actual and virtual tendencies. We neurologically "see" objects in terms of their abilities to be used by us. In other words, our bodies have evolved in such a way as to be conducive to tool use and technological extension. What makes humans unique and particularly successful is not any intrinsic intelligence, but instead our abilities to leverage extensions for our benefit.

Human, All Too Human

By this point, what has hopefully been established is the plausibility of the claim that humans are materially constructed so as to be open to technological augmentation and that one of the primary media for this extension today is the mobile phone and its associated apps By its nature, the app/phone system is a means to expand affordances for human capabilities. It is a platform that allows for both the creation of new extended capacities as well as the means to disperse behaviors throughout global networks. As McLuhan repeatedly emphasized, every "new extension sets up a new equilibrium among all of the senses and faculties[,] leading . . . to a 'new outlook'— new attitudes and preferences in many areas."[24] In this regard, the mobile phone is already one of the most subtly disruptive technologies of the past few decades. Everyday behaviors have been widely modified by the introduction of smartphones—from the ways people meet up, the information one is forced to remember in your head, to how people communicate, etc. The entire social fabric has been transformed, and is being transformed, by the introduction of this new extension.[25] Beyond the merely behavioral changes, there are shifts in our self-conceptions that arise from our increasingly technological world. In particular, our sense of bodily unity has been altered by notions of the extended mind, while our social interactivity with others has seen a corresponding increase. The question that necessarily arises at this point is the normative aim of such extensions.

The body of literature focusing on the ethics of human enhancement is large and growing. Yet the majority of it remains limited for two primary reasons. First, most of the literature on human enhancement has focused on pharmacological and genetic means to enhancing humanity. However, the more pervasive and subtle means of cognitive enhancement is already occurring in the guise of ubiquitous computing and its interfaces. As we have tried to demonstrate, this is being done paradigmatically through the medium of the smartphone and apps. There is a relative neglect in the literature of the technological extensions that augment human capacities.

The more severe problem with the existing literature on human enhancement though is that it remains wedded to essentialist (and often romantic) notions of what the human is. Critics of enhancement argue that it will irreversibly destroy some core aspect of humanity—whether this is the "gift" of life,[26] the normative basis for communicative rationality,[27] or even just some mysterious 'Factor X' that makes humans human.[28] Proponents of enhancement are often no better, though—their arguments typically rely on arguing that enhancement will retain all the comforting and familiar human elements, but just improve them without significantly altering them.[29] That enhancement and augmentation may lead to a phase transition in the nature of humanity rarely occurs to the proponents. This debate has religious resonances insofar as the advocates maintain that some soul-like aspect will transcend our fleshy origins, and the opponents maintain that some human essence must be kept. Both rely on a religious division between the essence of the human and its physical embodiment. By contrast, the concept of the body without organs flattens this dualism, with the mind merely expressing some of the capacities in the body. Changing the body therefore means changing the capacities which means changing the "human."

What is needed is a non-religious form of experimentation—a rejection of the idea of perfection, a rejection of any belief in transcendence, and a rejection of immortality dreams as unmitigated ethical goods.[30] As Braden Allenby and Daniel Sarewitz remind us, "the history of our species is the history of redesigning ourselves, of fuzzing the boundaries of our inner and outer worlds."[31] In an age where technology increasingly permeates everyday phenomenology, and science increasingly impinges on our innermost existence, the question of redesigning ourselves becomes more and more significant.

The Body with Auxiliary Organs

In light of what has been argued here, the classical idea of the body as the locus of human thought is no longer capable of being sustained, nor is the idea that social media is some retreat from the "real world." The ethics appropriate to such an emerging age of sociotechnical blurring needs to reject both a presupposition of enclosed individuality and reject a presupposition of some innate human quality. Among materialist thinkers, Deleuze and Guattari's work offers the best conceptual resources for thinking through what sort of ethics might emerge from a post-human shift. Their manual/manifesto for such an ethics takes shape in the essay "How Do You Make Yourself a Body without Organs?" The body without organs (BwO) is the virtual aspect of every actualized entity. It is the possibility space set out by the capacity for the entity to vary and be transformed—it is the preindividual excess at the heart of every individuated entity.[32] "The BwO is what remains when you take everything away. What you take away is precisely the phantasy, and signifiances and subjectifications as a whole."[33] The BwO is the body without individuation; it is a set of pure capacities for variation which reveals that the figure of the human is always already becoming-other. As Gilbert Simondon argues, there is no essence to the human—it is rather a psychosocial individualization that prolongs the already ongoing vital individualization of an organic body. Psychosocial individuation responds creatively to the problems faced by the body within its environment.[34] This also clarifies the relation of the BwO to Freud's epigraph on "auxiliary organs"—the latter seems to oppose the former, insofar as Freud praises auxiliary organs whereas Deleuze and Guattari appear to argue against organs. Yet in fact "the BwO is not at all the opposite of the organs. The organs are not its enemy. The enemy is the organism."[35] Freud's auxiliary organs are therefore not in contradiction with the BwO. In fact, the auxiliary organs are an exemplary means to construct the BwO precisely because they allow the body to experiment, to vary, to construct, to adapt, and to develop. Technological enhancement via auxiliary organs accentuates the normative goal of experimenting with the organism. Ultimately, this is what the BwO is about: the liberty to experiment and resist oppressive mechanisms of individuation. More specifically, what is required is a form of accelerationism: a project of self-transformation which aims to unbind any and all necessities in life with the goal of transforming them into malleable tools that let us construct further means for generating freedom. Beyond just the Deleuzo-Guattarian project of taking apart organisms, bodies, and identities, this form of accelerationism aims to actively construct freedoms—employing technology and reason in order to transform and surpass physical, biological, economic, and political necessities. Experimentation here is marshaled in the name of constructing freedom.[36]

We must be careful here though. Too often, commentators on the BwO have taken this normative imperative to experiment as arising directly from the ontological claim.[37] Such a reading, however, relies on the mistaken transference of an ontological description into a normative necessity, when in fact ontology cannot dictate such normative ends. Yet what the body without organs does reveal is that the essence of the human is not to be found in any actualized attributes. In relation to the literature on human enhancement, the concept of the BwO reveals that the primary ethical questions over human enhancement are mistaken insofar as they hinge on the question of whether "the human" as some set of specified traits should be advanced or whether the human should instead be conservatively maintained. The important questions are not about resistance or expansion—they are about experimentation, but experimentation as a political practice, not an ontological necessity.

One can see in Deleuze and Guattari's own work this eventual recognition that ontological deterritorialization was not sufficient for valorizing deterritorialization as an ethics. The shift from *Anti-Oedipus* to *A Thousand Plateaus* was precisely the shift away from reading ethics off from ontology. From the championing of unbinding every unity (the body, the organism, the community, the state, etc.), Deleuze and Guattari would take a much more cautious approach in their later works.[38] While the BwO describes a particular ontological condition, there are nevertheless different means to constructing a BwO (which is equivalent to de-constructing an individuated entity). The risk is that some means of constructing the BwO are dangerous in that they threaten to destroy the very basis of the BwO (turning into what Deleuze and Guattari call a suicidal BwO which eliminates the basic supports for experimentation). In their words, "You have to keep enough of the organism for it to reform each dawn; and you have to keep small supplies of significance and subjectification, if only to turn them against their own systems when the circumstances demand it, when things, persons, even situations, force you to."[39] Their call is for experimentation, but experimentation that recognizes the limits of unbinding and deterritorialization—neither too quick nor too severe—but always with an aim at destratifying and removing constraints. As Deleuze writes, it is always the case that "politics is active experimentation, since we do not know in advance which way a line [of flight] will turn."[40] With regard to technological augmentations the ethical imperative is therefore to experiment, to create, and to explore the possibility spaces opened up by technological prostheses like the app/phone platform. This is in contrast to those who would simply aim to conserve a human nature and decry the progressive shift of society into technological media. It is also in contrast to those who think that technology can simply accentuate existing human capacities without drastically changing us in the process. Instead it is about exploring what it *could* mean to be human. It is necessarily about ruthlessly taking various necessities that impose themselves upon us (physical, biological, cognitive, etc.) and employing technology to free ourselves from these. Artists, designers, and creators will move beyond the profit-oriented logics of the market in order to uncover the disruptive potentials of these new sociotechnical assemblages. What should be supported and encouraged is the creation of new ways of interacting and experiencing that these extending technologies can make possible. This imperative needs to elude any remnants of comforting human conceits—the future portends a radically different idea of the human, and artists can indeed be the first to work this out and accentuate the disruptiveness.[41] The phone platform today forms the basis for these extended human abilities, but the future promises tablet platforms, augmented reality glasses, heads-up displays in contact lenses, interactive projections, and eventually biologically embedded technology. We may know not what a body can do, but with the ability to change cognition and experience via these new technologies there is an increasing scope for us to explore precisely what the human assemblage can do.

Acknowledgment

Thanks to Alex Williams for comments on an earlier draft of the essay.

Notes

1. Sigmund Freud, *Civilization and Its Discontents* (Norton, 1989), 42.

2. It remains to be seen if augmented reality glasses will become the primary material means in the near future; though the analysis here will hold for them as well.

3. For a popular account of the material infrastructure of the Internet itself, see Andrew Blum, *Tubes: A Journey to the Center of the Internet* (HarperCollins, 2012).

4. "Global Mobile Statistics 2012" (http://mobithinking.com).

5. Ibid.

6. Thanks to Benedict Singleton for this point.

7. Annabelle Gawer, "Platforms, markets and innovation: An introduction," in *Platforms, Markets and Innovation*, ed. A. Gawer (Elgar, 2009), 2.

8. Carliss Baldwin and C. Jason Woodard, "The architecture of platforms: A unified view," in *Platforms, Markets and Innovation*, ed. A. Gawer (Elgar, 2009), 26.

9. Thanks to Alex Williams for this point.

10. Perhaps the best fictional treatment of this future is Charles Stross' *Accelerando* (Orbit, 2005), which presents an accelerationist techno-fantasy world, with minds increasingly shaped and devoured by their surrounding app interfaces.

11. Rachel Metz, "Augmented reality is finally getting real," August 2, 2012 (http://www.technologyreview.com).

12. Moustafa Alzantot and Moustafa Youssef, "CrowdInside: Automatic construction of indoor floorplans," September 17, 2012 (http://arxiv.org/abs/1209.3794).

13. Marshall McLuhan, *Understanding Media: The Extensions of Man* (MIT Press, 1994).

14. Ibid., 9.

15. Edwin Hutchins, *Cognition in the Wild* (MIT Press, 1995).

16. Andy Clark and David Chalmers, "The extended mind," in Clark, *Supersizing the Mind* (Oxford University Press, 2008).

17. Richard Menary, "Introduction: The extended mind in focus," in *The Extended Mind*, ed. R. Menary (MIT Press, 2010), 21.

18. John Sutton, "Exograms and interdisciplinarity: History, the extended mind, and the civilizing process," in *The Extended Mind*, ed. Menary, 205.

19. It always needs to be recalled that the capacity for rational thought is causally reducible to the body (though not logically reducible). This formulation is James O'Shea's in *Wilfrid Sellars: Naturalism with a Normative Turn* (Polity, 2007).

20. Ray Brassier, "The view from nowhere: Sellars, Habermas, Metzinger," *Identities* 8 (2011), no. 2: 7–23, at 13.

21. Thomas Metzinger, *The Ego Tunnel: The Science of the Mind and the Myth of the Self* (Basic Books, 2009), 104–105.

22. Ibid., 78–79.

23. Ibid., 167.

24. McLuhan, *Understanding Media*, 125.

25. Ian Bogost, "The cigarette of this century," June 6, 2012 (http://www.theatlantic.com).

26. Michael Sandel, *The Case Against Perfection: Ethics in the Age of Genetic Engineering* (Belknap, 2007).

27. Jürgen Habermas, *The Future of Human Nature* (Polity, 2003).

28. Francis Fukuyama, *Our Posthuman Future: Consequences of the Biotechnology Revolution* (Profile Books, 2003).

29. John Harris, *Enhancing Evolution: The Ethical Case for Making Better People* (Princeton University Press, 2007); Julian Savulescu and Nick Bostrom, *Human Enhancement* (Oxford University Press, 2010).

30. For evidence of techno-utopianism's historically religious basis, see David Noble, *The Religion of Technology: The Divinity of Man and the Spirit of Invention* (Penguin, 1999); Steve Fuller, *Humanity 2.0: What It Means to Be Human Past, Present and Future* (Palgrave Macmillan, 2011).

31. Braden Allenby and Daniel Sarewitz, *The Techno-Human Condition* (MIT Press, 2011), 16.

32. Here we follow Manuel DeLanda's reading of Deleuze's work as an ontology of complexity theory. See DeLanda, *Intensive Science and Virtual Philosophy* (Continuum, 2012).

33. Gilles Deleuze and Felix Guattari, *A Thousand Plateaus*, 151.

34. Muriel Combes, *Gilbert Simondon and the Philosophy of the Transindividual*, 28.

35. Gilles Deleuze and Felix Guattari, *A Thousand Plateaus* (University of Minnesota Press, 1987), 158.

36. Thanks to Benedict Singleton and Alex Williams for conversations that developed these points.

37. The literature on enhancement also tends to remain bound to a judgment of enhancement from the perspective of the liberal individual. While the BwO risks suggesting this as well, it must crucially be recalled that the BwO operates at a preindividuated level. It cannot be adopted by any liberal paradigm without doing severe violence to the concept.

38. Though for a critique that laments this shift, see Nick Land, *Fanged Noumena: Collected Writings 1987–2007*, ed. R. Mackay and R. Brassier (Urbanomic, 2011).

39. Deleuze and Guattari, *A Thousand Plateaus*, 160.

40. Gilles Deleuze and Claire Parnet, *Dialogues II* (Columbia University Press, 2007), 137.

41. This also happens to be McLuhan's position on the artist—that figure which is the first to discern the social ripples of a newly emergent technology. See *Understanding Media*, 18.

7

Must We Burn Virilio?
The App and the Human System

Dock Currie

Perhaps unwisely, the brain is subcontracting many of its core functions, creating a series of branch economies that may one day amalgamate and mount a management buy-out.

—J. G. Ballard, "Project for a Glossary of the Twentieth Century"

All these psycho-dramaturges of body-art, body-alteration, body-modification (with biurgy and the plastic surgeons of the genome waiting in the wings) are introverts: they set out their own body as a narcissistic territory and strive to exhaust its possibilities, with no other project than this pathetic, clownish inventory.

—Jean Baudrillard, *Cool Memories IV*

By the time soft-engineering slithers out of its box into yours, human security is lurching into crisis. Cloning, lateral genodata transfer, transversal replication, and cyberotics, flood in amongst a relapse onto bacterial sex.
Neo-China arrives from the future. . . . Nothing human makes it out of the near-future.

—Nick Land, *Meltdown*

The app is not a program; it is a hulking wound in our nervous system, and it is the synthetic flesh that grows in its place, and it is crawling. This piece highlights a kind of *traverse* of the app that ought to be of concern as much to contemporary ontologists as to philosophers of technology. That is, with the advent of mobile technology, we have seen, in our lifetimes, the locus of technology's *macht* shift from the sedentary body of the *desktop computer* user to the nomadic body of the networked subject. Indeed, because this shift entails a movement inwards, in toward the body, this traverse can be seen, therefore, as a kind of encroachment. Paul Virilio refers to this movement, this encroachment, as an "endocolonization"[1]—that is, not the extensive colonization of terrestrial space but rather the intensive colonization of the body proper. We used to come to it, sit down, bang out words, the endless buzz of your 28k modem, MSN Classic, MSN 2.0, AOL, "You've got mail," ICQ—literally, I seek you, I sit down, I log on, I seek you—now they come to you, now it comes to you. The app is the history of this introversion, the history of this endocolonization, it traces not the development of software but the traverse, the crawl, the collapse of distance. The figure of our age is the "if-he-were-a-young-man" Bokonon watching his arms being consumed by Ice-nine, "grinning horribly and thumbing his nose at you know who."[2]

We have had a computer with a graphic user interface since 1983, we have had a computer with a desktop—the abstract representation of "where you work"—since 1983. Until now these things were synonymous. Apple's Lisa was a commercial failure, but the Apple picked up the pieces with the Macintosh and we have been part and parcel of Vannevar Bush's Memex "world of desks" ever since. Now Microsoft is hell bent on killing the desktop, sending it the way of DOS, making it one of the strange vestigial anecdotes of computing technology, the way tech-heads laugh about the keyboard on PCjr, Apple Newtons, the way their 486s rattled like a jet engine, and the inscrutable Microsoft Bob. Microsoft proposes in its stead, ostensibly, an environment of all apps, an app field: Metro, the visual constellation of the tablet. But the erasure of the desktop, as the basis of our comportment toward mobile devices—and hence as the basis of our comportment toward computing generally—is not merely different, new, a progression, but is rather requisite for and endemic of the traverse. The desktop is itself the last bastion of an outmoded comportment, an outmoded signifier, literally the desk, down, out there. The app is in here, in the blood, in the head, ping-body, third arms, biopunks, Eduardo Kac, Dave Asprey, Stelarc—the community of biohackers are on the warpath and they will not settle for anything less than prosthetic ubiquity: the radical sublimation of man by technology. As Arthur Kroker writes, "when the digital eye blinks for the very first time, when the augmented iris is streamed, networked, and vectored, an indispensable ethical preparation has already taken place, namely a prior human willingness to identify itself with its technological future with sufficient intensity to override any remaining (human) quibbles concerning . . . what's lost with the coming-to-be of the fully realized universe of augmented reality."[3]

The app is the harbinger of every kind of invasion, war machines handheld, ocular, cellular, genetic. Every function that an app performs is an instance of what Kroker calls "vampire metaphysics,"[4] from Yelp to Google Maps our architectural desire-lines are reduced to a series of nodal sites, from Camera+ to Instagram our aesthetic field is mediated by a five inch screen, from Boxcar to Teuxdeux our social systems have been irrevocably codified as a determinate set of messages and notifications. You want to do something? There's an app for that.

In drawing out the means and ends of the traverse, the app and its crawl, in delimiting what comprises it and where it is taking us, Paul Virilio warns us in no uncertain terms of a figure so isolated and narcissistic that it can only termed "planet-man."[5] This anthropocosmically insular being—for whom connection to the earth, its circulations and systems, is no longer sufficient— is so wholly enamored with the immanence of the app, and has so thoroughly acquiesced to the logic of the traverse, who has been so wholeheartedly swept up by an ontological horizon of the pure sign of technology (technological/ metaphysical enframing) and ontic endocolonization by machines, that he is, as Virilio writes, "no longer aware of any expanse at all."[6] Indeed, Virilio, in locating his figurative "planet-man," is especially critical of the work of the performance artist Stelarc, a Cypriot Australian for whom the mantra "the body is obsolete" has structured the breadth and nature of his performances and works. Stelarc acknowledges the rapid acceleration of contemporary tele-technological society, but rather than believing with Virilio that contemporary tele-technological society ought to range to the cognitive and physical limits of the body, Stelarc's performative work gestures toward how the cognitive and physical limits of the body—its "biological inadequacy"[7]—might be surpassed in the body's drawing in and utilizing the technical mediation which would otherwise render it obsolete. Through a series of performances in which he variously has had a prosthetic third arm—industrial and machinic— attached, a cell-cultivated ear sown into his arm, and had nascent and cutting-edge electronic connections made to his nervous-system, Stelarc professes to be a proponent of the technical extension of the body—this is what he professes, but this is not what he is. Rather Stelarc's project is to design ways that technical extensions may eventually comprise the body itself, entirely replacing and making redundant the fleshy configurations of "man" that can, by his reckoning, no longer keep up with the technics to which they have given rise. This is the *telos* of the app, subcontracting agency to technologies that purport to fill an already existent need, all the while acquiescing to take on the needs it generates itself as our own, as originary and intransient. As Stelarc notes,

> In the technological terrain, technologies, discourse, the body, all of these elements of interactivity are speeded-up, the "feedback loops" become increasingly invisible because they become increasingly immediate and subliminal . . . to the point where we may have to consider the moment in time where we realize that an ergonomic approach to designing technology to match the body becomes superseded by the necessity to redesign the body to match its machines: creating more effective inputs and outputs and interfaces with these new technologies.[8]

Today we contemplate the lack of an app capable of addressing a specific human need, tomorrow we will contemplate the lack of a human capable of addressing a specific need of the app—the Latin *applicationem*, a joining or attaching oneself to. "Stelarc is not responsible for this, he is a victim of the situation," as Virilio notes, "he believes himself to be a beneficiary of this vision, but what he really is, is a prophet of doom."[9] And in so painting Stelarc as a naive and hapless conjuror of the planet-man, Virilio therefore would have us understand the ontological and philosophical terrain of Stelarc's rejection of the body as an invasive and dangerous frontier, and Stelarc himself as deluded, narcissistic, and nihilating. Stelarc as the vanguard of a kind of app-being: a bionautical lemming, venturing to the ends of the traverse, traversing to the end of venturing.

The fundamental issue is the withering away of physical distances, or more appropriately the atrophy of meaning within "distance"—having been subjected to the relative instantaneity of contemporary tele-technological figurations, the traverse of the app to the body and its inevitable implication in the drone flesh of the biopunk *telos*. As Virilio writes,

> Like some gigantic implosion, the circulation of the general accident of communication technologies is building up and spreading, forcing all substances to keep moving in order to interact globally, at the risk of being wiped out, being swallowed up completely . . . we have closed the door behind us thanks to the rapidity of interactivity, and we will build from within the perspective of an earth that is too small.[10, 11]

So, too big (and too fast) for our geographical britches, then, the "difference" between locations becomes ostensibly immaterial. The value of distinct locations as other places, is emptied out—as Virilio writes, "these places will all equal nothing,"[12] as though they were simply different paintings on the walls of—ultimately—the same room. The notion of compression, therefore, implies an air of relevance for not only the logistical and technological acceleration of transmissions and the visual colonization inherent in the traverse, the crawl, but also for what is historically within our field of perception: what is present to us and what is not. It is the latter—that which is gracefully and considerately not present to us—which Virilio would have us understand to be in increasingly short supply, i.e., the "confinement under an open sky,"[13] as Sylvère Lotringer puts it, concerns not only the political and architectural realities of "globalization [as/at] the speed of light"[14] but moreover concerns the growing inability to liberate oneself from the instantaneous presence of everything; concerns our growing inability to hide. When was the last time you checked your Samsung, your Linked-In, your Facebook, your MySpace?

And yeah, I know you don't use MySpace anymore, but what about your band's account? Why haven't you checked in on Foursquare?

This claustrophobic immediacy—"a type of general arrival in which everything arrives so quickly that departure becomes unnecessary" (what Virilio refers to as absolute "dromospheric pressure").[15] As Adrian MacKenzie writes, "in [Virilio's] view, speed induces a kind of stasis. . . . Instantaneity, or general arrival, obviates real movement."[16] Or rather the appreciable difference between two sites is inversely proportional to the velocity of travel between two sites, insofar as the compression of distance belies a contraction or collapse of difference. Indeed, where Deleuze locates the event as being a fold, a differentiator of difference, Virilio's differentiating of difference is more appropriately located in the folds inherent to the space itself. It depends on our distances being, put simply, fundamentally and intrinsically distant. To appreciate our distances as distances depends, in other words, on the difference as difference inherent to their being, among other things, experienced as neither geographically nor architecturally the same. That said, to forget the essential difference inherent to difference does not simply result in the dissolution of space, but rather the dissolution of both space, as it occurs with or without us, and time as well. As Virilio writes, "such an end implies forgetting spatial exteriority as much as temporal exteriority ('no future') and opting exclusively for the 'present' instant, the real instant of instantaneous telecommunications."[17]

The app is the ceremonial codification of this instantaneity. The fact that we today hold it, literally, at arm's length will be historically regarded as a very quaint and indeed exceptionally brief last drag of a much longer traverse. That is, the app represents technology's becoming, as Michael Hardt and Antonio Negri write, "ever more 'democratic,' ever more immanent to the social field, distributed throughout the brains and bodies of the citizens."[18] Microsoft's Metro, following Apple, demonstrates that the broader market of computing is now being largely informed by the needs and desires of mobile technology, whereas the desktop, like the desk, was something one could walk away from, the app is not. Where would one walk? It would have to be quite far to get less than four bars on your iPhone, at least if you are on the big three.[19]

Indeed this emptying out of the meaning of movement has very real effects for our ability to be with each other—and the possibility of an "other" at all—in a contemporary tele-technological society. To quote Bernard Stiegler:

> [W]hat becomes of the exterior milieu with the advent of modern technics, when the equipment of ethnic groups, the "membrane" within which they form their unity, acquires performances such that each group finds itself in constant com-

munication with the quasi-totality of the others without delay or limits in distance? What happens when there is no longer any exterior milieu as such, so-called
"physical" geography being saturated with human penetrations, that is, technical
ones, and the principle relations of interior to exterior milieus being mediated by
a technical system having no "natural" remainder in its wake.[20]

Indeed, what Stiegler here calls the "quasi-totality" of our all possible
individuals and milieus finds itself as the sole delineated system—the
destruction of distance having eliminated the possibility for regional ontology whatsoever—and contributes to the withering away of particular uni-
ties, as determined by the form or constitutive makeup of their particular
"membrane." In other words, the technical mediation of the difference in
both spatial and temporal expanse has the effect inhibiting or negating any
possible reconfiguration of vantage; that is, the colloquial notion of "seeing
things from a different perspective" is here foreclosed and circumscribed
by the impossibility of ulterior station—"the physiology, origin and end of
our perception of the world"[21]—and, as a result, the dearth of *differing views*
understood literally in the sense of the places from which one might most
essentially view. You do not look work *at* a desk now, you do not work @
anywhere really—"at" is the outmoded content that the app rejects. "In the
costly acceleration towards global power, signifying processes take on a new
function: to mourn the loss of any proper place, any possibility of orientation," as MacKenzie notes, "'mental confusion' regarding locality (temporal
and spatial), and a collapse of the distinction between reality and fiction are
sometimes celebrated, and sometimes lamented by humanists and posthu-
manists alike."[22] You are where your apps are because our apps have become
the locus of creative and organizational power, your apps are where you are
because the appropriation of creative and organizational power demands
the appropriation of the body proper and the installation of a commensurable visual field, devoid of spatial particularity, and their becoming colonized;
as Virilio notes, "the loss or, more precisely, decline of the real space of every
expanse (physical or geographical) to the exclusive advantage of no-delay
real-time teletechnology, inevitably leads to the intraorganic intrusion of
technology and its micromachines into the heart of the living."[23] The app
implies its own fleshy imbrication, how could it not? We are indeed participating in this kind of endocolonization by machines at ever finer registers
of proximity, the ready-to-hand networked smartphone being merely the
intermediary stage in the realization of the app. The app is not concerned
with our movement, as it moves with us, it is only concerned with its movement, the traverse, the crawl, siege warfare, plotting new taxonomies of relation should it succeed in eroding the already threadbare membrane of the

human body. This movement—"[in which] the disorienting experience of speed leads inevitably to a rupture of the living interiority of the body"[24]—is the contentious terrain upon which proponents of such a coming together of man and machine champion the body's having always-already been implicated in the use and utilization of technical objects, while opponents fear the coming to presence and reification of the proto-fascistic war-machine that was gestured toward so lovingly by Marinetti and the Italian Futurists. As Virilio writes, "technology now aspires to occupy the body, to transplant itself within the last remaining territory—that of the body."[25] The app is the movement of this occupation, technology becoming distanceless, evacuating the distance between us, evacuating the distance between us and it, consuming the space between us and its content, our bodies.

Stelarc is in the business of implants and prostheses—"the revolution brought on by all sorts of miniaturization, nanotechnologies, machine-microbes, the machines you can swallow[,] electronic drums, memory stimulators, accelerators,"[26] as Virilio notes—both adding to and subtracting from his body so as to, as far as Stelarc is concerned, highlight possible re-configurations. The result, however, is that his work serves to entrench further (and in fact aestheticize) the organic limits and limitations of the body as such, to dramaturgically advocate for the obsolescence of the body, to propagandize for the complete and unmitigated endo-colonization of the body by technology. He is drafting the constitution of app consciousness, he is negotiating the terms of surrender. In subjecting himself, his (dis)embodied Cartesian whole, to technical mediation, Stelarc seeks to become, as he phrases it, "a genetic sculptor, restructuring and hypersensitizing the human body; an architect of internal body spaces; a primal surgeon, implanting dreams, transplanting desires; an evolutionary alchemist, triggering mutations, transforming the human landscape."[27] Though what he nonetheless becomes, in Virilio's eyes, is the material of yet another sculptor's design, i.e., neither the sculptor nor the architect nor the surgeon nor the alchemist, but rather simply the hubristic victim of—as MacKenzie puts it—that "conjunction of biotechnology and teletechnology [that] reflects a critical phase or discontinuity in the increasing speed of technology."[28] Stelarc is the perfect emissary of the app insofar as he identifies the demands placed upon us by the incessant acceleration of global techno-culture as coextensive with the need to develop further as a species.

In other words, we are not the proto-types, for Stelarc, of the post-humanity he is in the movements of inaugurating. As Sadie Plant notes,

> while the notion that technologies are prostheses, expanding existing organs and fulfilling desires, continues to legitimize vast swathes of technical development,

the digital machines of the late twentieth century are not add-on parts which serve to augment an existing form. . . . Quite beyond their own perceptions and control, bodies are continually engineered by the processes in which they are engaged.[29]

This is why the relatively benign object of the handheld ought to be an object of suspicion—the possibility that their development may see us and our bodies obsolete with respect to them in ways that we yet do not understand.

The point here is that Stelarc's work gestures less toward what the body can do with the mediation of and by technical objects, and more toward what the technical objects can do when not mediated and indeed constrained by the mortal flesh of the body as such. The technics which were our only Promethean gift, in the figurations of Stelarc's manipulations and alterations, serve to obviate the very organism that they were prosthesis to; where Virilio was hoping for the cavalry, Stelarc is ushering in the coup. And, in succumbing to such technical mediation, the body is subjected to precisely the kind of stasis that would otherwise necessitate its prosthetic enhancement. In other words, technical mediation supplants the function of the body and, in so doing, fosters precisely the kind of sedentary being which would require technical mediation. As MacKenzie explains: "implants, endo-corporeal prosthesis and perhaps biotechnology more generally flow for Virilio from the artificially induced immobility of living bodies."[30] Stelarc's pronouncement that the body is obsolete—his "rhetoric about escaping genetic containment"[31]—is based on a kind of obsolescence, therefore, that an acceleration of technological enhancement has itself given rise to. The failure of Stelarc's project is the failure of Theseus's ship, then, insofar as the beings that will one day develop in our stead are not self-same with, nor do they even derive from in any substantive sense, the beings who would otherwise wish to develop. Indeed Stelarc here most essentially wishes to attain "escape velocity" by manifesting, as David Wills notes, "a speed that has the body crashing through into its own unrecognizable or catastrophic otherness."[32]

Stelarc's line of flight, whether he understands or acknowledges it, is the dissolution of any meaningful aspect of humanity in favor of exactly the delimited sphere of things that we are not. As Massumi explains, "Paul Virilio, so obstinately wrong about so many aspects of Stelarc's work, got this one right: Stelarcian suspensions approach the body-as-object in order to 'negate' it."[33] In other words, the modularity of Stelarc's body, his being-modular, is a "thirst for annihilation" in Nick Land's terms, a will to nothingness, the death drive sped up and provided with all the nihilating resources of contemporary technology. Here, again, his semantic Cartesian acrobatics absolutely and unmitigatedly fail: the brain is insufficient to keep up with the technics it has developed—and so must be reconfigured to the point of being unrecognizably distinct—and the body is insufficient for the environments that this new brain might want to meander through and hence is "eviscerated and stuffed"[34] to the point at which any aspect that "was once body" becomes only incidentally figured therein. "The suspended body expresses nothing of need or use, nothing of symbolic or semantic value," as Massumi explains, "as a sensible concept, it is an underdetermined one from the point of view of function and meaning."[35] When articulated properly, and in less Cartesian terms, Stelarc is here an ostensible anti-corporealist, insofar as corporeal form figures as essentially meaningless, incidental as it pertains to the environment that our future selves might take up—whether actual space, wherein, as Dery notes, "immobilized in cybernetic networks and immortalized by means of replacement parts, Stelarc's posthuman teleoperators would reach across the solar systems to sift alien sands through robotic fingers,"[36] or in the virtual space of the app, wherein our existence would be mediated by, and manifest as, forms that otherwise bear absolutely no connection with our corporeal, embodied, fleshy incarnations.

Stelarc himself writes "I am not interested in human states or attitudes or perversions. I am concerned with cosmic, superhuman, extraterrestrial manifestation."[37] His art is, in other words, an attempt to nihilate the embodied subject in favor of the future of wholeheartedly alternate beings—as MacKenzie explains, he "embraces incessant upgrading of technical competence and equipment, and gleefully anticipates the fateful dissolution of existing human orientations"[38]—as though his art were performing a kind of *suicide of the Neanderthals*. And indeed to the extent that we are embodied, corporeal, incarnate beings, Stelarc's project is such that we do not figure thusly in his post-human future. As MacKenzie has it, "the local, including embodied subjects, must then be figured as a remainder, as a residue of whatever has not yet been captured and translated into modern, universal terms."[39] The desktop was an object of human design, its space became cluttered or pedantically organized by the whims of its consumer, its digital analog carried this resonance, the space of the app is almost unfiltered in this respect—what affect could emerge from a direct mediation between need and function? The virtual is a cover story for the disappearance of a spatial buffer between leisure time and work time, the app represents the kind of visual field which lacks a differentiation between work space and any other kind of space, it only acknowledges or respects body-space, the space it aspires to imbricate itself within or consume. As Virilio notes, ominously,

> the technosciences are getting their teeth into a weightless man-planet whom nothing can now really protect, neither ethics nor biopolitical morality. . . . Instead

of escaping from our natural biosphere, we will colonize an infinitely more acces-sible planet—as so often in the past—that of a body-without-a-soul, a profane body, on behalf of a science-without-a-conscience that has never ceased to profane the space of the body of animals and slaves, the colonized of former empires.[40]

The app does not merely superimpose itself upon the visual field, for example, it supplants it: Google Maps does not contribute to the psycho-geography of the city, it becomes the psychogeography of the city. "The ideal sphericity is no longer that of a terrestrial globe," as Virilio writes, "but [rather] that of a virtual sphere expanding and swelling up in all directions (according to all the possible trajectories) so that the real sphere of the full world deflates and decreases lamentably, losing, with its dimensions, its sub-stantial value."[41] This is what Brian Massumi means when he refers to "the self network," in the sense that we realize ourselves to—in gesture of our reduction of everyone and everything to app content—be exhaustive of "what is" and hence begin to region the material that is left in the confla-tion of our physiology, handheld included, with geophysical expanse. "The self-network is a worlding of the human," as Massumi writes, "the moon's limit. Or maybe not. Having counteracted earth's force of gravity, the posthu-man body-world is in its own orbit: the becoming-planetary of the human."[42] This material Massumi would have us understand to be in keeping with the process of individuation in the work of Gilbert Simondon. Or rather, if geo-physical distance and the body as such are indeed collapsed as distinct, it is articulated in Massumi's work as the prefigurement of a further individua-tion, that of the individuation into the space of the virtual. That is, as Mas-sumi writes, "the transformative field of bodily potential is 'preindividual' (or better, 'transindividual')."[43]

But the planet-man, the networked subject, the wielder of the smartphone, is in fact the very exhaustion of the transindividual! Abandoning terrestrial expanse means abandoning its "bodily potential" as well, and in performance of Stelarc's suspensions and his line of flight away from the "obsolete body" he is not only isolating himself from the world, but denying the very medium or substance of transformative potential that he would otherwise like to fos-ter. That is, the terms under which "the body-self has been plugged into an extended network," as Massumi writes, "as fractal subject-object, the body is the network—a self network."[44] Indeed the possibility of a vital individua-tion in the work of Simondon is radically irreconcilable with the unchecked acceleration inherent to a re-individuation of the sort implied by Stelarc and made explicit by Massumi, a breaking down of meaning within space toward the ends of a wholesale replacement of the actual with the virtual. As Simon-don himself writes, "vital individuation would come to filter into physical individuation by suspending its course, by slowing it down, and by rendering it capable of propagation in an 'inceptive state.'"[45] The potential inherent to individuation is a process for Simondon of stepping out of step with the "logics of speed," as they are for Virilio, that determine the ekstasis of the living—in very broad terms—from the non-living. As MacKenzie notes, "the contrast between living and non-living emerges through the delays, or desynchronizing processes that living ensembles unleash in themselves."[46] No delay, real time, the app is the secret entropy of the techno-social assemblage, polar inertia, so fast it evacuates speed.

There must, in other words, be a distinction between, on the one hand, the promethean codetermination of the organism and its technical component, and the replacement of the organism itself by the "will to technology" that their acceleration of technology gives rise to on the other. Stiegler puts it this way:

> There are indeed "catastrophic" effects in the evolution of technical systems, which precisely concern the passage of one system into another (or, following Simondon, the passage from one stage of concretization to another) . . . but this in no way contradicts the continuity hypothesis, which holds that the dynamic of evolution is systematic and therefore permanent, as thinking is for Leibniz, and that no transformation (by borrowing or invention) can take place without ulterior consequences that extend the effects, even if the moments during which these effects are concretized take place suddenly and provoke a brutal reorganization of the technical milieu and, by counterreaction, of the interior milieu.[47]

Indeed, Massumi tips their cards in this respect—to the extent that he and Stelarc are playing the same hand—when he writes that "the obsolescence of the body that Stelarc waxes long on must be produced."[48] Produced? Yes, indeed, produced, not allowed to develop, evolve, determine on its own accord, but rather evinced, constructed, willed into being. Stelarc here figures as the ostensible sorcerer's apprentice, dabbling in a magic that he cannot understand, attempting to provoke a radical rearticulation, the consequences of which he has not the faintest idea. As Stelarc writes, "Virilio calls me 'some kind of techno-Shaman, pseudo-mystical, ecstatic non-thinking, non-rational being . . . he reports that I have a naive view of technology. Now that was the thing I took most umbrage to, because these are ideas that have emanated from interfaces, from direct experiences."[49] He goes on to indeed accuse Virilio of being the one who is naive in the face of technology, but his argument—that because he has "felt" technology through obviously mediated experience that he is in something of a privileged position to speak to these issues is wildly naive and optimistic. Would we trust a junkie, in the throes of a binge, to understand the consequences of more junk were he to make the same argument?

Stelarc would indeed like his work to be taken as, in a sense, apolitical, having no particular political resonance in its being purely scientific, purely experimental—this is wildly unrealistic. Indeed, as Keith Ansell-Pearson writes,

> the collapsing of *bios* and *technos* into each other is not only politically naive, producing a completely reified grand narrative of technology as the true agent and *telos* of natural and (in)human history, but also restricts *technics* to *anthropos*, binding history to anthropocentrism, and overlooks the simple fact that the genesis of the human is not only a technogenesis but equally, and more importantly, a bio-technogenesis.[50]

The destructive, anti-corporeal, extrotopian-come-endotopian bent that both Stelarc and Massumi have placed themselves on—that is, "escape velocity" as the telos of the isolated and narcissistic "planet man"—forgets this "simple fact" and celebrates not our relation to technics and their being constitutive of our makeup, but rather our being surpassed by technics and our becoming irrelevant in the face of their development. Virilio, much to the protest of techno-centric escapists like Stelarc and Massumi, is no mere conservative reactionary. Rather, Virilio is only conservative to the extent that he would ultimately prefer to conserve some embodied, corporeal form that springs from the *bios* of humanity in some originary sense beyond the mere fact of technics being one aspect thereof; he is only reactionary to the extent that he sees, better perhaps than do Stelarc and Massumi, that in the stripping these otherwise extraneous aspects from the constitution of the beings who are to come, we figure only as remainder—nothing is left of "the human" in the line of flight that Stelarc gives rise to. The app crawls toward human cognition to occupy it, to change the standard by which cognition matters, not so much delete it as demonstrate it to be superfluous with respect to the standard it sets. Burying inwards from our Blackberrys and Samsungs, the app does not mean to be so much parasitic as parasitoid. It does not, in other words, approach its host that they might consume together—para-sitos—it approaches its host with a view to its own survival and, at best, an indifference toward the survival of the host.

The fulcrum upon which *bios* and *techne* pivot has shifted from the literal and digital desktop to the spaceless instantaneity of mobile technology, the app its hieroglyph—this is more than simply the mobile screen, rather the immobile subject, always located in application: the locus computing power seemed to have shifted outwards, out into the street, out onto the laptops on the trains, it looked like it was radiating outwards but it wasn't, it's not, it's collapsing, it's imploding inwards. Sabine Gruffatt writes, incisively, that "this is the tendency of an app—or mobile media in general—toward a spatio-temporal totalitarianism"[51] but it is more than this—it is not spatio-temporal totalitarianism it's a totalitarianism which banishes the spatio-temporal, its belief or practice being unlawful. The app attaches itself and migrates ever inwards as contemporary technology allows for, it deletes the space between you and your application, and hence deletes the time as well. Consumers are reduced to users, users to nodal operators, nodal operators to nodes, knowledge of duration supplanted with mastery of instantaneity, the app registers proficiency at relay as merit—re-post, share, re-tweet, re-ply. Our "obsolete bodies" are called upon merely to provide the brute gray matter of their otherwise circuit-borne assemblages. The app is only a program if we're the hardware.

Notes

1. Paul Virilio, *Negative Horizon: An Essay in Dromoscopy* (Continuum, 2005), 58.

2. Kurt Vonnegut, *Cat's Cradle* (Dial, 2010), 287.

3. Arthur Kroker, "Three theses on Virilio now," in *Virilio Now: Current Perspective in Virilio Studies*, ed. John Armitage (Polity, 2011), 172.

4. Arthur Kroker, *The Will to Technology and The Culture of Nihilism: Heidegger, Nietzsche, Marx* (University of Toronto Press, 2004), 49.

5. Paul Virilio, *City of Panic* (Berg, 2005), 122.

6. Paul Virilio, *Politics of the Very Worst* (Semiotext(e), 1999), 43.

7. Stelarc, "Extended-body: An interview with Stelarc," in Arthur and Marilouise Kroker, *Digital Delirium* (St. Martin's Press, 1997), 197.

8. Stelarc, in Ross Farnell, "In dialogue with 'posthuman' bodies: Interview with Stelarc," in *Body Modification*, ed. Mike Featherstone (Sage, 2003), 139.

9. Paul Virilio in Virginia Madsen, "Critical mass (an interview with Paul Virilio)," *World Art* 1 (1995): 80.

10. Paul Virilio, *Open Sky* (Verso, 1997), 71.

11. Paul Virilio and Sylvère Lotringer, *Crepuscular Dawn* (Semiotext(e), 2002), 89.

12. Ibid., 63.

13. Ibid., 75.

14. Paul Virilio, *Virilio Live: Selected Interviews*, ed. John Armitage (Sage, 2001), 197.

15. Virilio and Lotringer, *Crepuscular Dawn*, 73.

16. Adrian MacKenzie, *Transductions: Bodies and Machines at Speed* (Continuum, 2002), 120.

17. Virilio, *Open Sky*, 24–25.

18. Michael Hardt and Antonio Negri, *Empire* (Harvard University Press, 2000), 23.

19. "Three corporations (Rogers Wireless, Bell Mobility and Telus Mobility) share over 94 percent of Canada's wireless market, and two dominate the Internet service provider market (Rogers and Bell)." Roberto De Vogli, *Progress or Collapse: The Crises of Market Greed* (Routledge, 2013), 155.

20. Bernard Steigler, *Technics and Time, 1: The Fault of Epimetheus* (Stanford University Press, 1998), 64–65.

21. "Critical mass," 80.

22. MacKenzie, *Transductions*, 66.

23. Paul Virilio, *Art of the Motor* (University of Minnesota Press, 1995), 100.

24. MacKenzie, *Transductions*, 121.

25. Paul Virilio, in Nicholas Zurbrugg, "'A Century of Hyper-Violence': Paul Virilio: An Interview," *Economy and Society* 25 (1996): 111–126, at 121.

26. "Critical mass," 81.

27. Stelarc, "Obsolete Body/Suspensions," in *Stelarc*, ed. J. D. Paffrath (JB Publications, 1984), 76.

28. MacKenzie, *Transductions*, 119.

29. Sadie Plant, *Zeroes + Ones: Digital Women + The New Technoculture* (Fourth Estate, 1998), 182.

30. MacKenzie, *Transductions*, 121.

31. Jane Goodall, "An order of pure decision: Un-natural selection in the work of Stelarc and Orlan," in *Body Modification*, ed. Mike Featherstone (Sage, 2003), 166.

32. David Wills, "Techneology or the discourse of speed," in *The Prosthetic Impulse: From a Posthuman Present to a Biocultural Future*, ed. Marquard Smith and Joanne Morra (MIT Press, 2006), 247.

33. Brian Massumi, *Parables for the Virtual: Movement, Affect, Sensation* (Duke University Press, 2002), 103.

34. Mark Dery, *Escape Velocity: Cyberculture at the End of the Century* (Grove, 1996), 162.

35. Ibid., 104.

36. Dery, *Escape Velocity*, 163.

37. Stelarc, in C. Carr, *On Edge: Performance at the End of the Twentieth Century*, revised edition (Wesleyan University Press, 2008), 11.

38. MacKenzie, *Transductions*, 121.

39. Ibid., 64.

40. Virilio, *The Art of the Motor*, 113–114.

41. Virilio, *The Virilio Reader*, 127.

42. Massumi, *Parables for the Virtual*, 128.

43. Ibid., 120–121.

44. Ibid., 127.

45. Gilbert Simondon, in MacKenzie, *Transductions*, 27.

46. MacKenzie, *Transductions*, 27.

47. Stiegler, *Technics and Time*, 64.

48. Massumi, *Parables for the Virtual*, 108.

49. Stelarc, "In dialogue with 'posthuman' bodies," 142.

50. Keith Ansell-Pearson, *Deleuze and Philosophy: The Difference Engineer* (Routledge, 1997), 182.

51. Sabine Gruffat, "Arduino-based Video Synth: An open source interface," *Journal of the New Media Caucus* 7 (2011), no. 2.

8
The App as an Extension of Man's Desires

Eric Kluitenberg

Imagine media with Gigabytes of imagination, instead of memory!
—from Peter Blegvad's stage play *On Imaginary Media*[1]

For all the practical purposes the multitude of apps available in the market-place and the commons can be seen fit for, there is yet something deeply phantasmatic about the app universe: a promise of new possibilities beyond the limitations of "life before the app." The use of the term became widely adopted after the introduction of Apple's iPhone and its software distribution point called the App Store. In contrast with "software" (a detached, level-headed, pragmatic designation for a work-related tool, usually statically located on a writing table in an office or a study), this snappy three-letter word indicates the portable Turing Machine that transforms the wireless communication devices we carry around with us everywhere into a seemingly endless variety of other media and tools.

Given the exponential success of these mobile devices and the continuous expansion of the "app universe" on what is ever more closely approximating a global scale, it seems justified to ask how it is able to hold millions of people under its spell. How do these media technologies inspire citizens to become consumers? What is the value investment that people make into these technologies, not just in monetary terms, but also in terms of their expectation of how these technologies will enrich their lives? If this question already seemed strangely elusive when considering the various lineages and rapid successions of media apparatuses, it becomes even more intractable when considering the immaterial life span of the app (which is generally short-lived but nonetheless often exuberant).

To account for the phenomenal expansion of the app universe, I suggest we need to shift attention beyond the practical purposes that many apps are undoubtedly useful for. The momentous shifts that happened and are ongoing in the media and cultural industries after the introduction of the new range of mobile media devices (smartphones, tablets, and portable media players) are only partly grounded in their ability to deliver practical solutions for mundane consumerist demands. A second and more ephemeral quality assumes a constitutive role for the success of apps: their ability to project imaginary solutions for potentially unattainable aspirations, which more often than not are of a transcendental nature. Shifting our attention to these ephemeral qualities can be highly elucidating for the puzzling state of affairs in the app universe. I will do so here by drawing on my ongoing research into what I have previously termed *imaginary media*.

An Archaeology of Imaginary Media

Imaginary media are machines that mediate impossible desires. This succinct formula opens up an unexpectedly complex field of signification. The exploration of this field started for me in private conversations with Finnish media archeologist Erkki Huhtamo as early as 1999, which continued and broadened in the next five years leading up to a series of public events staged in 2004 at De Balie (a center for culture and politics in Amsterdam) under the heading "An Archaeology of Imaginary Media."[2] The project started as a suggestion to various proponents of the emerging field of study called *media archeology*—most notable at that time Erkki Huhtamo and Siegfried Zielinski—to shift attention in these "archaeological" explorations, temporarily at least, away from the media apparatuses and toward the imaginaries that were constructed around and ascribed to these apparatuses: the visions and dreams, the propaganda, the nightmares and obsessions, the desires and ecstasies. For this project, we decided to narrow our focus to communication apparatuses (understood in the widest sense) and direct our attention to the quest for the ultimate communication medium. This helped us to draw a boundary with all sorts of other imaginary machines that might perhaps be equally fascinating, but would lead us too far from the human motive of seeking connection to the other, which seemed pertinent to us.[3]

As the project developed, we noted a persistent recurring aspiration toward the unattainable in emerging media genres, a desire to overcome the separation of ordinary life from this aspired but unattainable mode of being (hence an impossible desire), and the projection of this desire onto evolving generation of media apparatuses (hardware and software). The following years of a succession of disastrous economic, financial, and technological failures: the crash of the "Asian Tiger" economies (1997–1999) that transformed Kevin Kelly's infamous analysis of the "Long Boom"[4] into the "Long Bust" (which, in retrospect, can be seen to continue to 2013); the dot com crash and implosion of Nasdaq in

March 2000; the failure of the New Economy ideology (the idea that economic growth cycles would extend endlessly because of continued technological innovation); and finally the European TelCom Crash (2002) which threatened to liquidate some of the most established national telecommunications companies in Europe[5] over exaggerated and unrealistic biddings on UMTS (3G) frequencies that were simply impossible to recoup from future 3G services. One would expect that after such an impressive catalog of failures the investment of belief (and money) would be somewhat tempered. However, we noticed only a temporary relapse of material and imaginative investment in the media machine, soon to be replaced by the next wave of excitement instigated by a new generation of media technology. This left us with the question of how to account for these recurrent waves of media frenzy, and the unceasing quest for the ultimate communication medium.

The Failure of the Phantasmatic Spell: A Lacanian Reading

Imaginary media are constructs that emerge in the interplay of what is imagined and what is actualized in media and technological development. Imaginary media can be purely imaginary constructs, non-existent objects or systems, symbolic markers or allegorical representations of substances or processes that are difficult or impossible to capture. Imaginary media can, however, also be actually existing machines. In the latter case the imaginary is not so much in the machine itself as in its signification, in everything that is ascribed to these machines by the subject, the user, the producer, the consumer, the marketer for different (conscious and non-conscious) reasons and purposes. Finally, the actualized machines can have functions, effects, ramifications, or stir up emotions, excitement, anxieties that the designers never intended for them and that could not have been imagined before they came into being.

The driving force for the development of these media, imagined and actualized, is desire, and desire, classically in the Lacanian formula, is predicated on a lack. Whenever this lack can be filled by a purposeful design the desire for its resolution can be seen to fade away quickly as that what was lacking before has now been fulfilled. The most enduring lack is therefore the one that cannot possibly be fulfilled, the lack that remains eternally unattainable. This sensation of a lack, in the Lacanian understanding, emerges out of the unsuccessful attempts of the subject to construct an equivalence between the contradictory emanations of the subject's body's internal apparatuses and drives, the exterior specular images the subject uses to construct a coherent self-image, and the articulations in a pre-existing symbolic system that the subject is born into.[6] Such fragile mechanisms of self-determination indicate the fragmented nature of the subject's sense of coherence and unity, which is continuously torn apart by the ruthless forces of coercion and libidinal compromise to which it is exposed. The fissures and cracks in the self-image and the failed attempts to construct equivalence between the subject's interior (corporeal) and external realities can only be covered over by phantasmatic images, which in the most literal sense hide the frightening reality of the subject's inherent disunity, fragmentation, and alienation. However, such phantasmatic images can only offer a temporary resolve. The sensation of a terrible lack of unity, coherence, and equivalence soon reemerges and sets in motion new futile attempts to steer away from the abyss of absolute existential anxiety. In the Lacanian account perhaps the most illusory image is that of love (the search for unity with the big Other). Any thing or process can become the object of such phantasmatic projections that aim to wash out this dark abyss of existential anxiety. In technologically saturated societies it is no surprise that technological objects become powerful projection surfaces for these phantasmatic images. Imaginary media can thus be seen as phantasmatic machines that displace such impossible (existential) desires.

Following this Lacanian reading, it should be clear that these displacements are always inherently incomplete. Some surplus desire remains, which needs to be fulfilled. It should already be clear that the phantasmatic pursuit of unfulfilled and unattainable desires constitutes a much more powerful motor for the development of new generations and lineages of media machines than the construction of purposeful and practical machines. Imaginary media attach themselves to the deepest existential human desires and anxieties. They displace the fear of solitude, darkness, and death, the separation in distance and time, the limitations and unstoppable decay of the human body, the divisions of class and gender, and the divide between the living and the deceased. Imaginary media populate the universe of dreams: it does not really matter whether the machines are hardware or software, as it does not matter if they are existent or non-existent machines. Further, purely imaginary machines never designed or intended to be realized may still come into existence, sometimes centuries later. Imaginary media blur the dividing lines between the imaginary and the actualized, and reveal the depth of their mutual investment.

The ongoing anArchaeology of imaginary media[7] can be seen then as an invitation to regard media as the extension of human desire, not merely the extension of the physical body, the nervous system, and the brain—the ultimate desire to overcome inherent limitations of human existence by means of technology.[8]

Intermezzo: Inspiration's Turtle

A: What more do you want? The sky's the limit with imaginary media.

B: All right then. . . . I want media that will make everything easy for everybody. That will lift the curse our first parents incurred for their catastrophic lapse in Eden. . .

A: You want media that will make bringing into being effortless?

B: And instant. Inspiration comes so slowly to us mortals, that's why in allegories she's depicted as traveling by turtle.

I want imaginary media that will put skates on Inspiration's turtle.

I want media that will remove all obstacles to the immediate gratification of my every whim.

—from Peter Blegvad's stage play *On Imaginary Media*

Apps as Imaginary Media

To return to our original question, what is it that holds hundreds of millions of people under its spell and can account for the phenomenal expansion of the app universe, we can begin conceiving of an answer by looking at the most obvious promise held out by the apps and the devices on which they run. They promise to make their users more efficient in a variety of daily tasks: professional communication, access to up to date information, logistics, stock taking, note taking, navigation, entertainment, leisure, and (of course) maintaining personal contacts and conducting private conversations. For all of these purposeful tasks a multitude of apps have been developed that offer more or less practical solutions to them. Beyond this obvious usefulness of the devices and their apps, their servile humility, there is one especially important promise that shines through each of these useful tasks: the suggestion that apps (and the devices they run on) offer agency to the individual, that they empower their users to be able to act and produce results in accordance with their private needs and personal intentions. Linking back to the Lacanian reading of imaginary media we can see the apps and their devices as machines that support the subject in its (ultimately futile) attempts to establish some form of equivalence between its own internal contradictory drives and impulses and the exteriorities to which it is exposed. And insofar as apps and mobile devices manage to project the phantasm of individual agency (which is inherently limited and compromised by a variety of material, institutional, and personal limitations), they are able to conjure up for their users the illusion that they have achieved a certain degree of sovereignty in their daily operations.

Here one of the specific peculiarities of the technological fix becomes visible. It cannot be denied that the new generations of mobile wireless devices (smartphones, tablets, media players, e-readers) offer a certain degree of agency to their users, not just in terms of access to a variety of services, greater communicative flexibility, and logistical support, but also in enabling users to "stage themselves," a mediation of self which is the topic of extensive study on its own. However, it is equally easy to see how pressing material, political, economic, and cultural conditions and forms of coercion do not disappear simply because of the introduction of new informational and communicative modalities supported by these devices and their apps. As a result, the phantasmatic projection washing out the apprehension of the actual conditions the user is immersed in, can only offer a temporary resolve for the sensation of a lack of agency. Curiously, it appears time and again that it is easier for the users of these devices and their apps to ascribe this lack of agency to a lack of technological proficiency and features of the devices (and their apps), which are promised to be resolved by the next generation or the next lineage of devices, rather than confronting the material, political, economic, and cultural conditions in which they are immersed.

Building on the insights obtained from the anArchaeology of imaginary media, a number of typologies can be constructed (provided they are suggested and used without any claims to or expectations of finality) that highlight the phantasmatic spell cast by imaginary media in operation. I will focus on two of these typologies in particular and relate them to the app universe: imaginary media/apps as *compensatory apparatuses* and imaginary media/ apps as *machines of transcendence*.

The App as a Compensatory Apparatus

Apps that allow users to live up to familial or professional expectations have been particularly appealing to consumers, as many of us tend to fall short of these expectations. Apps can be successful here if they can address these shortcomings, or be seen by their prospective users to be able to address them. Of particular interest here is the vast category of so-called productivity apps.

Leaving aside the all too obvious critique of productivity apps that they suggest a false ideal of productivity in an always-on real-time economy (where sovereign enjoyment, or simply having more time for the *oikos* might be higher ideals to aspire to), a simple détournement, accomplished by inverting the stated purpose of some of the most familiar categories of these productivity apps, can reveal their (phantasmatic) compensatory function more clearly. Task managers are popular apps, for which an abundant variety of offerings is available. They help you to stay "on top of things," which implies that the prospective user clearly is not "on top of things" before using the app. The value proposition toward the prospective user of the app that it will enable her/him to manage a complex chain of tasks more efficiently indicates a lack of control over assigned tasks, and a lack or failure of oversight and handling of the task load. A simple solution to this problem would be to reduce the task load, but obviously there are pressing reasons why this simple solution cannot be adopted, mostly related to material, economic, and sometimes political constraints. Such forces of coercion and repression clearly indicate a lack of individual agency.

Similarly, scheduling apps provide solutions for keeping track of an overload of appointments and agreements with others (implying social coercion), or simply act as compensatory tools for forgetfulness. Mind mapping apps can be read as compensatory tools for unfocused or poorly structured thought processes. Another popular category are apps that force the user to stop working on their devices, and with their other productivity apps, because without them the user would work ceaselessly at the expense of her or his own mental and physical health. Health apps themselves have become a popular category, purporting to help users retain a healthy condition, but can also be read as sign posts of a compromised health condition in need of compensatory procedures.

In the sphere of leisure the profoundly popular category of gaming apps provides an ample supply of the phantasmatic. Gaming apps figure in both typologies of the imaginary app, that is, as compensatory apparatuses and as (soft) machines of transcendence. As compensatory apparatuses they allow users to excel at activities they are not particularly good at or skilled in, most prominently sports. The sports apps allow the user who might be entirely inept at various forms of physical agility to assume mastery of a variety of sports disciplines. The user can creep into the skins of great contemporary sports heroes or historical figures that still loom larger than life. The compensatory function of the app for that which we lack in life in terms of exceptional skill—in this case, sportive activities, among them playing tennis, soccer, baseball, snowboarding, driving race cars, and riding motorcycles—is clearly evidenced in the sports app.

The App as a Machine of Transcendence

Gaming apps take on a more transcendental quality by allowing users to engage in activities, spheres, and realms that are principally inaccessible in their daily lives: historical scenes, large-scale combat operations, space travel, or immersion in fantasy worlds. More than a compensation for a lack of skill or ability at something that is in principle part of their daily living environment, these games project the phantasm of being able to transcend the inherent limitations of human existence, bridge any distance, defy physical harm and even the threat of death, toss aside the social codex (particularly so in combat games, but the *Carmageddon* games would also figure in this category), or immerse into a universe beyond reason or logical constraints. In short, what these transcendental games afford is the phantasmatic transgression of the constraints that define the life experience of the vast majority of the global population. Hence, its almost universal appeal and its highly profitable value proposition come as little surprise. There are, however, apps that draw on similar (impossible) desires for transcendence of inherent constraints of daily life experience that present themselves as merely practical and functional tools, and can thus be read on both levels: the practical and the existential.

Communication apps are the software apparatuses most close to our original study into imaginary media, which focused on the quest for the ultimate communication medium. Communication apps, such as social network clients, messaging services and related applications perform a clear practical purpose—to distribute messages to a more or less defined and demarcated set of receivers (one or more depending on the channel it operates through). However, focusing exclusively on the information transfer aspect of these applications misses an important set of only partially conscious purposes these apparatuses serve to fill. I have argued previously[9] that these forms of privatized communication are primarily characterized by phatic forms of communication—that is, forms of communication that primarily serve social or emotive purposes, not the transfer of information. The two principal functions that this type of communicative behavior serve are marking presence (especially in quasi-public forums, social networks for instance), and establishing connections in one-to-one or one-to-some communicative exchanges.

Here the abolishment of the threat of privation of social contact and connection should be recognized as the principal motor driving the behavior. Edmund Burke, in *A Philosophical Enquiry into the Origin of Our Ideas of the Sublime and the Beautiful* (1757), already recognized that one of the greatest existential threats is constituted by the "terror of solitude," which is brought about by the privation of social contact. There is "scarcely a terror more powerful" than the terror of solitude, he claims, perhaps only eclipsed by the existential terror of death itself. It is privation of social contact that brings about the existential threat of the terror of solitude, and it is only when the privation of social contact is abolished, when a new connection is established, that this threat is put at bay, at which point the subject is engulfed by a wave of delight. The experience of this delight is what Burke describes as the sublime, one of the most profound existential experiences a human being may have.[10]

For the Twitter-feeder both aspects, the marking of presence and the delight of connection come into play more or less simultaneously. Tweeting marks the existence of the subject within a wider quasi-public context—theoretically anyone can gain access to the feed even if few ever will. Receiving a reply to a tweet or viewing another's tweets reconfirms the connection of the subject to the social world, regardless of whether this construction is imaginary or actual. With the abolishment of privation of social contact the existential threat of solitude is put at bay, at least temporarily, as a result of which the Twitter subject is engulfed with delight.

There is nothing illusory about this communicative exchange. The fact that the exchange is constituted through entirely standardized interfaces supported by formalized (network) protocols does not diminish the actuality of the experience in any way. However, if the experience would be limited exclusively to online exchanges, the fulfillment of the desire for the abolishment of privation of social contact is clearly only partial. Inevitably, some surplus desire for connection remains unfulfilled here (particularly the physical, embodied aspects) that can never be entirely covered over by the phantasmatic image the communication app projects (and thus a market potential for a next generation of apps is automatically created).

Remarkably, despite the strong presence of spiritualist media around 1900, when attempts to establish communication with the "departed" in the "afterlife" by means of new media technologies held a strong public appeal, in the app universe spiritualist apps still seem to be largely absent (disregarding a few rather isolated exceptions such as the Ghost Radar). Given the widespread interest in the "beyond" elsewhere, it would have seemed a self-evident constituent of the app universe. One cannot help but wonder, is this a policy issue of app distribution channels, or rather an as yet unfulfilled market opportunity?

The App as an Oscillator Between the Imaginary and the Realized

Like other media and technologies, the app continuously oscillates between the imaginary and the realized. Both apps and devices serve practical purposes, which are often at least partially fulfilled. However, they attach themselves to other domains as well that remain eternally elusive and unattainable, but that can be highly desirable for the average user. Such impossible desires can only be addressed by imaginary and phantasmatic constructs that cover over the fissure between the desired and the attainable.

The imaginary in apps is not just situated in the stated purposes of the producer of the app or the marketing apparatus that has been built around it (delivering impossible promises), but also resides within the significations that the users ascribe to the app or device. The latter holds true for both prospective as well as actual users. It is only when the frustration engendered by the failure of the medium to deliver on its impossible promise exceeds the power of the phantasmatic spell that the "magic" of the medium (the app or device) is broken for the user and the quest to fulfill the subject's impossible desires moves elsewhere.

The imaginary is a driving force for actual development of apps and media, but a purely phantasmatic solution will not suffice to keep the user under its spell. Rather, it is the delivery of partial solutions by the actualized imaginary apps and media apparatuses that guarantees their continued success. Something is delivered to us, but ultimately fails to satisfy entirely. In our anArchaeology of imaginary media we found this recurrent pattern throughout media and technological history, evidencing to us how much the imagined, the desired, and the actualized feed into and off each other in media and technological development.

My Imaginary App

What do I want from imaginary apps that current apps can't deliver? In Peter Blegvad's brilliant imaginary stage play *On Imaginary Media* the discussion about what the protagonists want from imaginary media that the plethora of existing media supposedly can not deliver, continues:

> *She:*   Tell me, what do you want from imaginary media that current media can't deliver?
> *He:*   I want immersion, initiation. I want to be torn to pieces, reassembled, resurrected, reborn—so that spirit may gain its truth . . .
> *Director (god vox):*   "Spirit gains its truth by finding itself in absolute dismemberment." —Hegel
> *He:*   What do you want from imaginary media that current media can't deliver?
> *She:*   Diderot's advice to painters was . . .
> *Director (god vox):*   "Illuminate your objects according to your own sun, which is not nature's sun. . . ." —Diderot
> *He:*   Ah, so you're an artist?

She: Of course. Everybody is. If extant media haven't established that fact already, imaginary media certainly will! I want imaginary media that will illuminate my objects according to my own sun. And project their reflection upon other minds.

As for me, I want an app that can make me dream, so that inspiration can come to me in my dreams, and "illuminate my mind with a sun, which is not nature's sun" (after Diderot). My dream app is not simply an app that inspires me by offering something "inspiring" to me, but an app that offers me instant inspiration, any time of the day (and night), for any task at hand that requires it, effortlessly!

I want an app that can deliver to me the generalized condition of "inspired-ness"—wake or sleep!

Notes

1. Peter Blegvad, *On Imaginary Media*, an imaginary stage play performed at De Balie, Amsterdam, February 5–7, 2004.

2. Documentation of the event series can be found at www.debalie.nl/archaeology.

3. See Eric Kluitenberg, ed., *Book of Imaginary Media: Excavating the Dream of the Ultimate Communication Medium* (NAi/De Balie, 2006). The book contains contributions by Erkki Huhtamo, Siegfried Zielinski, Bruce Sterling, Zoe Beloff, John Akomfrah, and others. The DVD contains the stage play *On Imaginary Media* by Peter Blegvad, written specifically for the occasion. (The play was conceived as an imaginary stage play that would never be performed, the performance was a reading of the text by actors, with all the nasty details of rehearsing, etc. – the actors were reading a stage play that would never materialize.) Remarkably, this project has continued to generate interest, theoretical reflection, and cultural production, and seems to has lost little of its original urgency over the past fifteen years. More recently, Jussi Parikka devoted a chapter of his book *What Is Media Archaeology?* to imaginary media as a mapping of weird media objects. See Jussi Parikka, *What Is Media Archaeology?* (Polity, 2012), 41–62.

4. See, for instance, www.wired.com/wired/archive/5.07/longboom.html.

5. France Telcom, British Telcom, Deutsche Telekom, and PTT Telecom in the Netherlands were some of the illustrious names that needed to be rescued with government bail-out packages in 2002. See www.economist.com/node/1234886 7 A.

6. See Jacques Lacan, *Écrits: A Selection* (Travistock/Routledge, 1977/1989). In particular, see "The signification of the phallus" and "The subversion of the subject and the dialectic of desire in the Freudian unconscious."

7. I borrow the term "anArchaeology" (of the media) from Siegfried Zielinski to denote a magical approach to technical media worlds that foregrounds the singular and the encounter of heterogeneous forces in the development of technical media. See Siegfried Zielinski, *Deep Time of the Media: Toward an Archaeology of Hearing and Seeing by Technical Means* (MIT Press, 2006), 258.

8. For an extended summation of the project, see Eric Kluitenberg, "On the archaeology of imaginary media," in *Media Archaeology—Approaches, Applications, and Implications*, ed. Erkki Huhtamo and Jussi Parikka (University of California Press, 2011).

9. See my essay "Media without an audience as posted on the nettime mailing list for net criticism" (October 19, 2000), available at http://amsterdam .nettime.org.

10. Edmund Burke, *A Philosophical Enquiry into the Origin of our Ideas of the Sublime and Beautiful* (Penguin, 1998 [1757, second edition, 1759]), 49–199. In particular, see Part I: Section XI *Society and Solitude*, Part II: Section II *Terror*, Section VI *Privation*, and Part IV: Section XV *Darkness Terrible in Its Own Nature*.

9

"Text and Walk without Fear":
Apps and the Experience of Transparency

Anna Munster

Not long after the release of the iPhone 3GS in 2009, a new genre of apps began to appear that were largely billed as "functional." Making the screen of a smartphone appear transparent so that one could look "through" or beyond the icons to the street below, these apps promised to allow the user to continue texting "without fear" of falling or bumping into a lamp post. Typical of such an app is Type n Walk.[1] The selling point of such an app is its prosthetic combination with the user's peripheral vision, providing the perfect technical assistance of just enough visual information for those who are simultaneously texting and walking to remain "safe" while out on the streets. Such apps have become increasingly popular with the spread of Android phones into the smartphone market, making the transparent experience possible for Google's operating system. The rallying cry "Text and walk without fear" has also proliferated in the wake of videos posted to YouTube that have gone viral of, for example, people texting while walking and falling straight into a fountain in a crowded shopping mall.[2]

Yet far from making the phone actually see-through, the app displays a real time digital video feed from its rear-mounted camera on the phone's screen. What the user sees, past the overlaid display of screen icons and the vector graphics of their text, is the ground below captured as *media material*. In the genre of functional apps, this media materiality is made less obvious, as the app plays less to a strategy for marketing games and other entertainments and more to usefulness. Hence it must claim the dissolution of mediation instead. A number of spin-off transparency-based apps have also been developed. One of these is Transparent Screens,[3] which allows users to select images of three-dimensional hands similar to their own to display onscreen while the phone is being held. (See figure 9.1.) The hand onscreen can be matched to the real hand underneath, quite literally producing an illusion of the part of the body that continues through the device. Such apps, although holding on to the image of transparency provided in their names, are sold under the entertainment category and come with disclaimers: "this app just let[s] you choose one of the existing hand themes and will not make your screen a real transparent screen."[4] Other apps that utilize the same functionality as Type n Walk—that is, they use smartphones' inbuilt cameras to stream media feeds to their screens—include the aptly named Mirror, now bundled as a utility with the operating system for iPhone 5. Here the app takes the camera feed from the front-mounted camera on the phone while simultaneously removing all other icons and graphics from the screen so as to seamlessly mirror back the space in front of the screen.

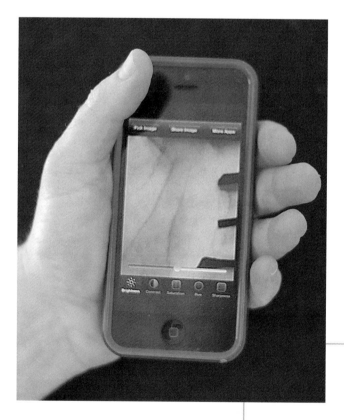

Figure 9.1
Using the Transparent Screens app. Image created by Anna Munster and reproduced with kind permission of the artist.

In all these cases of transparency, from "seeing through" to seamlessly "reflecting," an optical illusion is being performed. The app, far from its claim to functionality, participates instead in a world the media produces of pure performativity and illusionism. This chapter will take the transparent screen app as its starting point for a discussion about the kind of optical illusionism that permeates the visual imaginary of apps. It will suggest that the overriding experience of the app in contemporary culture is conveyed by just such transparent and reflective illusionism; that is to say, an entire sense of magic permeates the smart device. In the first instance, this sense of magic harks back to the illusory optics of nineteenth-century theatrical magic in which magicians caused objects to seem to appear and fade away onstage. In the second instance, such a theater of magical illusions morphs into the very genesis of contemporary media, first witnessed in the transition of theatrical magic to cinema late in the nineteenth century. This is what Tom Gunning has circumscribed as the mixed media genesis of film out of a "cinema of attractions."[5] The app, then, cannot be understood as a stripped down version of software functionality, heir to the infamous "killer app" which, in marketing terms, describes any program that is so desirable or functional that it ascribes core value to an entire technology. An example of this would be something like a word processing application, which for many years gave desktop computing its main value and purpose for the business and domestic markets. The app, I am suggesting, does not fundamentally derive its *experiential* force and desirability from the functionalism it facilitates for smartphones. Rather, the app rediscovers and reiterates a particular set of forces prevalent throughout media: the sophisticated interplay of revelation and trickery, which was so prevalent in the crossover from stage magic to the early optical illusions of cinema late in the nineteenth century. This is not to suggest, however, that we should consider the app as yet another installment in the history of *mediation*. I am not arguing that the app is a software remediation of early cinema, in the same sense that Jay Bolter and Richard Grusin have argued that all digital media remediate earlier media via the twinned logics of immediacy and hypermediacy.[6] Indeed I do not think that apps are media as such, or at least not media as we have previously known it and thought about it. I do not intend to simply conduct a media archeology of the app here, going back to the beginnings of a device's technical or media origins in order to rediscover forgotten aspects that will lead us to understanding of how it functions *as* media in the contemporary moment.[7] Nor do I intend to analyze the app and its illusionistic forces as an example of the oscillation between window and mirror that Bolter elsewhere has suggested is a feature of computer mediation itself.[8] Instead, as I have already intimated, I want to think about illusionism as a force specific to a range of modes of presenting and enacting images and the visual, a force that courses through both media and software. Unless we are able to grapple with this question of the forces of media and technical things we will not be able to account for why it is that phones and apps have become as experientially powerful, desirable, and affective as they have in contemporary culture. It is clear that the arrival of the app signals a phase in which the phone moves deliberately away from being functional to becoming a highly charged haptic fetish. Why? I don't think we can begin to account for the constant handling, addressing, touching, and fumbling we perform every day with our smartphones via a myriad of useful and useless applications if we stop at excavating their secret technical histories or theories of their digital (re)mediation. For neither of these approaches touches on the ways in which the app on our phone has become a mode for both affecting other technologies and others in general and for the way the phone affects us. I want, then, to begin to trace out a way of conceiving media, software, and devices as material concentrators and mobilisers of aesthetic forces and relations that are at once also social and political. By aesthetic I mean to suggest that these forces work at the level of immediate and affective experience; that is, at the level of sensory perception. But I also want to suggest that the sensory is by no means an autonomous realm. On the contrary, it is via the sensory or aesthetic that we are also immediately conjoined with the micro-politics of everyday media life.

Genealogies of the Disappearing Screen

Transparency is, of course, not peculiar to smartphones or the magic of apps. Indeed, virtually every computational graphic interface designed for con-sumer *and* high-end use from the 1960s onward has sought to make its inter-face visually disappear. As Søren Pold has argued, this particular aesthetics of transparency comes out of an engineering rather than aesthetic tradition and has continued throughout the design concepts and practices of human-com-puter interaction (HCI).[9] Bolter and Grusin argue that the will to transparency in media has a much longer history harking back to the culture of Renaissance visual perspectivalism.[10] Although Bolter and Grusin provide an important context for understanding continuities in historical and contemporary forms of visual culture, Pold's situating of the transparent user interface within an engineering mindset has more traction for understanding apps that make the smartphone screen interface become windows to see through. This is because what is at initially at stake for disappearing the smartphone screen is—as Type n Walk and Transparent Screens tout as their selling point—a notion of enhanced utility: "in the broader cultural and social understanding of the computer, the tendency has been to understand the interface as transparent, preferably invisible, for the benefit of a mimetic model of the task one is working on."[11]

From the mid 1980s to the 1990s, virtual reality (VR) seemed to take the transparency of the interface to an extreme in its desire to eradicate interfaces altogether. Brenda Laurel's design for dramatically engaging virtual worlds is well known as the point in which a (classical) theater tradition meets HCI, as the user no longer faces off against a computer with a visible screen but is instead richly immersed in a fully three-dimensional graphic world.[12] Yet VR is much less a part of this same engineering genealogy of transparency; instead, it tends to emphasize rich perceptual or media aspects of user experience. But it is precisely the seductive lure of the immersive computational graphic world that must be overcome in order to text and walk without fear. The branch of interface design that subtends this re-entry of interfaces as transparent windows leading us back to the real physical world is augmented reality (AR). That branch emerges in direct opposition to the disappeared interfaces of virtual environments, which, in effect have ensconced users in a paradigm in which they can literally no longer see reality. AR, by way of contrast, rescues the user from an aesthetic fantasy and returns them to the engineered, practical world: "While immersed, the user cannot see the real world around him. In contrast, AR allows the user to see the real world, with virtual objects superimposed upon or composited with the real world."[13]

As we can see from Azuma's early survey of where AR was at in the late 1990s, it began as a kind of composite notion of a mixed world in which computation and physical reality related to each other in a layered manner. This is in keeping with the idea of augmentation as a kind of "add-on" to the world. But more recently, AR, especially in applications designed for use in smartphones and handheld devices, sees itself as a set of HCI convergences in which ultimate transparency between computation and reality has been attained. This can be seen from proclamations on websites such as Augmentedreality.org: "The way we experience the world will never be the same. We no longer interact with computers. We interact with *the world*."[14] In this imagineering—a union of imaginary futures with engineering traditions—AR will no longer be computational at all but simply part of life's embedded utilities in a realization of the world as deeply informatic. Without the slightest trace of irony, AR is now conceived as a means of disappearing computing altogether, providing us with full access to engage with the world. The handheld device running current AR apps is not so much a window onto the world or a layer superimposed onto reality. Rather, it disappears the screen interface in order to more easily conjoin with some modality of the user's perceptual apparatus. In highly customized AR examples such as Sean White and Steve Feiner's SiteLens prototype from 2009, a mobile laptop with GPS, camera, and inbuilt sensors could be used to render visible certain invisible environmental factors (such as carbon dioxide levels in the atmosphere) and dynamically merge these with a "transparent view" of the very environment through which the readings were being taken on (i.e., through the device).[15] SiteLens, then, is an example of an AR system that no longer sees augmentation as computational per se but rather as a means for directly "jacking in to" the user's visual perception and cognition systems: "interacting with aspects of a physical site that do not have a natural or perceivable visual representation."[16] At a more basic computing level, Type n Walk, enacts the same experience of transparency as the disappearance of computing while nonetheless undertaking a computational task. In these apps the screen disappears so that computing can attempt to merge seamlessly into proprioception, that extrasensory area of perception in which we use our moving bodies to create, interact in, and relate to space. This conjunction of computation with perception seemingly allows us to compute without interacting with the computer. Instead we are interacting directly—that is, walking—with the world.

There is a sense in which we always remain aware of the extraordinary effort spent in attempting to secure such technological disappearance acts. Even reviews in technophile magazines such as *Wired* have noted that these apps' claims to utility might be far-fetched: "Of course, it won't work. Anyone who would write e-mail while walking is obviously too self-absorbed to pay attention to the world around them. Let them walk under a bus."[17] Augmentation always has to deal with its own embodied relations in the world. In a handheld mobile device such as the iPhone, the view of the physical world appearing on the screen when using text and walking apps and actually texting is the ground below. The back-mounted camera on the phone would usually be picking up a feed of the ground being walked upon by the person holding the phone and texting. This, of course, means that static vertical objects such as lamp posts, potential obstacles in the person's path of movement ahead and not necessarily picked up in time by the camera feed would still pose a problem for walking without fear! Such apps, I will argue, are always too caught up in performing their own illusions and as such are subject to the contingencies of actions as these unfold in the world. But as we shall also see, this does not mean we should expose them for the illusionistic media that they are. Illusionism is not at all what it seems.

Illusion, Invisibility, and Stage Magic

As I suggested at the beginning of this chapter, apps that trade on transparency already spill into the entertainment category. The Transparent Screens app that allows users to choose an image of part of a hand to appear on the screen thereby smoothing the visual gap between technical device and the "real world" revels in its own performativity, declaring itself to be an "Awesome Creative Application."[18] There is already a sense here that transparency does not simply provide a utilitarian service to the user but might just be a gimmick. It is as if these were more like gags that one might buy on the front counter of a magic shop, or the whoopee cushions and x-ray glasses that were once advertised in comic books.

I summon these associations deliberately because Transparent Screens is an app that self-consciously asks the user to perform an optical illusion—the dissolution of the smartphone screen into the hand holding it from behind. This connects it to a long history of such disappearing acts whose genesis can be traced back to nineteenth-century theater. Making the visible invisible by means of a sophisticated technical apparatus is a stage magic illusion still regularly performed where a magician such as David Copperfield makes the Statue of Liberty vanish before the audience's eyes. Interestingly enough, the appearance and disappearance of onstage optical illusions had its genesis in the live phantasmagoria shows of technicians and scientists such as Henry Dircks, an engineer from Liverpool, and John Henry Pepper, a chemistry professor from London.

At the core of the Pepper's Ghost image developed by these two Victorians was an actor, usually positioned in a pit at the front of the stage, whose image was projected through a 45° angled mirror upward and on to a transparent sheet of glass on the stage. (See figure 9.2.) With clever stage lighting, the stage background and foreground would merge and the image on stage appear to be a three-dimensional ghost floating in mid-air. Here actual transparent material, glass, is deployed along with the optical deceit of disappearing stage depth through projection and lighting in order to perform the simultaneous illusions of making visible (ghost) and invisible (stage set). Although an exact tracing of the history of appropriations and borrowings between the more technical phantasmagoria and magicians who also performed large stage acts of appearance and disappearance is murky,[19] the lines between the "technical" and the "magical" were themselves decidedly fuzzy when it came to conceiving of and performing illusions in the middle of the nineteenth century. For scientists and engineers of the Victorian period, the technical performance of illusion was testament to the wonders of mechanics; something to be celebrated rather than hidden in the rhetoric of utility.

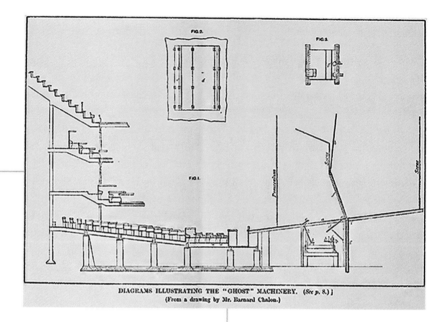

DIAGRAMS ILLUSTRATING THE "GHOST" MACHINERY. (See p. 8.)]
(From a drawing by Mr. Barnard Chalon.)

Figure 9.2
Diagram of the technical apparatus necessary for producing Pepper's Ghost on stage. Source: frontispiece of *The True History of Pepper's Ghost and All About Metempsychosis* (Cassell and Company, 1890) (public domain).

In tracing a genealogy for apps that exploits transparency back to phantasmagoria and stage magic, I do not mean to simply offer a "better" history of software. In the first instance, I am interested in just this early fuzziness between engineering and magic, which, in the very different sociotechnical atmosphere of post-World War II cybernetics, turns into a sharp distinction between utility and entertainment. If optical illusions involving the projection of the image have a history of performance that is not just magical but also celebrates technical accomplishment then perhaps the engineering tradition was never so far from the magical. In the second instance, phantasmagoria and stage magic also share the podium with the emergence of early cinema as a number of media theorists have pointed out.[20] If we are interested in where transparency might intersect with media histories, the convergence of magic, technical performativity and cinema, the end of the nineteenth century seems to offer fertile ground. This period is particularly rich since stage magicians such as Georges Méliès migrated from theater to making films. In his 1896 film *Escamotage d'une Dame au Theater Robert Houdin* (*The Vanishing Woman*), Méliès first used stop-frame animation to make a woman seen seated on a chair one moment disappear the next, when a drape is placed over her and then removed.

Would these shared histories, technical performances, and stage sets be enough to account for the carryover of the kind of magic we continue to encounter in the transparency illusions apps perform on our contemporary phones? Although I think that much can be made of such a media archeological approach, especially insofar as this suggests a loosening of distinctions between the categories of engineering and entertainment, I do not think this is enough to account for the affective pull of apps that perform optical illusions nor of how such apps coincide with the obsessive pull phones have as handheld devices. Transparent Screens, for example, is an app not only embedded in the magic of optical illusions but in the embodied conjunction of the visual and the haptic: "its [*sic*] amazing how close feeling [*sic*] this app gives you."[21]

Illusion as Optical Force

This closeness does not lie in the *resemblance* between an imaged hand and the user's actual hand but, as I will now suggest, a different kind of proximity: the sense in which it enacts touching the feeling of seeing. By this, I do not mean to suggest, as has been argued with respect to both interactivity and mobile devices[22] that the haptic has now become the predominant modality for relating to digital media. There has been a tendency in recent critical discussion of new media to associate the visual with regimes of representation that are now disappearing ("old media" such as cinema and television) and the haptic with a coming cultural and theoretical paradigm of affect. This seems to me to be an opposition that is too uncomplicated for the kinds of convergences, jumps, and relations that contemporary media enact. Instead, I am more interested in discovering how the visual can itself be understood affectively; that is, as a particular kind of force that helps to compose contemporary technical objects as heterogeneous composites of perception, sensation, and technicity.[23]

This means thinking about the visual as perceptual event rather than as an epiphenomenon of media themselves. Illusions are optimal material for thinking through what is happening when we visually perceive because, as psychologists, neuroscientists, and philosophers of embodied cognition all agree, illusions draw attention to aspects of looking that we tend to take for granted.[24] Illusions are winding their way back from the periphery of vision to taking center stage as an optical force. Equally important for understanding how illusions might be situated not just more centrally in perception but as major players in a more complicated history of media—that is, one which doesn't so dramatically distinguish between playback and real time—is an understanding of how illusions function within magic's histories. Dan North has argued that it is a mistake to suggest that magicians such as Méliès confounded their audiences through optical deceits.[25] Instead he suggests that spectators at magic shows, who also became the early audiences for cinema, were not passively duped by illusions but optically "colluded" with the magician.[26] They brought contextual knowledge to the magician's performance, often of how illusions had been performed elsewhere, which provoked the performer to expand upon and develop the trick in new ways. And importantly in this context they brought an embodied acuity to magic shows through which they developed their perceptual attunement to the illusion, strengthening its reception and its force.

By turning to the perceptual aspect of the visual via the illusory, we can enhance our understanding of how any visual media—live or prerecorded—function. This does not mean that we throw away "the cultural" or "the social" if we take a particular notion of media out of the mix and opt for understanding the perceptual event of vision as a way to think through the forces at work when apps make their screens transparent. As Brian Massumi has argued, media never easily fit into typologies that suggest mediation can be reduced to a (technical) imposition upon one sense or another: "Theorists have argued endlessly about what defines a medium. Is a medium defined by the material support, say celluloid for cinema? If so, is digital cinema then not cinema? Is a medium defined by the sense modality the product presents itself in—sound for music, vision for cinema?"[27] The smartphone, with its excessive pull toward being touched and its swathe of apps that play to the power of optical illusion, disrupts just such a typology. Media, especially those that so clearly foreground their perceptual recombinations and recompositions, must, as Massumi argues, be thought as events occurring in and of embodied experience. What is novel, forceful, affective, and evental about transparent apps and smartphones is the way they conjoin the haptic and the visual as a new aesthetic-technical event of "feelingvision."[28] A good deal of the force experienced in wanting to touch a device with a screen comes from just that novel aesthetic event of conjoining the tactile with the visual, which recomposes relations between the senses. Apps such as Transparent Screens give us that relation right up front—the sensation of literally holding vision as the imaged hand on screen is held in (media) relation with our actual hand holding this image.

We could say, then, that the transparent screen here would not so much participate in performing an *illusory* transparency, if by this we mean that transparency is itself a myth perpetuated by media. The "myth" of transparent media analyzed by Bolter and Gromola, for example, is that we are coerced by digital media and their representationalist histories to look through the screen at the world beyond and forget the materiality of mediation. And yet transparency in apps takes on a range of appearances from the utilitarian to the entertaining suggesting that transparency and mediation/materiality cannot be so easily opposed. There is the sense in which the dissolution of the screen in the Type n Walk variety of apps does do something different *perceptually*. In these cases, and in spite of the claim of such apps to the synchronization of vision and movement, the experience produced is instead of a holding apart. The entire purpose of such apps is dedicated to the noninterference of the screen (the visual) with walking (the proprioceptive) so that each activity might be conducted separately yet simultaneously. Here we see through the visual dimension (the screen) to the kinesthetic dimension in the movement of our feet below on the pavement. But, as we do, we also miss the potential for any relational aesthetic event sparked by a novel recomposition of the arrangement of the senses relative to each other. It is not so much that Type n Walk is utilitarian but that it is habitual, repeating the ways in which media act to enforce habitual patterns of perception by making movement conform to the habits of looking. As Massumi suggests: "When in the course of everyday life we march habitually and half-consciously from one drop of life to the next, we don't attend to the ripples. We see through the semblance to the next, not letting it appear with all its force."[29]

Transparency understood as a media event and enacted by an app such as Transparent Screens gives us a different sense of what media might be—this is media as an experience of forces felt as they come together and conjoin in embodied ways. What we feel immediately is the mediation, the relating of vision and touch together in direct conjunction with each other. The political dimension of such an event is experienced at a molecular level, where something feels different, where something aesthetically novel ripples through the device: the hand holding it, the eyes looking at it, *as* relation. We are not fooled by the illusion of the hand; we are looking at the hand holding (of) images as a new way of arranging the relation between the visual and the tactile and of creating a new kind of media material: the hand-held image. What we sense in this media event, then, is just that new quality of the mobile-tactile image, held momentarily as conjunction in front of our eyes. This "event" of mediation is not the same kind of mediating that occurs when someone sees through a smartphone to ensure that their vision continues to govern/control/mediate their movement on the streets below. In this kind of mediation, the app that makes the screen transparent does nothing but reinforce our habitual modes of wandering fearlessly through the city, device in hand, without seeing much at all. We might succeed in carrying out two actions—text and walk without fear—but the opportunity to experience their relating, the event of walking-in-to-sight, has fallen by the curbside.

Notes

1. Coactive, Type n Walk (iPhone application, 2009–2012) (http://www .type-n-walk.com).

2. "Girl falls in mall fountain while texting" (http://www.youtube.com).

3. Rajaseekur Battu, Transparent Screens (IPhone app for IPhone 3 and later) (https://itunes.apple.com).

4. Ibid.

5. Tom Gunning, "The cinema of attractions: Early film, its spectator and the avant-garde," in *Early Film*, ed. T. Elsaesser and A. Barker (British Film Institute, 1989).

6. Jay David Bolter and Richard Grusin, *Remediation: Understanding New Media* (MIT Press, 2000), 53.

7. Here I am boiling down a series of diverse approaches that have been termed "media archaeology" by its proponents, such as Jussi Parikka and Erkki Huhtamo in "Introduction: An archaeology of media archaeology," in *Media Archaeology: Approaches, Applications, and Implications*, ed. Huhtamo and Parikka (University of California Press, 2011), 2. As Parikka suggests on page 2 of *What Is Media Archaeology?* (Polity, 2012), media archeology is a non-formalized set of theoretical techniques for excavating history in order to run parallel lines of the old, the new, and the possible. I am not unsympathetic to this project, but, as I shall suggest in this chapter, the point is not to simply rediscover a past but instead to unleash potentialities in technologies so that they we do not just end up with histories or presents but with *differences* in our current cultural landscapes.

8. Jay David Bolter and Diana Gromola, *Windows and Mirrors: Interaction Design, Digital Art and the Myth of Transparency* (MIT Press, 2003), 9.

9. Søren Pold, "Interface realisms: The interface as aesthetic form," *Postmodern Culture* 15 (2005), no. 2 (http://muse.jhu.edu).

10. Bolter and Grusin, *Remediation*, 24.

11. Pold, "Interface realisms."

12. Brenda Laurel, *Computers as Theater* (Addison-Wesley, 1992), 33. I have written in more detail elsewhere about Laurel's relations with both theatrical models of representation and HCI. See Anna Munster, *Materializing New Media: Embodiment in Information Aesthetics* (Dartmouth University Press, 2006), 127–129.

13. Ron Azuma, "A survey of augmented reality," *Presence* 6 (1997), no. 4: 355–385, at 355.

14. Augmentedreality.org, "About," 2013 (http://augmentedrealityevent .com).

15. It seems that SiteLens remains at the prototype stage and is not in commercial development. Further information can be found at http://www1 .cs.columbia.edu/~swhite/projects.html.

16. Sean White and Steve Feiner, "SiteLens: Situated visualization techniques for urban site visits," in *Proceedings of the SIGCHI Conference on Human Factors in Computing Systems* (ACM, 2009), 1117.

17. Charles Sorrel, "Application makes iPhone disappear," 2009 (http:// www.wired.com/gadgetlab/2009/05/application-makes-iphone-disappear).

18. Battu, Transparent Screens.

19. Jim Steinmeyer, *Hiding the Elephant: How Magicians Invented the Impossible and Learned to Disappear* (Da Capo, 2004), 41–43.

20. See, for example, Tom Gunning, "'We are here and not here': Late nineteenth-century stage magic and the roots of cinema in the appearance (and disappearance) of the virtual image," in *A Companion to Early Cinema*, ed. A. Gaudreault, N. Dulac, and S. Hidalgo (Wiley-Blackwell, 2012); Matthew Solomon, *Disappearing Tricks: Silent Film, Houdini, and the New Magic of the Twentieth Century* (University of Illinois Press, 2010). Gunning argues that, contrary to cinema being seen as a new medium that departed from the traditions of theater, early cinema (1895 to around 1910) was enmeshed with fairground and vaudeville apparatus, means of distribution, and forms of display. Gunning also demonstrates that the entire tradition of special effects cinema that began with the films of George Méliès during this same period comes to us through his, and other, magician's original stage show magic, which invented sets and theatrical mechanisms for producing illusions and phantasmagoria on stage. Solomon makes a parallel argument, showing that Houdini's famous disappearing tricks influenced the development of techniques for editing and jump cutting in early cinema (*Disappearing Tricks*, 60ff.).

21. Battu, Transparent Screens.

22. See, for example, Rachel Lee, "Haptics, mobile handhelds, and other 'novel' devices: The tactile unconscious of reading across old and new media," *CTheory* 31 (2012) (http://www.ctheory.net/articles.aspx?id=697).

23. Here I am invoking, although not in its full force, the Simondonian notion of technicity, which refers to the becoming-technical of an object as a mode of conditioning technical invention. This is opposed to the common sense idea of an individual technology as something itself instantiating a full-fledged form of "the technical." Gilbert Simondon's emphasis is on the way in which the technical object both comes to be individuated within a particular kind of technical "mentality"—artisanal, industrial, and so forth—but also on the potential for its destabilization and reinvention as something else. For a discussion of a Simondonian approach to the technical object, technical mentality, and technicity, see Brian Massumi with Arne de Boever, Alex Murray, and Jon Roffe, "'Technical mentality' revisited: Brian Massumi on Gilbert Simondon," *Parrhesia* 7 (2009): 36–45.

24. There has been widespread recent interest in magical illusions among neuroscientists; see, for example, Stephen Macknik and Susana Martinez-Conde, *Sleights of Mind: What the Neuroscience of Magic Reveals About Our Brains* (Holt, 2010). But, following a common understanding of illusion, Macknik and Martinez-Conde see this as a visual mismatch between perception and "reality" (103). Alva Noë, in *Action in Perception* (MIT Press. 2004), has, on the other hand, used the "fact" of optical deceits in everyday visual perception to develop a sophisticated understanding of the ways in which vision is always conjoined with other embodied activities such as the movement of eyelids in involuntary saccades through to the ways in which we scan objects, hence moving our heads, in order to perceive volume in objects.

25. Dan North, "Illusory Bodies: Magical performance on stage and screen," *Early Popular Visual Culture* 5 (2007), no. 2: 175–188.

26. Ibid., 175.

27. Brian Massumi, *Semblance and Event: Activist Philosophy and the Occurrent Arts* (MIT Press, 2011), 96.

28. Massumi, taking up Michael Chion's work on cinema, remarks that what is novel about film is not that it is a visual medium but that it is produced out of the relational effect of conjoining auditory and visual experience such that one cannot be reduced to the other. Hence cinema operates as "audiovision." See Massumi, *Semblance and Event*, 95–96.

29. Massumi, *Semblance and Event*, 51.

III Economics

10
App Worker

Nick Dyer-Witheford

A new and enigmatic figure has recently appeared in North America's anxious dreams about jobs, prosperity, and the very fate of global capitalism: that of the app worker. Within a few years of Apple opening its App Store, rumors of a burgeoning "app economy" began to spread through IT, business, and job-finding websites, through company prospectuses, and through app-making-for-dummies manuals.[1] Stories of young men abandoning day jobs or school to make millions writing apps proliferated in the media, and enthusiastic business reports declared that apps were "where the jobs are."[2] These were among the very few sparks of light in the general darkness of the post-2008 slump. Even as Occupy Wall Street seized city squares across North America, apps promised a revival of capitalist growth.

Today, it is estimated that there are more than half a million software application workers in the United States, many of them developing software for mobile devices, and the numbers are anticipated to increase rapidly in the next several years.[3] Yet the nature of work in the app economy—the remuneration, the conditions, the prospects, and the long-term significance—remains contested and controversial. Focusing on the value networks of the North American smartphone industry, the epicenter of the app explosion, this chapter discusses the crowdsourcing of app development by giant platform providers, the technological and subjective resources it mobilizes, the labor processes it activates, and the conflicts it generates. Distributed app development is, I suggest, an apparatus in which "immaterial labor" is captured by "cognitive capitalism," a highly successful mechanism that might, however, become increasingly unstable in a context of world labor markets and algorithmic automation.

Value Networks

The cover of the December 1, 2012 issue of *The Economist* depicts a colossal under-sea struggle. Apple, Google, Facebook, and Amazon are portrayed as giant squids battling to the death, entangled in each other's tentacles. With a cheerful ruthlessness, this image dispenses with any illusions that the digital is the domain of the small or beautiful. The article's title, "Survival of the Biggest," conveys the complexity and the reach of the corporate entities that dominate the networks. The image of squirming, suction-cupped tentacles suggests a concept that is crucial for understanding the app economy: that of the value network.

The value network revises an older concept: that of the "value chain," which described how a dominant capitalist enterprise organizes subordinate aspects of the commodification process, dispersing each value-adding activity to global locations and organizational forms that optimize labor costs, access to raw materials, or proximity to markets, and then links the chain in a continuous, integrated sequence.[4] The original form of the value chain of headquarters research, design, and marketing in the high-wage areas of the global economy subcontracts manufacturing, assembly, and back-end office functions to newly industrialized territories, where they can be rapidly scaled up or down, while resource extraction or waste disposal are sent to abyssal sacrifice zones. In the last two decades this has become a standard process for producing cars, cappuccino, and cell phones. Value chains can, however, become both very complex, and very volatile, so some analysts prefer to avoid the linear (and oppressive) connotations of "chains" and instead speak of value "networks," highlighting the "intricate links—horizontal, diagonal as well as vertical—forming multi-dimensional, multi-layered lattices of economic activity."[5]

This is the case in the mobile communications sector, where there are always "several actors intervening along the value chain" and "roles are changed, combined and exchanged."[6] Before the smartphone, the most powerful organizers of value networks in the cell phone industry were telecommunication carriers, such as Verizon, AT&T, and Sprint in the United States or Bell, Rogers, and Telus in Canada, which concentrated mobile data access in carrier-provided "walled gardens."[7]

The smartphone, a phone doubling as a computer, disrupted this power, replacing the dominance of the carriers with that of the creators of operating systems and development tools—Apple, Google, Research In Motion, Nokia, and Microsoft. These "platform providers"[8] arrayed around themselves the other components of a smartphone value network—the carriers (who continued to be important because they subsidized the costs of popular smartphones in order to sell customers phone plans), the production of the handset on which the operating system must run, and the development of software applications to run on the platform.

To illustrate the flexibility of value networks, we can contrast Apple and Google. Apple typifies a vertical model of "platform integration"[9]: it makes iOS (the iPhone operating system) compatible only with other Apple devices, designs the iPhone handsets, has them manufactured according to its specification by subcontracted electronic assembly companies, and uses the reputation of this high-design handset to attract large subsidies from carrier companies. Although Apple's outsourcing of app development might seem to breach this verticality, its App Store reasserts control, subjecting apps to a stringent approval process and giving Apple a cut of sales. This is, therefore, a model in which the value tentacle drags revenues directly to the platform provider through every stage of production and sale.

Google's smartphone value network is more horizontal. Its open-source Android operating system has been adopted by a wide variety of tablet and smartphone producers, including those of handset giants such as Samsung, who control their own manufacturing processes. Google's own Nexus devices are not central to Android, as the iPhone is to iOS. The Google Play app store neither exercises the same rigorous vetting process as Apple's nor garnishes revenues from apps sold through it. However, this generosity is predicated on Google's strategic position as the world's dominant search engine. Disseminating Android broadly benefits Google by increasing Internet traffic generally, and, specifically, traffic from devices providing instant access to its advertising-supported search functions.[10]

The conflict between Apple and Google currently dominates the North American smartphone business, even as other contenders, among them Microsoft and RIM, strive to edge in, but victory in these corporate battles depends on success in another arena: that in which platform providers struggle to exploit labor in the process of app development.

Distributed Development

When in 2007 Apple announced it would open the iPhone to outside app developers this was hailed as a radical step for a corporation previously known for its exceptional secrecy—akin, one journalist remarked, to a virtuoso violinist's "letting a toddler play with his Stradivarius."[11] In fact, third-party software development has been a long-standing feature of the computing industry; ensuring an attractive range of applications for an operating system, whether a personal computer or a mobile phone, usually exceeds the resources and abilities of a single company. The balance of power between the parties involved has, however, varied, from the ascendancy of Microsoft at its peak vis-à-vis hardware makers, to subordination of independent video game developers to console companies. Apple's crowdsourcing departure, which was followed in short order by Google's similar institution of its Android Market (rebranded in 2012 as Google Play), was enabled by two factors, one technological and the other involving laboring subjectivities.

Technologically, crowdsourcing was made possible by the by the decreasing costs and the increasing power of computing. Smartphones are themselves a manifestation of this tendency, but so too is the increasing accessibility of authoring devices. So many people have been willing to try their hand at app work because the initial risk of becoming an developer is low; platform providers distribute inexpensive software development kits (SDKs), downloadable to a Mac or a PC, including authoring tools, libraries, debuggers, and handset emulators ($99 for the iPhone; not available for Android), and these can be supplemented from other third-party business-to-business sources, providing instruments not only for programming but also for cross-platform adaptation, ad networks, user analytics, crash reporting, and back-office functions that can transform a home into a virtual app factory.

Crowdsourcing apps also, however, depend on a special form of labor power integral to the computer software industry: youthful, predominantly male, technically wizard, skeptical toward corporate suits, outside the union traditions of industrial labor, and ideologically, in varying proportions, libertarian and entrepreneurial. This has been a stratum indigenous to computer software creation. From the original hackers to the open-source movement to Web 2.0 enthusiasts, it has expanded alongside the diffusion of computer technology and the dissemination of object-oriented programming skills through work, play, and educational institutions. The brilliance of Apple's app strategy was to invite this technically creative labor power into its value network on wider basis than ever before, by means of what would become known as the "mobile application distributed development process."[12]

This process involves "three main components."[13] First, developers build apps for a platform using SDKs made available by platform providers. Second, the developer publishes the app on a portal (which may be may be "decentralized," with developers freely uploading and distributing apps to customers, or "centralized"—that is, maintained by platform providers who act as middleman, determining policies governing app uploads and sales, and charging fees or taking a cut of developers revenues). Third, the customer downloads the app to a handset. In this process, developers may get revenues from a variety of sources: directly from the sale of apps, or indirectly from advertising for which their app serves as a vehicle (the most popular but least lucrative method), or from fees for "in-app" sales. In "freemium" apps the two functions are combined, with the limited free functionality of the app serving as an advertisement for paid additional content. Apps are thus either commodities or commodity accelerators—that is to say, either they are sold to smartphone users or they are given away only in order to speed the circulation of other commodities.

Apple's crowdsourcing of app development was acclaimed as a radical democratization of software production. Steve Jobs, however, was more hardheaded. When asked about the point of opening the App Store, he replied "Sell more iPhones."[14] Mobile apps present a classic "two-sided market": popular products attract consumers, and consumers are attracted to popular products.[15] This creates "stickiness"; the customer gets accustomed to a platform and the apps associated with it, and becomes "locked in," reluctant to incur "switching costs" of time and effort to become familiar with another system.[16]

Thus the battle between platform providers for primacy in smartphone markets is very much fought out over app offerings—as demonstrated by the fracas between Apple and Google over map apps, or the problems faced by RIM in launching its new Blackberry with a limited app library. However, in other two-sided markets, such as those for video games and credit cards, corporate leaders have traditionally used "loss leaders" (e.g., selling consoles below at or below cost, offering low interest rates) to "kick start" the virtuous circle of product popularity and consumer attraction.[17] The genius of Apple's App Store was that by charging app developers for use of its portal it extracted, rather than sacrificed, revenue from this process.

What allows large platform providers to capitalize on app development in this way is their control of the strategic bottleneck of distribution. To make money, developers must build apps for popular platforms, and customers like platforms with plenty of apps. Although in principle developers could publish on decentralized portals, the sheer volume of app production (with about 700,000 apps now available from each of Apple's and Google's stores) means that they face a problem of "discovery"—that is, of making their apps visible and easily available to users. In this situation, appearance on a branded portal, such as the App Store or Google Play, is all but necessary for survival. Though platform providers and app developers need each other reciprocally, the power is very much with the former.

According to one successful app developer, "the company is, in a sense, another arm of Apple's research and development program." The difference between app developers and the relatively small number of software engineers employed by Apple at its Cupertino campus or by Google at its Googleplex is, however, that while those elite employees earn about $100,000 per year, platform providers get the work of hundreds of thousands of app developers for nothing—in fact, Apple, which has probably made cumulative revenues of $7.15 billion from its 30 percent cut of App Store since its introduction in 2008, charges them for the privilege.

Splendor and Misery

And yet the allure of app work is that it *is* possible to make living, even a fortune, at it, because app workers *do* receive incomes—not from platform providers, but as wages from app-development companies or from the revenues of their own micro-enterprises. The actual incomes and conditions of app workers are, however, a matter of increasing controversy: reports of "appillionaires" clash with tales of virtual pauperization.[18]

Success stories of companies (for example, Rovio, the maker of Angry Birds) and of individuals (for example, Nick D'Aloisio, the teenage designer of the popular news app Summly) abound. Websites for people seeking jobs in information technology assert that "IT professionals who can develop applications for mobile devices are hands down the hottest commodity . . . these days."[19] However, a *New York Times* investigative report cast a more skeptical look at app work.[20] It featured a couple who gave up jobs and cashed in assets to set up an at-home app business, to which they devote innumerable hours, only to find themselves indebted and impoverished. The story ends with them clinging pathetically to the dream by maxing-out credit cards to buy two of the latest iPhones. The report concluded that the "gold rush" opportunities present at the start of the app economy are drying up in an over-crowded market.

These contradictions highlight the extreme unevenness of the app economy and the very different forms app work can take. One important recent analysis (Wright 2013) breaks down of US employment figures for app workers, distinguishing independent and salaried app developers.[21] Salaried app developers make half again or twice as much as independents. There is also a big gap in earnings between those at the top of salaried employment and those at the bottom. Indeed, this difference between salaried and independent developers is almost certainly larger than the study suggests, because many independent developers make so little that they don't identify app work as their full-time job.

Salaried app workers work as employees for app-development companies, or for businesses that regularly generate apps to promote their products. Such companies are by no means small. One perennial hope of digital optimists has been that that networked distribution will undermine the oligopolistic control characteristic of large companies and replace it with a "long tail"[22] of small entrepreneurs serving niche markets, an idea repeated in discussions of the app economy.[23] Unfortunately, what evidence there is does not support this idea. One study found that of the total revenue generated from paid app downloads and in-app purchases in the App Store in the first twenty days of November 2012 half was split among just 25 developers, who dominated the charts by offering multiple products.[24] All but one were game developers, including giants such as Electronic Arts, Gameloft, Rovio, and Zynga. Only 2 or 3 percent of the top 250 publishers on the App Store or Google Play were "newcomers" breaking into "a business dominated by incumbents."[25]

To date there have been no major studies of salaried workers employed by the large companies, only anecdotal accounts.[26] There is, however, some circumstantial evidence. Games are among the most successful apps, and game developers top the app sale charts. In the games industry, scandals about working conditions resulted in extensive "quality of life" studies by professional associations. Combined with salary reports, these portray an industry in which skilled programmers and designers can make high salaries, but which is also characterized by long working hours (especially at crunch time), resentments about arbitrary differences in compensation, a sense of burnout, and high turnover. A 2012 study suggests that while "many employees in this industry get intrinsic satisfaction from their work . . . this carrot is not sufficient to develop and maintain a happy and productive workforce in a sustainable, mature industry."[27] In view of the hegemony of game developers over app development, it would be surprising if conditions in that industry were very different.

Thanks to an invaluable study by Birgitta Bergvall-Kåreborn and Debra Howcroft,[28] we have a far better sense of the low end of app development. They conducted sixty interviews with app developers in the United States, the United Kingdom, and Sweden—permanent employees, freelancers, entrepreneurs, and "sideliners"—who had published at least one app for Android or iPhone. Some had developed apps outsourced by a third party, but the majority owned their own work, either as self-employed developers or as employees of small start-up companies. Most were male, with a technical college education. The survey describes an app-development communities clustered in cities, connected by face-to-face contacts and virtual forums, working in small teams at a frenetic pace and often for long hours, driven by the needs of rapid development, first-mover advantage, incremental releases, and updates, and the need for continual improvement in professional and technical skill.

Although developers generally own the products they have developed and the associated intellectual property, "they do not own the distribution channel, which is key to disseminating their artefacts."[29] Consequently they are subject to the discipline, and the vagaries, of the platform providers. This is particularly intense for iPhone app developers, for whom Apple's control over the acceptance of apps is a source of "great frustration." Problems with platform owners over issues of "control, transparency and consistency" are, however, general. The rivalry of these companies and the need to design for competitive platforms add to these troubles. App developers are constantly inconvenienced by the incessant changes of technological conditions occasioned by patent wars involving Apple, Samsung, and Google, and in many cases the litigation is aimed to inhibit app development by competitors.[30]

Though the aforementioned research does not provide data about the incomes these developers garner from their work, such data are available from other sources. A survey of 252 small developers selling through the App Store found that in their enterprise lifetimes 4 percent had made more than $1 million, 25 percent had made more than $30,000, and 25 percent had made less than $200.[31] Another survey found that only 12 percent of app developers had earned more than $50,000, and that 80 percent hadn't generated enough revenue to support a stand-alone business.[32] A third survey, from the US technology company Giro, found more than half of the respondents made less than $500 a month from developing apps. Some 75 percent of 352 respondents either held another job or did app development only as a portion of their main job. On the "much more rare" high end of the spectrum, about 5 percent of app developers, most of them working for large app firms, made more than $20,000 a month.[33]

In summary, it appears that app development is creating a small number of rags-to-riches stories and a layer of well-paid but probably pressured and insecure jobs for salaried employees at development companies participating in a boom of mobile-phone work. App development is also providing skilled freelancers with attractive contract work. Washing around the base of the app economy is, however, a large pool of aspiring independent app makers—small start-up companies and their employees—for whom software development, far from providing a secure livelihood, rather offers yet another variant on the themes of precarious, intermittent, unprotected low-wage work that has come to characterize the post-industrial capitalist economies. This provides the platform providers with a vast reservoir of digital talent and speculative effort. As Bergvall-Kåreborn and Howcroft remark, quoting a smug *Business Week* article about crowdsourcing, mobile app distributed development might be more appropriately termed "milking the masses for inspiration"— a "milking" that, they observe, raises important issues about the exploitation of "immaterial labor."[34]

Immaterial Labor and Cognitive Capitalism

"Immaterial labor" is a term coined by Michael Hardt and Antonio Negri,[35] Paolo Virno,[36] and others to designate labor in which the scientific, symbolic, and social aspects take precedence over manual exertion. In an era of high-technology production, they argue, living labor, far from being eclipsed by machinery, becomes ever more important—"knowledge, information . . . a relationship or an emotional response" emerge as the leading sources of capitalist value creation.[37] This concept of immaterial labor is distinguished from familiar accounts of "knowledge work" by its radical conclusions.

Writing in the context of an *altermondialiste* movement in which independent media centers, free software, and digital commons blossomed alongside street demonstration, Hardt and Negri saw in immaterial labor a radical potential, immanent to a context of computers and networks, for workers to escape capitalist command. The increasing importance of horizontal cooperation in production, the difficulties of measuring intellectual labor, and the impossibility of controlling intellectual property all subvers the extraction of surplus value. As communication, cognition, and affect come to the fore, production depends less on "direct labor" and more on the "general intellect" or "social brain"[38]; immaterial labor appears as attribute of a new collectivity, a "multitude."

This proposition was subsequently elaborated in the theory of "cognitive capitalism" formulated by Carlo Vercellone[39] and Yann Moulier-Boutang,[40] whose work, while sharing Hardt and Negri's orientation to worker autonomy, nevertheless recognized that capitalist enterprises were developing new means to harness and contain it. Control over a diffuse, intellectual workforce cannot, they suggest, take the form of Taylorist command. Instead, it increasingly withdraws from direct management of the production process, and instead exercises an indirect power, based on ownership of intellectual assets, in the way a landowner might extract revenues from tenants of a piece of land. Vercellone uses the analogy of the "putting-out-system" in which pre-industrial capital would provide tools and materials for artisanal workers to produce commodities in their own homes which they are compelled to sell at disadvantageous rates to large capital because of its control over supplies and markets.

App development is a case in point. To make a successful app—be it the astronomy guide Star Walk, the samurai game Infinite Blade, the money-saving Gas Buddy, the music-writing Hyperscore, or the romantic lure Crazy Blind Date—demands a combination of technical, affective, and social skills: the capacity to conceive a useful and attractive virtual micro-device; to design its graphic, textual, interactive and animated content; to program software;

to work with digital tools, often in teams requiring complex group cooperation; and to catch and hold the attention of customers in a crowded digital landscape. It is thus exemplary of the manifold, self-directed competencies of immaterial labor.

Apple and Google create some apps in-house but do not directly employ the majority of this immaterial labor force. Rather, they build app stores for developers, whom they supply with kits for making apps for their operating system. If they charge a fee to place an app in the store, or takes a cut of sales, this is manifestly a form of technological rent. But even where entrance to the store is free the platform developer benefits because the app increases the use value of the smartphone, and hence enhances potential exchange value the platform provider can extract from it—either directly, by increased sales of proprietorial operating system (Apple) or indirectly, from increased advertising revenues (Google). The relation of platform providers to app developers this conforms to the situation, described by the theorists of cognitive capital, in which "direct command over production tends to be substituted by command over markets."[41]

Hardt and Negri's original claims about the autonomous, re-appropriative capabilities of immaterial labor seem, however, to be contradicted by the relative ease with this system for the capture of app developers' labor has been imposed. In 2011 an "Android Developers' Union" website, with the slogan "Sharecroppers unite," targeted Google's Android App Market, demanding a bigger cut of app payments, better app promotion and payment options, public bug tracking, removal appeals, improved liaison with the platform provider, and "algorithmic transparency" about how apps appear in searches.[42] The following year, another website, that of the "App Developers Union," listed grievances against Apple, including the company's toleration of cloned applications and its inadequate response to a "patent troll" company that threatened developers with lawsuits, and called for a reduction in Apple's cut of each app sale.[43] So far these initiatives seem to have gained very little traction, surely because the distributed system for developing mobile apps militates against app producers' recognizing one another as workers with shared interests antagonistic to capital. It allows enough hope for success to ensure that developers compete with one another rather than collaborate against the platform providers. It is also ensures that independent app developers identify themselves not as workers but as freelance entrepreneurs who work "for themselves"—the discursive construction of app work that dominates manuals and media reports.

An alternative understanding would be that the platform providers' control over the app-development process places independent developers in the increasingly large category of nominally self-employed contractors who, in fields ranging from software to plumbing and food services, actually constitute a floating proletarian labor force for large companies dominating supply chains and distribution networks. This is, however, precisely the self-perception that is repressed by cognitive capital's replacement of direct Taylorist command with "indirect mechanisms based on the imperative to deliver, the prescription of subjectivity, and a pure and simple coercion linked to the precarisation of the wage relation."[44]

Beyond Immaterial Labor

For the moment, then, the cognitive capital of the giant platform providers faces few serious challenges from app labor. The tensions latent in crowd-sourced distributed software development may, however, be heightened by the unfolding of its own destabilizing dynamics, and in particular by globalization and automation.

Theories of immaterial labor and cognitive capital have been criticized for overlooking the persistence of material labor, which, far from disappearing, has been offshored to low-wage zones—a process whose dimensions, in regard to smartphones and other digital devices, can be summed up in one word: Foxconn. These criticisms are important not only for their political demand to recognize the dependence of "cyborg" work (such as app development) on "slave" foundations,[45] but also as a reminder that the same dynamics that gutted manufacturing in the global northwest are now in play in software development. Well before the iPhone, software industries in India were undermining any notion that immaterial labor would remain the preserve of already-advanced capital. The working class of Asia is as keen to climb the value chain of capital, escape manual labor, and adopt more immaterial (and better-paid) forms of work as were earlier generations of workers in North America. App development can be offshored, as has occurred in other software areas. Even if offshoring is constrained by the local and cultural-context-bound nature of some app development, it is clear that the major areas of smartphone expansion will be in Asia; even Apple will only succeed if it can "meet the Chindia price."[46] The world labor market promises to subject the North American platform providers and app developers to ever-increased competitive pressures, with unpredictable outcomes.

At the same time, apps are a manifestation of a problem that mainstream economists long thought laid to rest: job-killing automation. For several decades, suggestions that technology might generate unemployment have been contemptuously dismissed. Today, however, a number of economists and computer scientists suggested that this confidence may have been mis-placed, as advances in artificial intelligence and robotization, assisted by mili-tary funding from the 9/11 wars, have been encroaching on the very areas of informational and affective work—"immaterial labor"—that once were thought to be unassailable bastions of the human against the machine.[47] Even studies skeptical of a net effect of automation on employment agree that it is eroding "middle class" jobs in favor of sharper class polarizations.[48]

If it is Apple that springs to mind when one thinks of super-exploitative factories, it is surely Google, the maker of Android, that springs to mind in the context of extreme automation, in view of its founders' interest in self-driving cars, drone-like office appliances, and singularity theory. Although app work might, in the short term, be seen as a counter to capital's tendency to drive humans out of the production process, apps are themselves part of this vector—in some cases directly linked to factory or office automation and in other cases indirectly feeding the process by downloading to "prosumer" mobile users those functions within highly automated production and dis-tribution systems that still require human decisions.[49] As software tools and programming techniques become more automated, app work is itself subject to this process. But even where humans remain critical for app development, this figures as temporary expansion in the very sector necessary displace larger numbers caught at the intersection of high tech capital's holy trinity of apps, algorithms, and automata. The development of a global labor market for apps, coupled with an approaching wave of labor-destroying automation, to which apps are integral, therefore suggests that our imaginations of an app-filled future should include the possibilities of a profound crisis, both of app work and of work in general.

Notes

1. Douglas MacMillan, Peter Burrows, and Spencer E. Ante, "Inside the app economy," *Business Week*, October 22, 2009.

2. Michael Mandel, *Where the Jobs Are: The App Economy* (South Mountain Economics LLC, 2012) (http://www.technet.org/wp-content/uploads/2012/02/TechNet-App-Economy-Jobs-Study.pdf).

3. David Streitfeld, "As boom lures app creators, tough part is making a living," *New York Times*, November 17, 2012.

4. Michael E. Porter, *Competitive Advantage: Creating and Sustaining Superior Performance* (Free Press, 1985).

5. Jeffrey Henderson, Peter Dicken, Martin Hess, Neil Coe, and Henry Wai-Chung Yeung, "Global production networks and the analysis of economic development," *Review of International Political Economy* 9 (2002), no. 3: 436–464, at 442.

6. Adrian Holzer and Jan Ondrus, "Mobile application market: A developer's perspective," *Telematics and Informatics* 28 (2011), no. 1: 22–31.

7. D. M. Síthigh, "App law within: Rights and regulation in the smartphone age" (research paper, Edinburgh University School of Law, 2012), 22; Nicolas Bär, "An Economic Overview of Internet Mobile Platforms," in *Internet Economics VI*, ed. B. Stiller et al. (University of Zurich Department of Informatics, 2012).

8. Holzer and Ondrus, "Mobile application market."

9. Ibid.

10. Bär, "An Economic Overview of Internet Mobile Platforms," 67–68; Kimberley Spreeuwenberg and Thomas Poell, "Android and the political economy of the mobile Internet: A renewal of open source critique," *First Monday* 17:7 (2012) (http://firstmonday.org).

11. Streitfeld, "As boom lures app creators, tough part is making a living."

12. Birgitta Bergvall-Kåreborn and Debra Howcraft, "Mobile applications development on Apple and Google platforms," *Communications of the Association for Information Systems* 29 (2011), no. 1: 565–580.

13. Holzer and Ondrus, "Mobile application market."

14. Streitfeld, "As boom lures app creators, tough part is making a living."

15. Holzer and Ondrus, "Mobile application market," 23.

16. Bär, "An economic overview of internet mobile platforms."

17. Holzer and Ondrus, "Mobile application market."

18. Chris Stevens, *Appillionaires: Secrets from Developers Who Struck It Rich on the App Store* (Wiley, 2011).

19. Matthew Levinson, "Six hot IT jobs that will pay well in 2012," December 7, 2011 (http://www.itworldcanada.com).

20. Streitfeld, "As boom lures app creators, tough part is making a living."

21. Joshua Wright, "Entrepreneurial Software Developers and the App Economy," January 24, 2013 (http://www.economicmodeling.com).

22. Chris Anderson, *The Long Tail: Why the Future of Business Is Selling Less of More* (Hyperion, 2006).

23. Sarah Perez, "Eat the rich: The app economy's middle class is booming," August 1, 2012 (http://techcrunch.com).

24. Owen Goss, "Results: iOS Game Revenue Survey," September 28, 2011 (http://www.streamingcolour.com).

25. Jessica Lessin and Spencer Ante, "Apps bloom into industry now worth $25 billion," *Globe and Mail*, March 4, 2013.

26. Mark King, "A working life: The app developer," *Guardian*, March 5, 2011.

27. Marie-Josée Legault and Johanna Weststar, "More than the numbers: Independent analysis of the IGDA 2009 Quality of Life Survey," December 2012 (http://gameqol.org).

28. Bergvall-Kåreborn and Howcraft, "Mobile applications development on Apple and Google platforms."

29. Ibid., 570.

30. Síthigh, "App law within."

31. Owen, "Results: iOS game revenue survey."

32. App-promo, "Wake up call—If you spend it, they will come," May 2, 2012 (http://app-promo.com).

33. Rani Molla, "Most app developers make less than $500 a month," October 4, 2012 (http://gigaom.com).

34. Bergvall-Kåreborn and Howcraft, "Mobile applications development on Apple and Google platforms," 568.

35. Michael Hardt and Antonio Negri, *Empire* (Harvard University Press, 2000).

36. Paolo Virno, *A Grammar of the Multitude: For an Analysis of Contemporary Forms of Life* (Semiotext(e), 2004).

37. Michael Hardt and Antonio Negri, *Multitude: War and Democracy in an Age of Empire* (Penguin, 2004).

38. Karl Marx, *Grundrisse* (Penguin, 1973).

39. Carlo Vercellone, "The new articulation of wages, rent and profit in cognitive capitalism," Queen Mary University School of Business and Management, February 29, 2008.

40. Yann Moulier-Boutang, *Cognitive Capitalism* (Polity, 2011).

41. Vercellone, "The new articulation of wages, rent and profit in cognitive capitalism."

42. Andevuni, "Android Developers Union," 2011 (http://andevuni.wordpress .com).

43. Charles Arthur, "Developers express concern over pirated games on Android market," March 17, 2011 (http://www.guardian.co.uk/technology/ blog).

44. Vercellone, "The new articulation of wages, rent and profit in cognitive capitalism."

45. George Caffentzis, *In Letters of Blood and Fire: Work, Machines, and the Crisis of Capitalism* (PM, 2013).

46. Derek Thompson, "What a new, cheap iPhone reveals about Apple's grand strategy," January 29, 2013 (http://www.theatlantic.com).

47. Paul Krugman, "Robots and robber barons," *New York Times*, December 9, 2012; Erik Brynjolfsson and Erik McAfee, *Race Against the Machine* (Digital Frontier Press, 2011).

48. David H. Autor and David Dorn, "The growth of low skill service jobs and the polarization of the U.S. labor market," *American Economic Review* 103.5 (2013): 1553–1597.

49. Vincent Manzerolle, "Mobilizing the audience commodity: Digital labour in a wireless world," *ephemera* 10 (2010): 455–469.

11

Dare et Capere:
Virtuous Mesh and a Targeting Diagram

Vincent Manzerolle and Atle Mikkola Kjøsen

A Capitalist Love Story

Commodities are attracted to money, argues Marx. Indeed, "commodities are in love with money."[1] But what appears as a love affair for things is a fetish between humans; love is exchange value. Hence, where commodities and money find love, their guardians must go; individuals are, after all, but personifications of economic categories—fleeting, repeating inhabitants of economic functions and forms.[2] Once upon a time this meant people journeying to downtowns, stores, plazas, malls, and other places where commodities used to gather in large numbers in hope of finding their significant equivalent. More and more, "because of the Internet and smartphones" (as the sublime and seductive rhetoric of the technological evangelist explains), commodities have begun to follow the money wherever it might be. In fact, commodities must now stalk money and, by extension, their guardians.

The circuit of capital—the basic metaphor of capital as "value in motion"[3]—describes a cybernetic love story based on the cyclical attraction between the economic forms of money and commodities, an attraction consummated at the moment of exchange. The story of courtship then immediately ends just where it began. This libidinal feedback loop is a metaphor for the movement of capital itself, and it captures the contradictions, tensions, and crises characteristic of any loving relationship. The ubiquity and instantaneity of personalized digital media, however, offer greater resources in algorithmic "matchmaking" for commodities that want to find their significant other: value in the form of money.

Inseparably tethered to digital information supply chains, though not central protagonists in the love story they make possible, individual users offer dynamic inputs of capta[4] that ensure the regular, often serendipitous reunion of commodities and money. As mere input and access points from the perspective of capital, apps are a crucial means of mediating and articulating the communicative, attentional, collaborative, and creative capacities of individual users. These capacities, through their conversion into capta, fuel the accelerated wooing between commodities and their equivalents.

In keeping with the theme of this edited collection, our contribution peeks beneath the "surface effects"[5] of apps to highlight the bursts and flows that coordinate and narrate the love story of equivalents. Our analysis emphasizes connectivity as *sine qua non* in supporting the miraculous and mundane features of app-centric media. Connectivity is an essential component in the procession of capital through its circuit, one that enhances the vector of capital's circulation and self-augmentation, offering up new points of connection between money and commodities. Ubiquitous connectivity (UC) is an increasingly dominant form of mediation within advanced capitalist economies, and apps are currently the most effective matchmakers in the courtship between commodities and money. Our task in this essay is to reveal how the app economy mediates this courtship, how this mediation opens up new diagrammatic modes of capta extraction and modeling that drive the guardians of money deeper into the "cash nexus."

The apps economy is not a collection of apps; rather, it is a social relationship between people that is mediated by buttons, diagrams, and algorithms. When money begins to attract commodities, money's guardians become targets—prey stalked by commodity capital.

A Virtuous Mesh

It is now commonplace to discuss apps as enabling mobile devices to become the remote control for our lives.[6] "The smartphone," Brian Chen writes, "is no longer just a portable computer in your pocket. It has become the remote control for your life. Want to flip off the living room lights, unlock your front door or get a reading of your blood pressure? All of this can be done through mobile apps that work with accessories embedded with sensors or an Internet connection."[7] The (potential) rise of the Internet of Things—through IPv6 and the proliferation of machine-to-machine (M2M) standards such as near-field communication (NFC), Bluetooth, and radio-frequency identification (RFID)—will connect all objects into potential communicative nodes within a vast, and prospectively virtuous, mesh of human and machine subjects. To human beings the mesh appears as if it is virtuous because it is based on the essential characteristics of ubiquitous connectivity: ubiquity, immediacy, and personalization.

Here "ubiquity" refers to both perceived and actual colonization of digital media devices and the technical capacity to remain connected at all times. The device is designed to be "always on" and "always on you." Through the harnessing of electromagnetism, everything becomes ubiquitous; everything is everywhere at once because electromagnetism makes any point on Earth, in principle, connectable to any other. Paul Virilio argues that ubiquity, the condition of being present everywhere at the same time, is tele-presence. The condition of ubiquity arrives when the physical displacement of matter is replaced by the continuous emission and reception of simultaneous information. This replacement ushers in a new form of proximity: an electromagnetic proximity in which events, people, and things are no longer confined to a specific spatial location, but are instead tele-present.[8] With ubiquity, the points of production and exchange are no longer places in space, but fields surrounding individuals in possession of smartphones and connectable tablets.

"Immediacy" refers to a perceived instantaneity enabled by the devices and infrastructure of ubiquitous connectivity, tending toward real-time, networked communication and a collapse of distance, be it measured in space or time. In spatial terms, "immediacy" refers to a perceived direct relation or connection, a proximal experience of nearness; temporally it refers to something current or occurring instantly without seeming delay or lapse in time.[9] More generally, "immediacy" highlights the tendency of digital media to accelerate the circulation of information; it describes the general condition of speed-up that is experienced phenomenally at an individual level, and at the level of capital's compulsive space-time compression,[10] to the point of voiding space and time in favor of the present moment.[11]

"Personalization" refers to the tendency of contemporary media to materially incorporate the identity, capta, and relationships of a particular user into an apps ecosystem (e.g., iOS vs. Android) through the extraction of capta from always-on devices. Personalization is a necessary corollary to ubiquitous connectivity; the former makes the latter more profitable. The necessary evolution of this commercial logic is to wed the identity of individual users (represented as an address: phone number, e-mail, user id, ip address, credit card number) with the hardware (SIM cards, NFC chips, unique device identifiers) of devices, and making this connection a prerequisite for provision of services (e.g., wireless connectivity, downloading apps, mobile payment, theft prevention, augmented reality, location-based services). Indeed, personalization of digital media is implicit in the terms "the filter bubble,"[12] "the daily you,"[13] and "monadic communication clusters."[14] Each of these terms attempts to capture how embedded learning algorithms (en)frame individuals into categories, make assumptions about identities and subject positions, and use these assumptions to customize content, services, and prices.[15] The logic of personalization is currently best articulated in the apps ecosystem and Web browsing[16]; however, as the built, physical environment becomes smart and connectable, individual behavior in geophysical space can also be tracked, recorded, and processed. It is personalization, rather than just their smartphones or tablets, that tethers individuals to supply chains, and that allows for better matchmaking of equivalents.

The mesh's virtuous appearance stems primarily from the "fact" that the features of ubiquitous connectivity appear to offer nothing but benefits to us; it increases our bourgeois freedom of choice in the use values that provide solutions to daily problems and needs, some of which we once didn't even know we had. We read—presented in the best marketing lingo that money can buy—that our lives will become much easier to live, more fulfilled, and less stressful. For example, the Speaktoit Assistant is "a virtual buddy for your smartphone that answers questions in natural language, performs tasks, and notifies you about important events." It "saves you time and makes communication with gadgets and Web services easier and less stressful."[17] With Locale (an app that makes your phone aware of your geographical coordinates), "you create situations specifying conditions under which your phone's settings should change. For example, your 'At School' situation notices when your Location condition is '77 Massachusetts Ave.,' and changes your Volume setting to vibrate."[18] And Fred Wilson, principal of Union Square Ventures, agrees: "I'm really taken with Locale. . . . The idea that I have an intelligent phone that configures itself depending on where I am is very powerful."[19] This app is nothing but virtuous, a project manager named Judy tells us: "I used to have this nightmare that my kids were sick at daycare but no one could reach me because my ringer was off. With Locale, now I don't have to worry!"[20] Wikitude, an augmented-reality app, promises to be your "third eye": "New in town? Want to know what's what? With Wikitude, you can explore the world around you with a simple glance. Thanks to Wikitude's millions of points of interest, you're sure to find something new and informative around you right now. . . . Got a taste for Thai tonight? Yum! Use Wikitude to not only find Thai restaurants near you, but narrow in on user reviews and opinions. 3am and need a taxi? Wikitude to the rescue! Want to visually see the tweets happening around you? Can do! Know what that money in your pocket is really worth? Check it with Wikitude! Wikitude is constantly adding new content to the app daily, ensuring you'll never run out of augmented experiences."[21] In this sense, the app economy epitomizes what the personal digital assistant (PDA) once promised in name only: a selfless aid whose sole purpose is to help us live better and more fulfilling lives.

In the virtuous mesh, participation is voluntary, often euphoric, but it requires users to "buy in" by purchasing devices, paying for services, and regularly using the panoply of "solutions to modern living" offered by app-centric media. Whether users accept these terms and conditions through informed consent or through willful ignorance matters little. The effect is the same: acceptance and support for the nominally voluntary basis of the virtuous mesh is to consent that your device to transmit capta about how you use the device, where you are, what you are doing, where you are going, and so on.[22] Proximal effects of connectivity are at once maximized yet increasingly obscured by the perceived simultaneity and invisibility of electromagnetic waves. Messages triggered by our movement through time and space—say, restaurant suggestions from Yelp or Foursquare sent as we move through midtown at dinnertime—provide an immediate utility that conceals the complex interweaving of capta flows, algorithmic processing, and commercial transactions that makes this event and this surface effect possible.

While at the level of individual users these surface effects are variously positioned as solutions to modern life, the qualities we have noted—ubiquity, personalization, and immediacy—have not evolved by accident. Let us therefore leave this world of screens, where everything takes place on illuminated surfaces, for the world of the machine and its micro-dramaturgy of temporal events,[23] which will reveal not only how capital circulates in the apps ecosystem but also how this circulation is produced.

The Targeting Diagram

Underneath what appears as a virtuous mesh of human and machine connectivity we find the pathways of capital's diagram. Wolfgang Ernst argues that the diagram is not a structure; in operation it is a process that unfolds according to the time and logic of the machine that the diagram represents. In this sense, the diagram is a technical term: "the diagrams of circuits and machines' functions, which are abstract descriptions of the operational principles of modern technology."[24] Far from referring to a stable, static machine state, the diagram is "a generative, active and articulating force expressed on the time axis" and is a guiding principle for the potential actions and connections a machine might take and/or make.[25] When, thanks to the connectivity enabled by spectrum technologies, the market is no longer a place but a field, the number of potential moments for equivalents to consummate their love is maximized.

The diagram, however, is also a heuristic tool: "a way to understand how society operates through the diagram of machines."[26] The circuit of capital (figure 11.1) can thus be understood as a diagram that abstractly describes the operational principles of the capitalist mode of production. Capital's operational principle is to reproduce its conditions as the results of its life process.

On this understanding, the capitalist mode of production is locked in society when "capital itself is already presupposed as the condition of its own production."[27] The circuit shows how the reproduction of capital is an iterative process that posits money (M), commodities (C'), capitalist social relations ($M—Lp$ and $M—Mp$) and a production process (P) as both conditions and results of capital's vibrant material process. Operationally, rather than as a static two-dimensional representation, the diagram of capital depicts how labor-as-value is distributed, how capital is accumulated, and how capitalist social relations are reproduced in generalized commodity societies. Capital's diagram is thus also an articulating force on the time axes of labor and circulation, but what is articulated is the domination of labor by capital and the real abstractions that mediate life in the capitalist mode of production. The fetish occupies the place of agency.

As with the technical diagrams that Ernst analyzes, capital's diagram also depicts events in motion: buying, selling, and producing. For capital, stasis is death, devaluation, and negation, whereas movement and acceleration is capital's becoming.[28] Ideally, capital circulates as it does in the mind: at the speed of thought, as one concept turns into the next.[29] When capital assumes a material form next to its economic one, however, it becomes subject to the laws of gravity, thermodynamics, and nation-states, and as such it cannot circulate boundlessly and without friction. As C. J. Arthur explains, capital must invest itself in matter—which may be resistant to it.[30] If matter resists, capital can slow down or get stuck in one of its economic forms, lie fallow, and be negated as capital, though when movements starts up again the economic form gains the social form of capital once again.[31] Capital's movement (its communication) depends on the economic and material form that it assumes, and transmission is always faster than transportation. When capital is in the form of digital objects, riding electromagnetic waves (as is the case with apps), it circulates right under the threshold of absolute velocity. If capital were to circulate at absolute velocity, it would negate its existence.[32]

When capital's diagram is executed as a material process in space and time, capital is nothing but the purposeful movement of matter in various economic guises. As a material process, capital assumes the form of a supply chain (see figure 11.2), comprising the integration of transportation, infrastructure, vehicles, packaging, warehouses, banking, and so on. In this context we can understand logistics as the time-related positioning of value-forms to ensure that commodities, labor power, productive capacity, and information are at the right place, at the right time, and in the right quantity.[33] All of this is to say that capital's representatives, be they humans or machines, work to realize the union of equivalents on a grand scale. Logistics

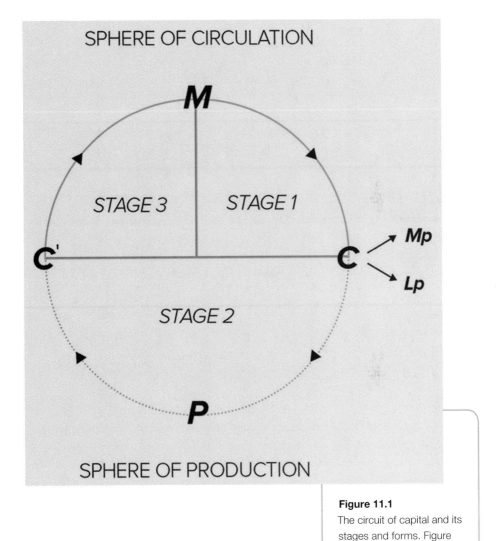

Figure 11.1
The circuit of capital and its stages and forms. Figure designed by Jordan Coop.

or supply-chain management is thus the science of capital's circulation—a science of acceleration compelling progressive reorganizations of space and time. The logistics of capital necessitate the adoption of newer and faster media: from metabolic vehicles to jet transportation, container shipping, and digitized commodities transmitted by tele-technologies operating at the speed of electromagnetic waves.

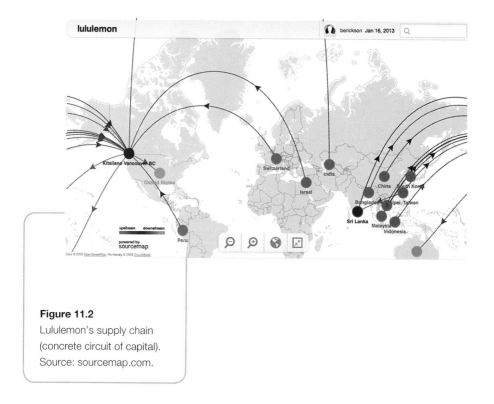

Figure 11.2
Lululemon's supply chain
(concrete circuit of capital).
Source: sourcemap.com.

Because all "independent circuits of individual capitals"[34] are concrete supply chains, the diagram of capital is also topological. Its various moments represent a set of spatial coordinates and temporal waypoints. Thus the individual points of the diagram of capital (figure 11.1) can be mapped onto locations in space (figure 11.2).[35] Thus M can refer to a corporation's headquarters as a center of calculation,[36] P to the point of production and C' to points of exchange (stores and other marketplaces). The functions M—L and M—Mp assume the existence and thus precise location of labor and commodity markets in space, while C'—M' relies on the existence of consumer markets. As figure 11.2 shows, the point of departure for Lululemon's individual circuit of capital is Vancouver. The company acquires (stage 1) the means of production and labor power from markets in Europe, Peru, South Asia, and Southeast Asia. With several points of production (stage 2) in various Asian countries and one in Canada, it sells in only four national markets: Canada, the United States, Australia, and New Zealand (stage 3).

The circuit, as a physically instantiated supply chain, has limited points of connection for commodities and money. They are confined to points, places,

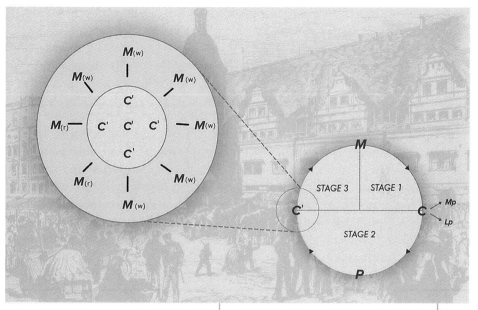

Figure 11.3
The marketplace/commodity as attractor.
Figure designed by Jordan Coop.

or locales—city centers, shopping districts, plazas, malls, and so on. Space is limited: only one store can occupy the location with the most consumer traffic, and inside stores shelf space is limited. Furthermore, it takes time for money to travel to the gathering places of commodities. The possibility of commodity-capital being sold at these places thus depends on the material infrastructure and the marketable appeal of locations that help to attract money, and their guardians. This form of connection between commodities and money in terms of specific but limited locations in space was the dominant mode of circulation before the 1970s' ICT revolution. Figure 11.3, an abstract representation of this type of connection, shows how commodity-capital (C') is the attractor for the money (wages or revenue) of consumers. M(w) designates wages and M(r) designates revenue that workers and capitalists respectively spend to reproduce themselves. C' represents various commodity capitals. The arrows indicate that money's guardians must go to where commodities are located—for example, a Lululemon store in Vancouver.

In the age of computation, telecommunications, and post-Fordism, capital increasingly circulates through the operative diagrams of digital devices, such as tablets, smartphones and the wider apps infrastructure. Capital ceases to circulate in geophysical space, instead traversing the topology of chip-set architectures and the paths of fiber-optic cables between server farms and continents and bouncing off satellites. In the case of apps, capital has ceased to move according to the geographical foundations of real space (roads, railways, etc.) in favor of the "tele-foundation of the global real-time communication system."[37]

It is by way of the operations of telecommunications that capital's circulation itself becomes diagrammatic as it traverses the space of electronics, or, in the words of Wolfgang Ernst, operates according to the intensive microtemporal dramaturgy of events inside computational devices. Capital's circulation comprises pulses, starting, and stopping—a creeping vector employing electromagnetism to close the gap (the "last mile"[38]) between commodities and money. In this process, capital's circulation becomes isomorphic with the technical diagrams of computational devices of smartphones, tablets and the Internet's backbone; the potential points of connection multiply, and are theoretically and technologically, for all intents and purposes, limitless (especially if IPv6 is adopted).[39]

The potential points of connection expand when the market ceases to be a place and instead becomes a field (see figure 11.4), as is the case with any app store. What increases are the potential points of connection between commodities and money. Figure 11.4 shows how the money of consumers ($M(w/r)$) is the attractor when the market is a field. The waves designate that a specific quantity of commodity-capital (C') is transmitted in the "last mile" to a trackable and locatable individual consumer, or, more precisely, to an always-on smartphone pinpointed in space. Thus capital's meeting places for equivalents in love no longer refers to specific locations in space (such as a supermarket, a mall, a corner store, or your home); it now refers to all the potential locations in space that a particular individual might occupy as it moves through geophysical space. When the market is a field, commodities can in principle be transmitted directly to individual consumers wherever they may be in the world.

By privileging money as the attractor, we are not arguing that the individual consumer is empowered, even though the virtuous mesh might give consumers and market evangelists precisely that idea. Rather, what has happened is that one abstraction has replaced another as the center of gravity of attraction.

With the increase in potential connections, the apps economy is the paradigmatic example of what political economists[40] and logistics revolutionaries[41] refer to as the change from a push economy to a pull economy, from

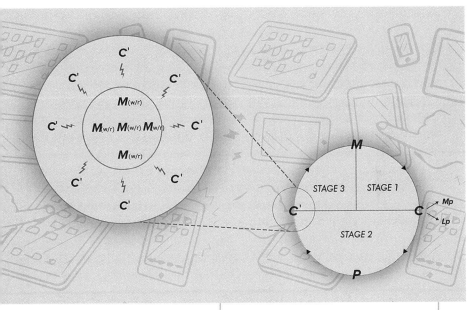

Figure 11.4
The market field/money as attractor.
Figure designed by Jordan Coop.

supply to demand, or (in epochal terms) from Fordism to post-Fordism.[42] In terms of the value form, there has been an inversion of polarity, from commodities to money being the attractor for circulation.[43] Instead of connecting with money in the limited points of connection afforded by physical stores in real space, capital has a virtually limitless field of potential connections in the form of vectors. Although malls are dying and the old bricks-and-mortar stores are going under as online and hybrid businesses are gaining more and more market share,[44] the storefront is omnipresent. The app stores of Apple and Google have such a tele-presence (that is, ubiquity in space) because of always-on smartphones and tablets. Ubiquitous connectivity renders the points of production and exchange to be potentially ubiquitous. Indeed, app stores are neither "here" nor "there."

Accessing these vectors, capital launches its digitized commodities (such as apps and downloadable content) directly at the consumer, in a manner similar to how anti-aircraft batteries attempt to intercept planes or missiles by tracking them in real time. With the app economy/ecosystem, capital has found a way to penetrate directly to the individual rather than going by way of a store located in a specific location in geophysical space. Through the closed supply chain of the app ecosystem, capital has gained a targeting system. This targeting system has the function of predicting who will buy what, where, and when. The system thus calibrates its predictive targeting by aggregating and processing capta extracted from the devices of individual consumers. Nearly all commercial apps extract capta from the individuals who have installed them. Although individuals expect Facebook, Google Maps, and other apps to collect some capta, even innocuous apps (such as Angry Birds and Brightest Flashlight) collect locational and device ID capta.[45]

Points of connection, transmission, and reception offer both opportunities for the exchange of equivalents and opportunities for the extraction of capta about the moment of exchange itself. This confirms what the prophet Marshall McLuhan observed: there is a "steady progression of commercial exchange as the movement of information itself."[46] The cybernetic actualization of this potential is the diagrammatization of capital.

Formerly anonymous and accidental moments of exchange in generalized commodity societies have been replaced with an abstraction, a "known/knowable" individual, produced by the technical capabilities of identifying and pinpointing consumers in space and time. It is through the ubiquity of capta production/extraction that capital enhances the vector (that is, its targeting system) of its circulation and makes the circuit diagrammatic.

Capta are used for the real-time calibration of coordinates, and subsequent extraction of capta allows for the further calibration of capital's targeting system so that commodity-capital can confront an equivalent in money with less friction and more accuracy. This calibration and this targeting occur by making assumptions about who the guardian of the money and the smartphone is. The (en)framing of individuals into categories that John Cheney-Lippold discusses is an excellent example of calibration; the category is the cross-hairs for delivering commodities, content, and advertising. Systemic categorization is a central technique in this targeting system, which ultimately aims for a target market of one.

Cheney-Lippold documents how algorithms using capta from Web-surfing behaviors are used to generate "statistical commonality models to determine one's gender, class, or race in an automatic manner at the same time as [mathematical algorithms] defines the actual meaning of gender, class, or race themselves. . . . It moves the practice of identification into an entirely digital, and thus measureable, plane."[47] For example, "gender becomes a vector, a completely digital and math-based association that defines the meaning of maleness, femaleness, or whatever other gender (or category) a marketer requires."[48] Similarly, pregnancy is a vector. By statistically analyzing point-of-sale capta, the Target Corporation is able to "predict" who is pregnant, because pregnant women buy specific commodities during each trimester. Using capta from such purchases, Target's marketers can send vouchers for commodities that they know a consumer will need as her pregnancy progresses.[49]

Although categories can change both offline and online, algorithmic identity-making represents a "continuous, data-centered manner that modulates both user experience (what content they see) as well as the categorical foundation of those identifications."[50] Users can be "made" more male or female if they browse content that is targeted to a particular gender. In this way consumption itself could be determined by what the individual consumer is presented with, which is only further proof that bourgeois freedom of choice obfuscates how individuals are determined as workers and consumers.

(Dia)Grammatization and the General Intellect

Although the virtuous mesh is only a surface effect, it has the particular function of translating human capacities into capta for the purposes of more effectively uniting the star-crossed lovers of this story. The virtuous mesh articulates us as communicating subjects for capital, but what is most important is the surface appearance of the apparatus that is used to extract our behavior, absorb it, and translate it into usable flows of capta. The concept of the general intellect has found renewed relevance, particularly in view of the seemingly virtuous nature of our networked surroundings. In the same way that industrial machinery absorbed the physical and intellective capacities of the worker in the sphere of production, our networked environment and digital devices absorb our sociality and movement through space and time as streams of capta, which are produced by the very nature of personalization and connectivity in the sphere of circulation (i.e., our cultural and communicative capacities). The sum total of this distributed process is a material expression of what Marx called the "general intellect," i.e., the process by which social knowledge becomes a direct force in production.[51] We argue that the general intellect has become a direct force in circulation as well. The role of the general intellect in the sphere of circulation is thus, in the words of Dodge and Kitchin, "conceptually about understanding a mass of consumers, in order to persuade individuals to consume in ways more profitable to business."[52]

According to Paolo Virno, the "general intellect manifests itself today, above all, as the communication, abstraction, self-reflection of living subjects."[53] This manifestation, however, occurs in a system of machines (as

Marx originally argued), and not as "an attribute of living labour" (as Virno insists).[54] With the rise of ubiquitous media, the body (as "understood/inter-preted" by our devices) becomes inseparable from a steady stream of digital capta. Indeed, the economy and the ecosystem of apps set this articulation in relief. Individuals gain capta-shadows that follow them, and often precede them, as they are (en)framed into categories of gender, race, place, time, and other demographic abstractions. It is these abstractions that subsume the communicativity and self-reflexivity of individuals into the general intellect; indeed, the general intellect consists in part of such abstractions.

When money becomes the attractor, and when capta about its guardian can be extracted, capital acquires a targeting system for its commodities. "The *general intellect* demands virtuosic action, precisely because a consistent portion of this intellect is not channeled in the machine system, but manifests itself in the direct activity of human labor, in its linguistic cooperation."[55] Virno is correct in that a consistent portion of laboring subjects is not subsumed into the general intellect—this is precisely the distinction between data and capta. But capital demands virtuosic action because it can extract capta from and about these actions—capta that then become part of the (machinic) general intellect. Because the general intellect can subsume only capta, and not data, it has to fill in the rest for itself by making assumptions about an individual's gender, race, consumption capacity, and so on. Capital must rely on abstractions about individuals based on a mass of consumers; the concrete individual, however, is a singularity that can never be fully captured and subsumed.

In the sphere of circulation, it is not surplus value that can be extracted from communicative and intellectual activities; it is capta, via the apps running on smartphones and tablets. Capta about these activities are, in turn, processed into abstractions that allow commodity capital to lock onto and fire at its target. The stakes are high: miss and love is lost. It is not surprising that the moment and activity in which capital is particularly interested is exchange itself. There is, therefore, an intense interest in producing apps that provide payment and financial services by telecommunications providers (e.g., the ISIS payment system used by AT&T and other companies), device/component designers (e.g., Apple's Passbook), and software developers (e.g., Google Wallet).

The subsumption of social and communicative capacities into the general intellect is similar, in effect, to what Bernard Stiegler refers to as "grammatization," which involves the "exteriorization of memory in all its forms" through a variety of technical organs[56] but mainly through communication devices that are closely integrated with the identity and the embodied spatio-temporal vector of an individual. Grammatization can thus be seen as serial or mass amputation—dissection—as more and more of the human being's senses, organs, and capacities are exteriorized, replaced by the meta-prosthetic of universal computing machines. Apps are anatomical; the app store or the buttons on your screen are, for all intents and purposes, mimetic of an Angus Beef diagram. Rather than showing where the various cuts of meat are located on a steer, apps show the various "cuts" of capta to the representatives of capital, specifically those that base capital accumulation on "big data."

The aim of customer profiling and personalization, and what these animated abstractions are used for, is to identify "people who poses the characteristics that make them a potential purchaser of a product, to encourage them to buy it, and to reward them for the purchase in order to maintain brand loyalty."[57] This invisible "captaveillance" is an embedded component of our social lives and relationships as they are increasingly mediated by digital networked technologies. The combination of personalization and ubiquity makes the widening circulation of capta a resource in the diagrammatic expansion and intensification of capital's vector.

The "targeting" mechanisms that underpin the modeling of consumer identity and consumer behavior also reveals the ontological presuppositions that have been central to cybernetics since that term was coined. As Peter Galison writes, "anti-aircraft fire control was the key to cybernetics. Faced with the problem of hitting fast maneuverable bombers with ground-based artillery, [Norbert] Wiener brought to bear his own established interest in feedback mechanisms, communication technology, and nonlinear processes."[58] Just as Wiener's proto-cybernetic anti-aircraft targeting system posited the "ontology of the enemy" as a composite servo-mechanical system that assumed that the pilot and the craft were inseparable in order to model the enemy's being, the diagrammatic coordination of equivalents frames the ontology of the consumer as a mobile relay point and an independent center of exchange in the sphere of circulation. Whereas the enemy offered a final "exchange" of fire (life/death), the virtuous mesh conceals the targeting functions that posit the user as a relay in an accelerating process of "matchmaking" between commodities and money. In the final instance, the target is itself always an imaginary entity, a projection born from a cybernetic system defined by a recursive exchange of capta.

The whole life of a society in which post-Fordist conditions of circulation prevail presents itself as an immense accumulation of capta. All that is lived can be statistically aggregated and analyzed. Ultimately, what resides on our portable devices, though seemingly innocuous, is the final anchor point that links the circuitry of computational capitalism to individuals, forcing us to draw individuals into the diagram of capital. The fetish is thus strengthened, and so is our subjection to the abstractions of economic categories and processes.

Acknowledgments

Thanks to Siobhan Watters, Lee McGuigan, and Julia Campbell for reading and commenting on a draft, Stacy Manzerolle for helping with the figures, and Jordan Coop for final design of the figures.

Notes

1. Karl Marx, *Capital*, volume I (Penguin Classics, 1976), 201–203.

2. Ibid., 92, 178–179.

3. David Harvey, *The Condition of Postmodernity: An Enquiry into Origins of Cultural Change* (Blackwell, 1989), 107.

4. To properly distinguish the relationship between potentiality and articulation in this process, we use Kitchen and Dodge's distinction between data and capta: "data is everything that it is possible to know about [a] person." By contrast, capta are "units that have been selected and harvested from the sum of all potential data." Rob Kitchin and Martin Dodge, *Code/Space: Software and Everyday Life* (MIT Press, 2011), 5. As Kitchin and Dodge explain, this distinction is based on the etymological roots of each term: the Latin root of "data" is *dare*, meaning "to give," whereas "capta," from the Latin *capere*, means "to take" (261). Through apps individuals give and capital takes capta that is consequently processed and used for capital's matchmaking of economic forms.

5. Friedrich A. Kittler, *Gramophone, Film, Typewriter* (Stanford University Press, 1999), 1.

6. See, e.g., Matt Cohler, "Great mobile apps are remote controls for real life," at http://techcrunch.com; William Webb, "The future of mobile phones: A remote control for your life," *The Independent*, May 14, 2007.

7. Brian X. Chen, "Smartphones become life's remote control," *New York Times*, January 11, 2013.

8. Paul Virilio, *Open Sky* (Verso, 1997), 13, 17, 25. See also Paul Virilio, *The Original Accident* (Polity, 2007), 26, 49.

9. John Tomlinson, *The Culture of Speed: The Coming of Immediacy* (Sage, 2007), 74.

10. Harvey, *The Condition of Postmodernity.*

11. Virilio, *Open Sky.*

12. Eli Pariser, *The Filter Bubble: What the Internet Is Hiding From You* (Viking, 2011).

13. Joseph Turow, *The Daily You: How the New Advertising Industry Is Defining Your Identity and Your Worth* (Yale University Press, 2011).

14. Kenneth Gergen, "Mobile communication and the transformation of democratic process," in *Handbook of Mobile Communications Studies*, ed. James Katz (MIT Press, 2008), 297–299.

15. See John Cheney-Lippold, "A new algorithmic identity: Soft biopolitics and the modulation of control," *Theory, Culture, Society* 28 (2011), no. 6: 164–181; Astrid Mager, "Algorithmic ideology: How capitalist society shapes search engines," *Information, Communication and Society* 15 (2012), no. 5: 769–787.

16. Cheney-Lippold, "A new algorithmic identity."

17. Locale product description page (www.twofortyfouram.com/product), accessed January 20, 2013.

18. Ibid.

19. Locale page on Google Play (https://play.google.com/store/apps/details?id=com.twofortyfouram.locale&hl=en), accessed February 4, 2013.

20. Ibid.

21. Wikitude (www.wikitude.com/app), accessed February 3, 2013.

22. For the purposes of analytic clarity, let us set aside questions of privacy and security, because in principle these are necessary concerns for commercial forces too (after all, perceived security risks and overt surveillance mechanisms scare consumers away). The goal is to have consumers, one way or another, opt-in to these processes. For this to occur, individuals must accept the basic "terms and conditions" (both in a legal and experiential sense) associated with ubiquitous connectivity. Such presumably voluntary processes help validate technologies and services of ubiquitous connectivity as necessary components of a virtuous mesh, one seamlessly embedded in everyday life and rapidly disappearing from direct oversight by all but the most technologically savvy users.

23. Wolfgang Ernst, ". . . Else loop forever: The untimeliness of media," presented at conference "Il Senso della Fine," Universita degli Studi di Urbino, Centro Internazionale di Semiotica e Linguistica, September 10–12, 2009.

24. Jussi Parikka, *What Is Media Archaeology?* (Polity, 2012), 132.

25. Jussi Parikka, "Operative media archaeology: Wolfgang Ernst's materialist media diagrammatics," *Theory, Culture & Society* 28 (2011), no. 5: 66.

26. Ibid., 65.

27. Karl Marx, *Grundrisse: Foundations of the Critique of Political Economy* (Penguin Classics, 1973), 715.

28. Ibid., 519, 536, 621.

29. Ibid., 548.

30. C. J. Arthur, "The fluidity of capital and the logic of the concept," in *The Circulation of Capital: Essays on Volume Two of Marx's Capital*, ed. C. J. Arthur and G. Reuten (Macmillan, 1998), 117.

31. Ibid., 107–108.

32. For a more detailed explication of the function of digital media in relation to capital's logic of acceleration, see Vincent Manzerolle and Atle Mikkola Kjøsen, "The communication of capital: Digital media and the logic of acceleration," *tripleC: Communication, Capitalism & Critique* 10 (2012), no. 2: 214–229; Atle Mikkola Kjøsen, An Accident of Value: A Marxist-Virilian Analysis of Digital Piracy, master's thesis, University of Western Ontario, 2010, 9–35.

33. A textbook definition goes as follows: "Logistics can be broadly defined as time-related positioning of resources ensuring that material, people, operational capacity and information are in the right place at the right time in the right quantity and at the right quality and cost." Alan E. Branch, *Global Supply Chain Management and International Logistics* (Routledge, 2009), 1.

34. Marx, Karl, *Capital*, volume II (Penguin Classics, 1978), 110.

35. With the advent of the Internet of Things, the separate topologies of aliquot parts of capital can be tracked in real time.

36. See Bruno Latour, *Science in Action: How to Follow Scientists and Engineers through Society* (Open University Press, 1987).

37. Paul Virilio, *The Information Bomb* (Verso, 2000), 9.

38. "Last mile" is a figurative term used within the telecommunications industry referring to the final stretch linking backhaul infrastructure and the user/subscriber. Historically, the last mile is usually the most costly, technically challenging, and often politically charged; see Michele Martin, "Communication and social forms: The development of the telephone, 1876–1920," *Antipode* 23 (1991), no. 3: 307–333. In our essay, it describes the field in which individuals are ubiquitously connected by wireless devices. More important, in assigning mobile devices IP addresses, "the last mile" refers to the final relay point in the diagrammatic circulation of capital.

39. IPv6 refers to a new Internet protocol, launched on June 6, 2012, that increases the number of existing addresses from 4.3 billion (with IPv4) to roughly 3.4×10^{38}. In so doing, this new protocol allows the assignment of Internet addresses to devices previously unconnected. IPv6 provides the basis for an "Internet of Things" in which virtually any device might be brought online. More information on IPv6 and the Internet of Things can be found at http://ioftthings.org.

40. Harvey, *Condition of Postmodernity*, 177.

41. Martin Christopher, *Logistics & Supply Chain Management* (Prentice-Hall, 2011), 104.

42. Harvey, *The Condition of Postmodernity*; Nick Dyer-Witheford, *Cyber-Marx: Cycles and Circuits of Struggle in High-Technology Capitalism* (University of Illinois Press, 1999).

43. The app economy is, of course, not the first example of money attracting commodities. It is an extension of mail order shopping combined with the postal payment of checks or money orders or wiring money in advance (Kitchin and Dodge, *Code/Space: Software and Everyday Life*, 184), and more recently hybrid online/offline stores of which Amazon is currently the paradigmatic example. However, in these cases the purchased commodity did not come directly to the individual consumer wherever it was located, but to a home or otherwise established physical postal address. The apps ecosystem thus enables exchange and consumption on the move, but with same-day delivery this could become a reality for even physical commodities, for example, by using drones to deliver directly to the consumer, as the case of the TacoCopter demonstrates. See http://elidourado.com/blog/tag/fedex.

44. Jeff Jordan, "The death of the American shopping mall," December 26, 2012 (http://www.theatlanticcitie.com/jobs-and-economy/2012/12/death-american-shopping-mall/4525).

45. Jialiu Lin, Norman Sadeh, Shahriyar Amini, Janne Lindqvist, Jason I. Hong, and Joy Zhang, "Expectation and purpose: Understanding users'

mental models of mobile app privacy through crowdsourcing," in *UbiComp* '12 (ACM, 2012).

46. Marshall McLuhan, *Understanding Media: The Extensions of Man* (McGraw-Hill, 1964), 149.

47. Cheney-Lippold, "A new algorithmic identity," 165.

48. Ibid., 170.

49. Charles Duhigg, "How companies learn your secrets," *New York Times Magazine*, February 16, 2012.

50. Cheney-Lippold, "A new algorithmic identity," 172.

51. Marx, *Grundrisse*, 704–706.

52. Kitchin and Dodge, *Code/Space: Software and Everyday Life*, 203.

53. Paolo A. Virno, *Grammar of the Multitude: For an Analysis of Contemporary Forms of Life* (Semiotext(e), 2004), 65.

54. Ibid.

55. Ibid.

56. Bernard Stiegler, *For a New Critique of Political Economy* (Polity, 2010), 34.

57. Kitchin and Dodge, *Code/Space: Software and Everyday Life*, 203–204.

58. Peter Galison, "The ontology of the enemy: Norbert Wiener and the cybernetic vision," *Critical Inquiry* 21 (1994), no. 1: 228–266, at 232.

12
Construction of the App Economy in the Networked Korean Society

Dal Yong Jin

With the rapid growth of smartphones and applications, Korean society has witnessed a dramatic change. While traditional information and communication technologies (ICTs) such as television, fixed telephone lines, and the Internet are still significant in the national economy and culture, smartphones and applications have swiftly become a new area that corporations and people desire to own and use. Many countries—Western and non-Western—have developed smartphones and applications (apps) to advance socio-cultural, technical, and economic growth. Korea is a world leader in both penetration of smartphones and use of apps. Both huge ICT corporations (including Samsung and LG) and small start-ups have invested in apps because apps have been lucrative ever since Apple launched the Apple Store after the tremendous success of the iPhone in 2009.[1]

The development of the app economy depends not only on infrastructure but also on software,[2] and the evolution of smartphones has consequently influenced the Korean software sector. The widespread use of apps has enabled people to engage in mobile games and online stock transactions and to search for information, from weather to maps; they have become essential for communication purposes as well as for entertainment activities. As was correctly observed in an Associated Press article, "a handful of smartphone apps that began as basic instant messaging services have amassed several million users in Korea in just a couple of years, mounting a challenge to the popularity of online hangouts such as Facebook as they branch into games, e-commerce, celebrity news and other areas."[3]

This essay explores aspects of smartphones and app services in Korea and their implications for the app economy. It analyzes the evolution of smartphones and apps in the socioeconomic milieu specific to the country, which is becoming part of the global information economy. It especially recognizes technology as a socioeconomic product that has historically been constituted by certain forms of knowledge and social practice; therefore, it discusses the role of people in the diffusion of app services and the implications for the networked society.[4]

Construction of the App Economy in the Twenty-First Century

Continuous dramatic improvements in ICTs, including the Internet and smartphones, are changing the ways in which knowledge is generated and communicated, and thereby the ways that firms operate, markets function, and economies develop. ICTs are providing a new electronic communication foundation or infrastructure for the economy, capable of transmitting all forms of information instantly over global networks.[5] As Manuel Castells notes, "one of the key features of information society is the networking logic of its basic structure, which explains the use of the concept of network society."[6] As Jan van Dijk points out,[7] "networks have become the nervous system of society." Emphasizing the network as one of the major systems in capitalism, Dan Schiller argues, "networks are directly generalizing the social and cultural range of the capitalist economy as never before."[8] What they commonly underscore is the major role of ICTs, in particular the Internet, in modern capitalism.

The notion of information economy should be readdressed, because some significant shifts are taking shape because of smartphones and apps. Until a few years ago, the bite-size software programs people loaded onto their mobile phones or tapped into on the Web seemed mostly to be silly games and pointless novelties.[9] However, smartphone apps have created new capital for ICT corporations and have changed the way business gets done. The app economy—that is, the range of economic activity surrounding mobile applications that encompasses the sale of apps, ad revenue from apps, and digital devices on which apps are designed to run—has evolved in just a few years.[10] The proliferation of smartphones has created an app-centric global marketplace, ushering in an app economy that is driving new business models and revenue streams across all industries.[11] The development of apps underlines that people are increasingly going online using smartphones and other wireless devices,[12] which proves the existence of a new pattern of media convergence with smartphones in the twenty-first century. People are keen to use smartphones because they integrate several functions, such as the Internet, telephony, and email, in a single gadget, and the convergence of old media (telephony) and the new media (Internet) in their hands has changed their daily lives completely.

Korea's smartphone revolution occurred relatively late. In November of 2009, when the iPhone was introduced in Korea, domestic mobile producers barely competed with it; however, the iPhone made Koreans aware of the significance of smartphones as the primary information technology for the national economy and the youth culture. The pace of the iPhone's penetration into Korea's tech-savvy market was about twice that of overseas markets that adopted the phone earlier, and an "iPhone effect" created a chain reaction in the mobile-carrier-centered market.[13] In fact, before the iPhone's arrival, the Korean companies Samsung and LG together claimed more than 80 percent of the domestic mobile market. However, at the end of November 2011, their combined domestic market share was estimated at 61 percent. Under these circumstances, Samsung tightened its ties with Apple's rising rival in the smartphone market, Google, with its Android-based Galaxy smartphone.[14] LG, the world's number-three maker of mobile phones after Samsung and Nokia, replaced its chief executive and jumped into the smartphone business.

Although Korea was a comparative latecomer to the smartphone revolution, the rate of the shift from feature phones to smartphones has been remarkable. Korea had 53.4 million mobile subscriptions at the end of November 2012, more than one subscription per person in the country.[15] The number of smartphone users exceeded 32 million by the end of November 2012, comprising 60 percent of total mobile phone users, an increase from around 470,000 (1.0 percent of total mobile phone users) in November 2009.[16] This was one of the fastest take-up rates in the world. In the United States, 50.4 percent of mobile subscribers owned smartphones in March 2012, up from 47.8 percent in December 2011 and up from around 21 percent in late 2009.[17] In China, the world's biggest mobile market, the smartphone penetration rate was 25 percent at the end of September 2013, up from 5.7 percent in 2009.[18] The figure in many developing countries is more than 50 percent.

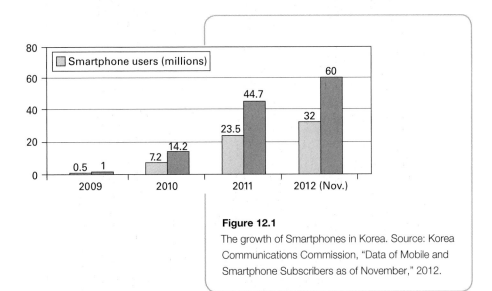

Figure 12.1

The growth of Smartphones in Korea. Source: Korea Communications Commission, "Data of Mobile and Smartphone Subscribers as of November," 2012.

Furthermore, Korea's mobile operators have rushed to offer faster data service by setting up a more advanced network technology, called Long-Term Evolution (LTE). SK Telecom (the country's largest mobile carrier by subscriber base) and LG UPlus launched LTE networks in July 2011, followed by a network from KT, the second-largest mobile provider.[19] LTE has become one of the most significant structural elements of the recent boom in mobile games, and this trend is expected to continue.

Major Characteristics of the Korean App Economy

The diffusion and use of smartphones and apps have been dedicated to shaping economic growth, business performance, and subscribers. Among the significant features of the Korean app economy in tandem with the evolution of smartphones are the ways in which smartphones access the Internet, the concentration of smartphones, and the dominant position of foreign operating systems.

Smartphones as Gateways to the Internet

Diverse elements differentiate the Korean app economy from other major markets, and the ways that people connect smartphones to the Internet are distinctive. To begin with, mobile access options are unique, ranging from using free Wi-Fi at a hotspot to getting a mobile broadband (e.g., 3G) network on a mobile device for "anywhere, anytime" Internet access. In Korea, among all the smartphone users, wireless Wi-Fi was the most common option to connect to

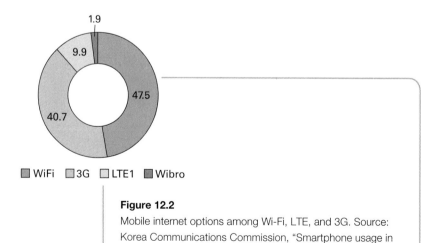

Figure 12.2
Mobile internet options among Wi-Fi, LTE, and 3G. Source: Korea Communications Commission, "Smartphone usage in the first half of 2012."

the Internet.[20] During the first half of 2012, Wi-Fi consisted of 47.5 percent of mobile Internet use, followed by 3G (referring to the collection of third-generation mobile technologies that are designed to allow mobile operators to offer integrated data and voice services over mobile networks) (40.7 percent), LTE (9.9 percent), and Wibro (1.9 percent).[21] However, several telecommunications service providers have rapidly developed LTE, and LTE will be the most common way to connect to the Internet. Korea is set to be the world's first major mobile market to migrate the majority of its subscribers to LTE networks.

Smartphone Brand Shifts

The Korean smartphone market has experienced a dramatic shift, again, since the introduction of the iPhone in November 2009. Only a year later, at the end of 2010, iPhones had 23.2 percent of the market, even though the two largest mobile makers, Samsung and LG, are based in Korea. However, this newfound success did not last long, and the iPhone's market share dropped to 12.9 percent in December 2011 to only 2 percent in the first half of 2012, mainly because of the strong presence of domestic smartphones. Samsung, in particular, has rapidly increased its market share, from 31 percent in 2010 to 56 percent in the first half of 2012. Thanks to the global success of Galaxy SIII in the second half of 2012, Samsung's market share soared. Meanwhile, LG and Pantech each had about 20 percent of the market. Although there were a few more foreign-based smartphone providers, including the Taiwanese firm HTC, their market shares plunged, and some of them, including HTC, had no choice but to leave the Korean market at the end of 2010.[22]

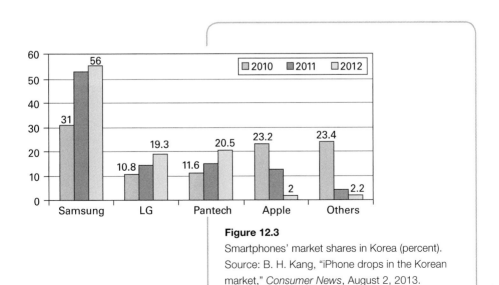

Figure 12.3
Smartphones' market shares in Korea (percent).
Source: B. H. Kang, "iPhone drops in the Korean market," *Consumer News*, August 2, 2013.

Thus, foreign brands have not been successful in Korea, except for the first year after the iPhone was introduced in the country. Some newspapers, including *Hankook Economic Daily*, have dubbed the Korean mobile market "the cemetery of foreign smartphones."[23] The quality of domestic smartphones has been greatly improved, and people receive timely services. However, subsidies provided by smartphone service providers are also crucial in the Korean market. In contrast with the iPhone, Korean smartphone service providers subsidize as much as $540, resulting in cheaper prices than for foreign smartphones.[24] Regardless of the fact that the Korean government has introduced smartphone price labeling since January 2012 in order to control this unfair market practice, it is ineffective because of over-competition among smartphone service providers.

Dominant Foreign Operating Systems

Paradoxically, the dominant power of domestic smartphone makers has resulted in the construction of a unique ecology in the operation system (OS) market, because foreign-based operating systems are dominant. Breaking down the smartphone market by operating systems, one finds that Android is the largest in Korea. Android had only 6 percent of the market in 2010; however, its share soared to as much as 89.7 percent,[25] while that of Apple's iOS plunged from 43.3 percent in 2010 to only 9.3 percent in October 2012.

Android and iOS seem to be everywhere in the world, and they have become hegemons in the smartphone industry. Of course, survey research shows compelling evidence of the growth of Android in the world. Android

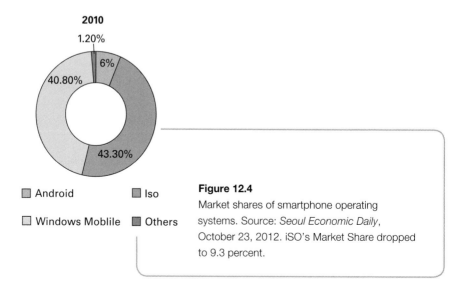

2010

1.20%

6%

40.80%

43.30%

☑ Android   ☐ Iso
☐ Windows Moblile   ■ Others

Figure 12.4
Market shares of smartphone operating systems. Source: *Seoul Economic Daily*, October 23, 2012. iSO's Market Share dropped to 9.3 percent.

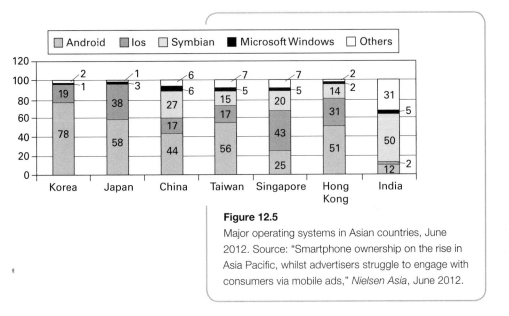

Figure 12.5
Major operating systems in Asian countries, June 2012. Source: "Smartphone ownership on the rise in Asia Pacific, whilst advertisers struggle to engage with consumers via mobile ads," *Nielsen Asia*, June 2012.

was the leader in 35 of the 56 countries that the research firm Canalys tracks around the world, achieving a global market share of 48 percent in the second quarter of 2011. Growth was bolstered by the strong Android performance of products from a number of vendors, including Samsung and LG in Korea, HTC in Taiwan, and ZTE and Hwazei in China.[26] Korea is the country with the greatest dependency on Android. As figure 12.5 shows, smartphones using the Android OS are more dominant in Korea's market than in other regional markets.[27] Although Korean IT corporations have advanced their own gadgets, they heavily rely on Western-based operating systems, including Android.

A Smartphone Apps Wonderland

The rapid growth in the use of smartphones has also increased the importance of applications, as they bring added value into the smartphone market.[28] There are many smartphone services that are using apps because apps give users the opportunity to keep their phones updated with the latest software and services. Among the significant apps are domestic search portals (e.g., Naver and Daum), messaging apps (e.g., KaKaoTalk), and free international calling apps (e.g., OTO and ACE) (figure 12.6). These apps are all free and can be found in the iTunes store or on the Android market.

As a reflection of the importance of the use of apps, Korea shows its unique smartphone environment in conjunction with apps. While people worldwide

Figure 12.6
Source: "Must have smartphone apps for living in Korea," at http://seoulistic.com.

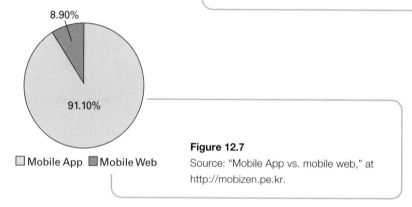

Figure 12.7
Source: "Mobile App vs. mobile web," at http://mobizen.pe.kr.

use their smartphones evenly between mobile app (50.7 percent) and mobile Web (49.3 percent) as of December 2011, Koreans overwhelmingly use smartphones for apps (91.1 percent) over Web (8.9 percent) in terms of their usage time for smartphones.[29] Although several users enjoy smartphones for Web searching, the majority of Koreans use them for apps, including mobile messaging, games, and maps. This implies that the Korean mobile culture revolves around apps instead of the Web, bucking the global trend.

In Korea, owing to the strong presence of domestic search engines (including Naver, Daum, and Nate), global search portals, such as Google and Yahoo, are not dominant players in the realms of either mobile search or Web search. Naver has rapidly become the primary player in the mobile search field, as it is in the Internet search area. Naver's market share in the mobile search area

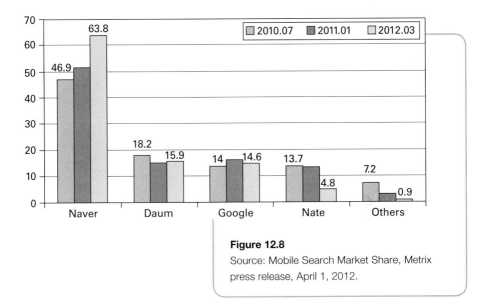

Figure 12.8
Source: Mobile Search Market Share, Metrix press release, April 1, 2012.

was 63.8 percent at the end of March 2012, up from 46.9 percent in July 2010 and 51.9 percent in January 2011. Daum, the second-largest portal, also had 15.9 percent; therefore, including SK's Nate, domestic portals had about 85 percent of the mobile search sector. During the same period, Google, despite being the largest global search engine, had only 14.6 percent of the market; Yahoos had only 0.8 percent.[30]

Google indeed falls short in Korea. No matter how powerful Google's search engine may be, it doesn't have enough Korean-language data to trawl to satisfy Korean customers. Naver's founders realized that when a person was searching in Korean there was hardly anything to be found. They set out to create content and databases so that a person searching in Korean would find high-quality content. Google and Yahoo are making efforts to catch up in this market. Google, for example, recently tried to improve its Korean home page.[31] Although Google and Yahoo are global leaders in search engines, they hardly penetrate the Korean market, because they are not willing to consider local people's preferences.

As will be detailed later, Koreans use Web portals to enjoy several apps, including mobile games, weather, and news; however, these two global leaders have focused on information search, which has made them less influential in Korea. Many global ICTs have appropriated globalization strategies in order to attract local customers.[32] Disney, MTV, STARTV, and other major media firms have embraced the motto "think globally, act locally," but so far Google has mainly pursued global standards in local markets. Google and Yahoo did not make any tangible changes in response to their failure in the Korean market. Yahoo decided to leave Korea at the end of 2012. Yahoo joined the Korean Internet market in 1997 and commanded an 80 percent share of all searches from within Korea in the late 1990s; however, it can no longer compete with domestic search engines. Google's share in the Web search market was only 2 percent in 2012.[33] With the exception of Android-based and iOS-based units, the smartphones and other apps used in Korea are primarily produced by Korean IT corporations.

Apps Embedded in People's Daily Lives

With a plethora of applications now available for smartphone users, it is not surprising that app use is high in Pacific Asia. Korea and Japan had the highest incidence of app use in 2012 (81 percent), while Korea and Singapore smartphone users had the largest numbers of regularly used apps (with medians of 55 and 47 respectively) (figure 12.9). Games were the most popular app category across Pacific Asia, except in Indonesia (where music and social networking apps were favored).[34]

Smartphone apps are popular among Koreans. While there are diverse reasons for the use of smartphones, apps are among the most significant factors for smartphone users. People use smartphones as alarms, for maps, for navigation, for music, for instant messenging, and for mobile gaming. According to a survey conducted in October 2012, about 42.4 percent of Korean smartphone owners use their phones to connect to mobile apps in Korea.[35]

Communication and mobile gaming are two major apps for Korean users. Previously, voice calling was the priority for 39.3 percent of users, while text messaging was the main use for 18.3 percent. Increased use of instant mobile messenger services, such as KaKaoTalk, has led to a decrease in the use of traditional text messaging: 68.1 percent of Korean users said they now use text-messaging services less than before, a jump from 41 percent in a similar survey conducted in July 2012. However, with the sudden popularity of mobile games since late 2012, the situation has changed. According to the Korea Communications Commission,[36] smartphone users downloaded 43.3 apps on average in the first half of 2012, and they used 11.4 apps daily. The most popular app type is mobile gaming (78 percent), followed by communication (55.8 percent), weather (51.7 percent), news (48.8 percent), and music (48.5 percent). Relatively small numbers of smartphone users download apps for education (17.5 percent) and e-books (14.3 percent), which means that the majority of smartphone users enjoy apps for entertainment or use them to get information, such as maps and navigation.

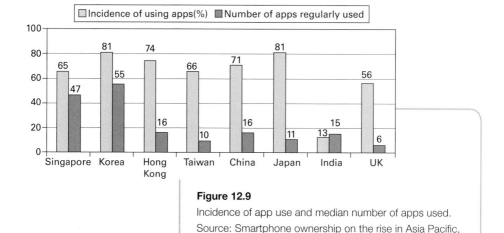

Figure 12.9
Incidence of app use and median number of apps used.
Source: Smartphone ownership on the rise in Asia Pacific,
whilst advertisers struggle to engage with consumers via
mobile ads," Nielsen Asia, June 2012.

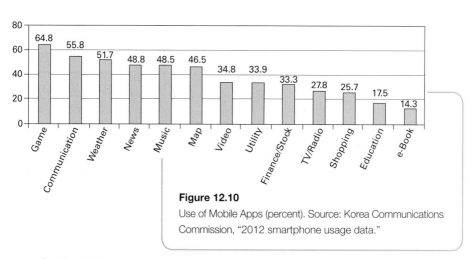

Figure 12.10
Use of Mobile Apps (percent). Source: Korea Communications
Commission, "2012 smartphone usage data."

October, 2012

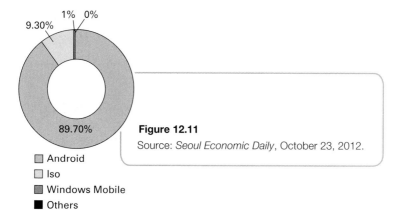

Figure 12.11
Source: *Seoul Economic Daily*, October 23, 2012.

- Android
- Iso
- Windows Mobile
- Others

KakaoTalk Fever

Mobile social networking sites (SNSs) have shown a unique trend. Regardless of the rapid growth of Facebook and Twitter as foreign-based SNSs in Korea, domestic mobile SNSs are dominating the Korean market. The leader among mobile SNSs in Korea is KakaoTalk, a mobile messenger application and a virtual machine platform that enables smartphone users to download services and other applications, including mobile games. Virtually everyone has in Korea this app, because it started as the go-to messaging service for any smartphone user. As Henry Jenkins points out,[37] people's migratory behavior in pursuing new trends has become a primary reason for media convergence, and the sudden boom of KakaoTalk has fundamentally been made possible by the changing pattern in people's smartphone use. KakaoTalk is a downloadable software application for mobile devices that allows its users to send and receive messages (including photos, videos, and contact information) for free, and it has become the most popular application for mobile games. Released in 2010, KakaoTalk reached 100 million registered users in August 2013. In August 2012, when it reached 57 million, about 24 million of them used it daily, and more than 3.4 billion messages were sent every day.[38] Among mobile apps in SNSs, KakaoTalk already had as many as 3.56 million users as of January 2011, followed by Nate and Naver. Domestic mobile apps are dominant. Twitter and Facebook are the only two Western-based apps in the realm of mobile SNS. KakaoTalk has become the most powerful mobile SNS in Korea.

Many users find KakaoTalk convenient because it provides both the function of online messenging (thus one can send and receive files and have a group chatting) and the function of normal text messenging. Many people use KakaoTalk not only for communication but also to update their profiles and photos. And KakaoTalk has played an indispensable role in generating a nationwide mobile gaming boom. Many Korean users were first exposed to mobile gaming through KakaoTalk. Once KakaoTalk started a mobile gaming service on its own app, in August 30, 2012, people immediately became so accustomed to using KakaoTalk services that they were unwilling to return to other platforms. Before then, no particular app provided exclusive mobile gaming services; however, when KakaoTalk began its service, many mobile game developers tried to get a contract with KakaoTalk because of its popularity as a smartphone app. Previously, smartphone users used KakaoTalk primarily for messenging; however, many of them now also use it as a mobile game app.

Smartphones and apps stimulate new youth culture in conjunction with KakaoTalk and mobile games, because many younger people in their teens and in their twenties have switched their major leisure activities, from online gaming to mobile gamin, for example. However, as the cases of KakaoTalk

Figure 12.12
Source: "Spotlight on Asian import messaging apps gaining traction stateside," at http://www.digitaltrends.com, 2012.

and other apps prove, the current app economy differentiates itself from the general notion of information economy because their primary benefit lies not in their intrinsic value but in their applications for other purposes.[39] Unlike previous mobile ICTs, smartphones support third-party software. The Korean app economy will continue to grow as application software and multimedia content can be provided more easily and reliably through smartphones.

Conclusion and Discussion

According to one survey conducted in October 2012, many Korean parents worried more about smartphone addiction (48.1 percent) than about Internet pornography (35.9 percent), and about 65 percent of the parents who participated in the survey reported occasional conflicts with their children due to smartphones and apps.[40] KaKaoTalk bullying is also a new side effect that the app economy faces. Though school bullying and/or cyber bullying are not new in Korea, many school gangs harass some students in school via KaKao-Talk due to its anonymity as well as non-face-to-face communication service.

Some students even snatch other students' smartphones for their own use in school. The victims of KaKaoTalk bullying usually have high monthly bills because bullies use their phones to download and enjoy apps.[41]

The app economy based on smartphones and apps service has begun to experience several negative effects. As Dan Schiller correctly argues,[42] as with the case of mobile phones, the world of smartphones and apps is also "not created to deliver us into an era of playfulness and personal freedom. It came to us, rather, as a complex historical extension of the domination and inequality that continue to define our divided societies." Meanwhile, another major issue is the concentration of the network power among only an oligopoly of mega telecommunications corporations. This raises a concern for governments with respect to the application of existing competition laws and/or direct industry regulation, as William Melody notes.[43]

Nevertheless, Korea's unprecedented app economy has fundamentally changed Korean society. Regardless of the fact that the smartphone revolution occurred relatively late, Korea's smartphone producers have made cutting-edge gadgets, and smartphone operators have rushed to offer faster data service by setting up more advanced network technology, known as LTE. Korea is about to be the world's first major smartphone market to migrate the majority of its subscribers to LTE networks. In addition, as the cases of KaKaoTalk and other apps exemplify, the current app economy differentiates itself from the general notion of information economy in that their primary benefit lies not in their intrinsic value but in their applications for other purposes.

Notes

1. Douglas MacMillan, "Inside the app economy," *Business Week*, October 22, 2009.

2. Dal Yong Jin, *Hands On/Hands Off: The Korean State and the Market Liberalization of the Communication Industry* (Hampton, 2011).

3. Associated Press, "Smartphones, apps all the rage in Asia's mobile market," September 18, 2012.

4. Lee Rainie and Berry Wellman, *Networked: The New Social Operating System* (MIT Press, 2012).

5. William Melody, "Markets and Policies in New Knowledge Economies," in *The Oxford Handbook of Information and Communication Technologies*, ed. R. Mansell, C. Avgerou, D. Quah, and R. Silverstone (Oxford University Press, 2009), 93.

6. Manuel Castells, *The Rise of the Network Society* (Blackwell, 2000), 21.

7. Jan van Dijk, *The Network Society*, second edition (Sage, 2006), 20.

8. Dan Schiller, *Digital Capitalism* (MIT Press).

9. MacMillan, "Inside the app economy."

10. Ibid.

11. "App economy under attack," August 20, 2012 (http://www.market wire.com).

12. Associated Press, "Smartphones, apps all the rage in Asia's mobile market."

13. You Kyung Lee, "Mobile big bang strikes S. Korea's smartphone market," Yonhap News Agency, December 20, 2010.

14. Ibid.

15. Korea Communications Commission, "Data of Mobile and Smartphone Subscribers as of November 2012."

16. Ibid.; Pyung Ho Kim, "The Apple iPhone shock in Korea." *The Information Society* 27 (2011): 261–268; "Smartphone users in Korea: 20M and rising," *Wall Street Journal*, October 31, 2011.

17. "America's new mobile majority: A look at smartphone owners in the U.S.," May 7, 2012 (http://blog.nielsen.com).

18. "China ships 347m smartphones by Sept," *China Daily*, October 30, 2013.

19. Ibid.

20. William Lehr and Lee McKnight, "Wireless Internet access: 3G vs. WiFi?" *Telecommunications Policy* 27 (2003): 351–370.

21. Korea Communications Commission, "Smartphone Usage in the First Half of 2012."

22. Ji Hyun Cho, "HTC to close Korean office on slow sales," *Korea Herald*, July 30, 2012.

23. S. W. Lee, "Korea is the cemetery of foreign smartphones," *Hankook Economic Daily*, May 29, 2012.

24. Youn Hee Jung, "Naver controls mobile as well" (http://www.zdnet.co.kr).

25. "iSO's Market Share dropped to 9.3%," *Seoul Economic Daily*, October 23, 2012.

26. "Android takes almost 50% share of worldwide smart phone market," Canalys press release, August 1, 2011.

27. Nielsen Asia, "Smartphone ownership on the rise in Asia Pacific, while advertisers struggle to engage with consumers via mobile ads" (http://jp. en.nielsen.com).

28. Man-Won Jung, "South Korea's future in mobile and wireless," *Asia-Pacific III* 2010: 8–9.

29. Nielsen, "Mobile app vs. mobile web," November 7, 2012 (http://mobi-zen.pe.kr/1154).

30. "Mobile Search Market Share," Metrix press release, April 1, 2011.

31. Yong Seok Hwang, Dong Hee Shin, and Yeolib Kim, "Structural change in search engine news service: a social network perspective," *Asian Journal of Communication* 22 (2012), no. 2: 160–178.

32. Anthony Fung, "Think globally, act locally: China's rendezvous with MTV," *Global Media and Communication* 2 (2006), no. 1: 71–88; Roland Robertson, "Glocalization: Time-space and homogeneity-heterogeneity," in *Global Modernities*, ed. M. Featherstone, S. Lash, and R. Robertson (Sage, 1995).

33. Y. K. Seo, "Worldwide famous Google and Yahoo cannot make its presence in Korea," *Kookmin Ilbo*, October 21, 2012.

34. Nielsen Asia, "Smartphone ownership on the rise in Asia Pacific, while advertisers struggle to engage with consumers via mobile ads."

35. Korea Communications Commission, "Smartphone usage in the first half of 2012."

36. Ibid.

37. Henry Jenkins, *Convergence Culture* (New York University Press, 2006).

38. "KaKaoTalk daily traffic hits 3 billion" (http://english.chosun.com).

39. William Melody, "Markets and policies in new knowledge economies," in *The Oxford Handbook of Information and Communication Technologies*, ed. R. Mansell, C. Avgerou, D. Quah, and R. Silverstone (Oxford University Press, 2009).

40. B. Y. Kim, "Parents shocked due to children's unusual behaviors," *Hankook Economy Daily*, October 29, 2012.

41. I. H. Ryu and H. M. Lee, "KaTalk bully causes a death," *Kyunghyang Shinmun*," August 23, 2012.

42. Schiller, *Digital Capitalism*, 173.

43. Melody, "Markets and policies in new knowledge economies."

13

What China's Netizens Want: Building Tech Ecosystems in the World's Toughest Market

Steven Millward

It is a testament to the strength and competitiveness of the Chinese Internet space that it is home to about a dozen Web giants. Many of those, displaying a typical fear of not having a thumb in each super-size pie of over 560 million Internet users[1] and 1.1 billion mobile subscribers,[2] have long since diversified into an astonishing array of areas—highlighting a marked difference to the Western model of more single-purpose online services. Who are these big online brands that are so familiar to the China's netizens? Let's look at four prominent names.

Baidu is China's leading search engine and advertising platform. Rather awkwardly, it has failed to define or jump upon the right trend social media at an opportune time; nonetheless, it has more recently excelled at mobile apps, and it has its own Android-based mobile operating system.

Alibaba is synonymous with e-commerce in China, especially for its eBay-beating site, Taobao. It tapped into the readiness of China's young Web users to use the Internet to change their lives and thereby turned the country into a nation of amateur shopkeepers and online shoppers. For eBay, the battle that began in 2004 was over two years later. Taobao took the lead in China's nascent e-commerce sector; it stands as a business lesson in failing to adapt to new and distinctive markets. The company, now valued at over $40 billion with 20 percent of it still owned by Yahoo, also runs Tmall, which serves as a virtual shopfront for medium-size businesses and global brands. To back all that up, there is also the Paypal-like e-payments platform Alipay. Alibaba, founded by a former English teacher named Jack Ma, is diversifying of late, investing more in mobile social apps. Ma once said that e-commerce is merely dessert for American shoppers, but for the Chinese it is the main course. That was seen in November 2012 when Alibaba's Tmall, on China's equivalent of America's "Cyber Monday," checked out a total of $3.1 billion in sales revenue in a 24-hour e-shopping frenzy; that was more money spent than on every single e-store in America on the same year's "Cyber Monday." And while America's online shopfest grows quite slowly, at rates of about 10 to 20 percent each year, Tmall processed $5.7 billion in sales on the same blowout day in November 2013. The online shopping market in China is not even saturated yet.

Tencent is China's largest Internet company, built originally around its QQ instant messenger, China's first ubiquitous social network. Tencent is emblematic of the diversity—and voracity—of Chinese Web companies, as it also has significant interests in e-commerce, online and social gaming, online ads, news and entertainment portals, online payments, and dozens of mobile apps. This is the firm that might accomplish China's first overseas social media success. With its mobile-only WeChat app, which is in the mold of Whatsapp or Kik, Tencent is first targeting Southeast Asia as a young and receptive market; it already has more than 300 million monthly active users.

Sina is more like an "old-school" online portal business. It might have faced the same rough path as the likes of Yahoo, except that it remodeled the essential concept of Twitter to create Sina Weibo, now China's hottest—and most controversial—social network. Sina Weibo (that second word is the generic Chinese term for "microblogging") is controversial insofar as it is a platform on which Chinese netizens are pushing the boundaries of what can be expressed on the Internet in China, often using it to decry local injustices and expose corrupt politicians (and, of course, share cat photos). Sina Weibo has evolved far faster than Twitter, quickly adding a virtual currency for use in casual social games. Sina is also looking quite tentatively to Southeast Asia for a broader user base; but the mandated media censorship of Sina Weibo could make it problematic to an overseas audience.

Most of China's tech giants have been quick to realize that the mobile Web is the future—insofar as "mobile" is just another screen from which online content will be consumed. While Indonesia, Vietnam, and other countries in the region have been slower getting onto the Internet and can largely bypass the era of the personal computer, China is alongside the West in having to cut the cords before committing to the mobile Internet. Indeed, mobile Web use surpassed that of desktop computers early in 2012 in the country.[3] China's major Internet companies (the ones that do not die off during this transition to a diverse array of new screens—not just mobile, but also Google Glass and whatever wearable tech will next define our interaction with our gadgets) at least have the benefit of possessing a strong range of products across social media, gaming, e-commerce, and other genres that can be adapted to mobile media and continue China's fast-paced digital evolution.

China's Smartphone Era

Smartphones will be the vehicle for this future more so than less responsive—and less entertaining—feature phones. In this respect, too, China is in step with Europe and North America in seeing its more affluent middle- and upper-income netizens make the leap to the mobile net. It is happening already. The IDC research group believes that China will ship in more than 450 million smartphones in 2014, up from an about 360 million in 2013.[4] And that is just a measure of new smartphones being bought, not a figure that represents the total number in hands and pockets across the country. But it is not an iPhone-fest. Most new smartphones bought run one of many flavors of Android. All available evidence suggests that China is nowhere near as close to its smartphone saturation point as is the United States in 2013, so there is room for yet more growth.

Figures from several research firms indicate that Samsung remained the top smartphone vendor in China from 2011 through 2013, thanks to the many variations of its Galaxy line-up. However, the Korean tech titan cannot be complacent, as China's own Lenovo is in second place. In Lenovo's home market, the brand is spearheading mobile growth as it diversifies from the slowly shrinking market for laptops and desktop computers. Close behind are ZTE and Huawei, also local brands. Toward the end of 2013, figures from a few different sources disputed whether Apple was in fifth place in the country or in sixth, as smaller Chinese brands like Coolpad and Xiaomi—specialists at cheaper smartphones for youngsters—crowd around and jostle Apple for position.

There remains room for disruption, even while sticking to the smartphone formula of a slim slab. The startup Chinese phone maker Xiaomi is leading this charge, shaking up the market with social media marketing razzmatazz and selling most of its phones online to keep costs down and prices low enough that a premium-feeling smartphone experience—as seen on Xiaomi's newest top-end phone, the Android-powered Mi3—is available to China's young, urban office workers, hairdressers, and Starbucks employees for less than a month's wage packet.

At first glance, Google's mobile operating system, Android, is the winner here. There are more Android phones as a proportion of smartphone owners in China than there are in the United States. But there are several reasons why that success hasn't spread across the rest of Google's ecosystem of products in China.

Google Hits the Great Wall—and the Firewall

Many people have gone from doing nearly everything in a Web browser on a laptop or desktop PC to curating a neat personal selection of smartphone

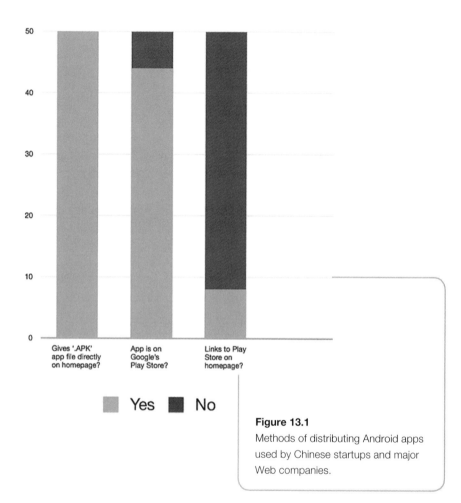

Figure 13.1
Methods of distributing Android apps used by Chinese startups and major Web companies.

apps. That transition gives Web companies new chances to innovate and get ahead. Good-looking, feature-rich, and stable apps are the best—if not the only—way to get China's young and wired citizens to stay with an online service. But for a Web company operating in China, other factors—uncontrollable, untouchable, unmentionable—can come into play.

Authorities in China seem to be trying to deprive Google of that apps explosion. A case in point is Google Maps. Usage of Google Maps for mobile phones has plunged in China in the past couple of years. Data from Analysys International for the third quarter of 2012 shows that Google's product— once the market leader in China—fell to sixth place.[5] Google's loss is—as with search—Baidu's gain. Data from the same source for 2011 show that Google Maps had 25.2 percent of the market for mobile mapping. In the third quarter of 2012, it was down to 9 percent. Baidu Maps has gone the other way, climbing from a share of 11.7 percent to 19.1 percent in the space of a year. But both these companies are still being bested by the Chinese firm Autonavi—Apple's online maps partner in China—which remains the market leader, albeit with pretty stagnant market share in the country. Figure 13.1 depicts the scene in full at the end of 2012.

What is holding Google back in mainland China? Google's first explosive confrontation with Chinese authorities in March 2010, when Google declared that it would no longer self-censor search results in line with what is demanded of all other Web and media companies in China, was the moment at which all Google's services became targets for blocks by authorities, and Google Maps was no exception. Access to the conventional Google Maps page has been obstructed by authorities ever since that first public clash. The same is true of Google.com and of the Hong Kong-based Google.com.hk, which replaced the shuttered Google.cn. Indeed, Google's international maps site—maps.google.com—is blocked in China most of the time, though the company's China-based site ditu.google.cn operates without any apparent interference from the "Great Firewall," China's meticulous system of Web censorship. Though Google retains offices in China and is seeing success among local app developers using AdMob to monetize their free apps, China is hardly a level playing field for Google. And since the 2010 incident it is no longer certain that any Google service will get to remain online in China. Even services with no outwardly controversial aspects, including Gmail and Play store (Google's central Android app marketplace), are hindered, throttled, slowed down, making it appear to users that Google's product is deficient in some way.

Not Playing Along with Google Play

But let's not cast Google as a martyr to online freedom of speech. Some of its products seem perfect for China and have been embraced warmly—especially Android, Google's largely open-source and highly extendable mobile operating system. But Chinese users have rejected other aspects of Google's services—particularly the Android ecosystem's official app store, called Google Play.

The app catalog, formerly dubbed the Android Market, is generally being subverted and/or ignored in China. But this time it's not about censorship or interference, exactly. Rather, the store has never really fitted in in China.

Instead, Chinese app developers are ignoring Google's marketplace, and smartphone owners are doing the same. Looking at dozens of popular Chinese apps, very few app developers even linked to the Play store from their respective homepages.[6] Many Chinese web giants and startups alike are still publishing to Google Play, but seemingly only as a minor distribution chan-nel. The Google Play store does not support paid apps in China, and many overseas developers choose not to publish their apps on it. As so often occurs in China, local services have spotted a market opportunity, filling the app gap with a mixture of piracy and legitimate, alternative app distribution. Dozens of alternative Android app stores have emerged in the past couple of years. A case in point is the game Temple Run 2, which is not in the Chinese version of the Google Play store but is easily available on other sites. The Baidu app catalog syndicates items from numerous third-party Chinese Android stores. Among the best of those are AppChina and Wandoujia.

It is an interesting example—to a corporation, terrifying—of a large mar-ket of consumers rejecting a product because it doesn't quite fit. Or, to be more precise, cherry-picking what's desirable, and discarding what's incon-venient. For Chinese smartphone owners, Google's approach to distributing Android apps wasn't quite flexible enough; but, with no penalty for not play-ing along (in contrast to the difficulty of "jailbreaking" an iPhone or an iPad), Chinese businesses swooped in to do things the way they knew Chinese neti-zens wanted them. Some local tech companies, noticing that Chinese phone owners have had difficulty syncing an Android device with a Windows PC, have created PC apps for that purpose. And in that app they have embedded an app store for good measure.

However, a plurality of app stores is the least of Google's concerns with regard to China. At least Chinese consumers are buying Android phones in great numbers, and local developers have the option of mobile ads as a means of monetizing apps for which they cannot charge.

Embrace Plurality

Another issue that Chinese netizens have with the Google Play store is that it involves partaking in the whole Google ecosystem, which requires a Gmail address. Chinese Internet users are not fond of being tied down. The West has one Twitter, but China has at least ten Twitter clones. (Two of those, Sina Weibo and Tencent Weibo, have been dominant, each with more than half a billion registered users.) With so many locally made apps to choose from, Chi-nese netizens and mobile users seem to have decided collectively that digital ecosystems are not their kind of environment.

Just as American Web users could comfortably survive online using only the creations of Silicon Valley, Chinese netizens have sufficient—and suffi-ciently mature—choices from local companies (except in terms of software platforms, given the huge reliance on Windows, iOS, and Android). With regard to e-commerce, social media, news, entertainment, and all the things that the Internet offers, China's Internet model shows that a country needs its own online brands as much as a country needed retailing or trading companies in centuries past. A nation in charge of its own Web-building strategies is one that keeps jobs and profits at home. Yes, it is unfortunate that this control is also exerted to extremes by authorities, even at the expense of free speech, putting a virtual gag on every netizen on its soil. Outside of those restrictions, China's powerhouse Internet industry, on which e-commerce shoppers were spending $40,000 per second on average throughout 2012, is an exemplar of the notion of being in the game, whatever the costs. Most of that e-commerce spending occurred via Chinese-owned e-commerce sites—mainly Alibaba, but also Amazon China. Countries that do not create big brands online will find profits going overseas and corporation taxes being avoided. Whether it is online or in malls, a country will generally earn more from its own homegrown firms.

So long as China's Web and business laws do not result in even greater isolation for the country's tech industry, it is a market where overseas players need to come in and match the skills, cunning, and local wisdom of Alibaba and Baidu. It is little wonder that few have managed to do so; it is no surprise at all that, amid all those strong and well-developed local apps and products, no entire ecosystem from Apple, Google, or Amazon has succeeded as a whole.

It is a clear warning to the tech giants that not every market around the world is keen on taking your ride; some prefer to hop on only when it is convenient for them. Is not that how it ought to be? Apps might be global, but an Internet company's strategy has to be local, reflexive, and well adapted. Perhaps more so than any other country, China gives Web firms a harsh lesson in this.

Notes

1. CNNIC data for 2012. Source: http://www.techinasia.com.

2. CNNIC data for China's three mobile telcos for November 2012. Source: http://www.miit.gov.cn.

3. CNNIC data for June 2012: http://www.techinasia.com/china-mobile -internet-users-statistics-behavior.

4. IDC data for smartphone sales in second quarter of 2013 and projected to 2014. Source: http://www.idc.com.

5. Analysys International data for mobile maps apps market share. Source: http://data.eguan.cn.

6. Survey of online distribution method of Chinese Android apps . Source: http://www.techinasia.com.

IV   Remediations

14
The Language of Media Software

Lev Manovich

From Media to a Metamedium

Outside of certain cultural areas, such as crafts and fine art, software has replaced a diverse array of physical, mechanical, and electronic technologies used before the twenty-first century to create, store, distribute, and access cultural artifacts. When you use Instagram, iPhone's Camera app, or Photoshop to edit an image, you are using software. When you use your mobile phone or tablet to tweet, post messages on Facebook, search videos on YouTube, or check flight schedules, you are using software. Your mobile phone comes with dozens of pre-installed software programs (i.e., apps), and it you want more you can choose from hundreds of thousands available on Apple App Store or Google Play.

And you are using software when you play a video game, explore an interactive installation in a museum, design a building, create special effects for a feature film, design a website, or carry out thousands of other cultural activities. Software has become our interface with the world, with other people, with our memory, and with our imagination—a universal language through which the world speaks, and a universal engine on which the world runs. What electricity and the combustion engine were to the early twentieth century, software is to the early twenty-first century.

One important category of software is what I call "media software"— programs such as Word, PowerPoint, Photoshop, Illustrator, After Effects, Final Cut, Firefox, Blogger, WordPress, Google Earth, Maya, and 3ds Max. These desktop programs enable us to create, publish, share, and remix images, moving image sequences, three-dimensional designs, texts, maps, interactive elements, and various combinations of these elements—websites, interactive applications, motion graphics, virtual globes, and so on. Media software also includes Web browsers such as Firefox and Chrome, email and chat apps, and other software applications whose primary purposes are accessing, organizing, and sharing media content (although they often also include some authoring and editing features). For example, the Camera app on my iPhone 5 allows me to capture photos, to share them via email, Facebook, and Twitter, to assign a photo to a contact, and to perform some simple editing (cropping and "auto-enhancing"). With Twitter, I can write new tweets, follow the tweets of others, and edit my profile. I can also chose from dozens of apps for working with video, music, texts, maps, and other media.[1]

These software tools for creating, interacting with, and sharing media represent a particular subset of application software (including Web applications). In view of this, we may expect that all these tools inherit certain "traits" common to all present-day software. If this is true, what happens to the modern understanding of artistic media, with their various properties and possibilities? Is it still meaningful to talk about different media at all? Do we now find ourselves in a brave new world of one single monomedium, or a "metamedium"?

The term "metamedium" was introduced by Alan Kay, a visionary computer scientist who, together with a number of other people working at the Xerox Corporation's Palo Alto Research Center (PARC), developed the concepts and technologies that are essential to today's media software. At the end of a 1977 article summarizing this research, Kay and his close collaborator Adele Goldberg call the computer "a metamedium" whose content is "a wide range of already-existing and not-yet-invented media."[2] In an article published in 1984, Kay added: "[A computer] is a medium that can dynamically simulate the details of any other medium, including media that cannot exist physically. It is not a tool, though it can act like many tools. It is the first *metamedium*, and as such it has degrees of freedom for representation and expression never before encountered and as yet barely investigated."[3]

In the 1980s and the early 1990s, the ideas from Xerox PARC found their way into AutoCAD (1982), Word (1984), PageMaker (1985), Alias (1985), Illustrator (1987), Director (1987), Photoshop (1989), After Effects (1993), and other commercial media authoring applications. (These personal-computer applications were paralleled by much more expensive systems for professional markets. The TV and video industries got Paintbox in 1981, Harry in 1985, Avid in 1989, and Flame in 1992.) With the growing popularity of smartphones and tablets as the new vernacular computing and communication platforms in the late 2000s, media editing capacities began to appear in apps for these platforms—thus disseminating the "language" of media software already learned by millions of culture industry professionals to billions of ordinary users.

Media-Specific and Media-Independent Techniques

Unpacking Kay's definition, I would like to suggest that the building blocks that make up the computer metamedium are the *different types of media data* and the *techniques for generating, modifying, and viewing such data.* Currently, the most widely used types of data are text, audio, vector images, and image sequences (vector animation), continuous-tone images and sequences of such images (i.e., photographs and digital video), 3D models, and geo-spatial data. I am sure that some readers would prefer a somewhat different list, and I will not argue with them. What is important for the present discussion is to establish that we have multiple kinds of data rather than just one kind.

The techniques for generating, modifying, and viewing the various kinds of data can be divided into two types, depending on the kinds of data they can work on:

1. *Techniques of media creation, manipulation, and access that are specific to particular types of data.* I am going to refer to these techniques as *media specific,* using the word "media" to mean "data type." For example, the technique of geometrical constraint satisfaction invented by Ivan Sutherland for Sketchpad around 1962 can work on graphical data defined by points and lines, but it would be meaningless to apply this technique to text. Another example: Today image-editing programs usually include various filters, such as "blur" and "sharpen," that can operate on continuous-tone images. But normally we would not be able to blur or sharpen a 3D model. More examples: It would be as meaningless to try to "extrude" a text or "interpolate" it as to define a number of columns for an image or a sound composition. Some of these data-manipulation techniques appear to have no historical precedents in earlier media—the technique of geometric constraint satisfaction is a case in point. Another example of a new technique is the use of evolutionary algorithms to generate still images, animation, and 3D forms. Other media-specific techniques do refer to earlier physical tools or machines—for instance, brushes in image-editing applications, a zoom command in graphics software, or a trim command in video-editing software.

2. *New software techniques that can work on any digital data (i.e., media-independent techniques).* Examples include being able to view the same information in different ways (for example, switching between file view and icon view on a PC or a Macintosh) and navigating through information hierarchically (for example, switching between viewing a single photo and all photos by a particular user in Instagram app). Other examples are hyperlinking, sorting, searching, network protocols such as HTTP, and various data-analysis techniques from artificial intelligence, machine learning, knowledge

discovery, and other subfields of computer science. (In fact, large parts of computer science, information science, and computer engineering focus on designing algorithms for processing data in general regardless of what the data represent—i.e., media-independent techniques.) These techniques are general ways of manipulating data regardless of what the data encode (i.e., pixel values, text characters, sounds, etc.). For instance, in the middle of the 1960s Douglas Engelbart and his colleagues invented "view control"— the idea that the same information can be displayed by a computer in many different ways. This idea is now implemented in most media editors and therefore works with images, 3D models, video files, animation projects, graphic designs, and sound compositions. "View control" has also become part of desktop and laptop operating systems (Mac OS X, Microsoft Windows, Google Chrome OS) and of mobile operating systems (iOS, Android). We use view control daily when we change the files "view" between "icons," "list," and "columns." (These are names used in Mac OS X; other operating systems may use different names to refer to the same views.) The general media-independent techniques also include interface commands such as "cut," "copy," and "paste." For instance, you can select a file name in a directory, a group of pixels in an image, or a set of polygons in a 3D model, then cut, copy, and paste these objects or their parts.

The arts give us many examples of media-specific techniques: think of editing techniques in cinema, ways of outlining a contour in painting, ways of creating rhyme in poetry, or ways of shaping a narrative out of chronological story events in literature. However, software "media-independent techniques" look less familiar. What are these techniques, and how can they work across media—that is, on different types of data?[4]

I will argue that "media independence" doesn't just happen by itself. For a technique to work with various data types, programmers have to implement a number of separate methods (algorithms) to cover all the types. Thus, *media-independent techniques are general concepts translated into different algorithms, each operating on data of a particular kind*. Let us look at some examples.

Consider the omnipresent "cut" and "paste" commands. The algorithm to select a word in a text document is different from the algorithm to select a curve in a vector drawing, or the algorithm to select a part of a continuous-tone (i.e., raster) image. "Cut and paste" is a general concept that is implemented differently in different media software depending on which data type this software is designed to handle. (In Larry Tesler's original implementation of universal commands concept done at Xerox PARC in 1974–1975, they worked only for text editing). Although "cut," "copy," "paste," and a number of similar "universal commands" are available in all contemporary GUI applications for desktop computers (but not in all apps for mobile phones), what they do and how they do it differ from application to application.

Search operates in the same way. The algorithm to search for a particular phrase in a text document differs from the algorithm that searches for a particular face in a photo or a video clip. (I am talking here about "content-based search," i.e., the type of search which looks for information inside actual images, as opposed to only searching image titles and other metadata the way image search engines such as Google Image Search were doing it in the 2000s.) However, despite these differences the general concept of search is the same: locating any elements in a single media object—or any media objects in a larger set of objects—that match particular criteria defined by the user. We can ask a Web browser to locate all instances of a particular word in a current Web page, we can ask a Google search app to locate all Web pages that contain a set of keywords, and we can ask the Twitter app to find all tweets that contain a particular hashtag.

Because of the popularity of the Web search paradigm, we now assume that in principle we can—or will in the future be able to—search any medium. In reality it is much easier to search media that have modular organization—such as text or 3D models—than to search media that don't have it, such as continuous-tone images, video, or audio. But for the users these differences are not important—as far as they are concerned, all types of media content acquire a new common property that can be called *searchability*.

Similarly, in the mid 2000s photo and video media began to acquire "findability" (a term introduced in Peter Morville's 2005 book *Ambient Findability*).[5] The appearance of consumer GPS-enabled media capture devices and the addition of geo-tagging, geo-search, and mapping services to media sharing sites such as Flickr (added in 2006) and media management applications such as iPhoto (added in 2009) gradually made media "location aware." This new property made possible apps, such as FourSquare and Instagram, that explore photos' spatial coordinates and named locations.

Another example of a general concept that, through the efforts of many people, was gradually made to work with different media types—and thus became a "media-independent technique"—is information visualization (often abbreviated as "infovis"). The name "infovis" already suggests that it is not a media-specific technique; rather, it is a general method that potentially can be applied to any data. The name implies that we can potentially map any data—numbers, text, network, sound, video—into a spatial layout to reveal patterns and relationships in the data. (A parallel to information visualization is data sonification, which renders data patterns as sounds.)

Inventing techniques to turn this potential into reality took decades. In the 1980s the emerging field of scientific visualization focused on 3D visualization of numerical data. In the 1990s the growing graphics capabilities of personal computers enabled larger numbers of people to experiment with visualization—which led to the development of techniques to visualize media. The first successful visualizations of large bodies of text appeared around 1998 (*TextArc* by W. Bradford Paley, 2002; *Valence* by Ben Fry, 1999; *Rethinking the Book* by David Small, 1998).[6] Visualizations of musical structures emerged in 2001 (*The Shape of Song* by Martin Wattenberg), visualization of a feature film in 2000 (*The Top Grossing Film of All Time, 1 x 1* by Jason Salovan). By early 2010, many mobile apps incorporated visualization into their interfaces. For example, Weatherphone (released for iOS in 2013) uses a few visualization techniques to present information about weather, as opposed to relying only on text and numbers.

Infovis is a particularly interesting example of a new "media-independent technique" because of the variety of the algorithms and strategies regarding what and how can be visualized. For example, Martin Wattenberg—whose work, in his own words, "focuses on visual explorations of culturally significant data"[7]—created visualizations of a history of Net art, of musical compositions by J. S. Bach, Philip Glass, and other composers, of the thought process of a computer chess-playing program, and of the history of Wikipedia pages. In each case, Wattenberg had to decide which dimensions of the data to choose and how to translate them into a visual form. But despite the differences, we recognize all these projects as information visualizations. They are all realizations of the same general concept: selecting some dimensions of the data and representing them visually through the relations of graphic elements.[8] They also all rely on the same fundamental capacities of software to manipulate numerical data and to map the data from one format to another. Finally, they all can be also understood as applications of computer graphics— as the generation of images from numerical data.

As the result of infovis work by Wattenberg and many other people in the 1990s and the 2000s, many types of data acquired a new common property: their structure can be visualized. This new property of media is distributed across various applications, software libraries, art and design projects, research papers, and prototypes. Today some visualization tools are included in media-editing software—for instance, Photoshop can display a histogram of an image, Final Cut and other professional video-editing software can visualize the color content of a video clip, and many media players (including iTunes) offer a music-visualization feature. Google Trends visualizes search patterns. YouTube and Flickr visualize viewing stats for video and photos.

Going through the thousands of infovis projects collected on infosthetics. com and other blogs about visualizations, one finds a variety of experiments in visualization of media such as songs, poems, and novels and of many kinds of data—two examples are the movements an artist's son, daughter, and cat in a living room over a period of an hour (*1hr in front of the TV* by bumblebee (flickr user name), 2008) and citations in science journals (*Eigenfactor.org* by Moritz Stefaner, 2009).[9] We can also find such projects in art exhibitions such as the Museum of Modern Art's 2008 *Design and Elastic Mind*,[10] SIGGRAPH 2009 *Info-Aesthetics*,[11] and MOMA's 2011 *Talk to Me*. In mobile space, fitness apps often use visualization to show patterns in exercise activities.

Visualization, searchability, findability—these and many other "media-independent techniques" (i.e., concepts implemented to work across many data types) go against our habitual understanding of media as plural (i.e., as consisting of a number of separate media). If we can now use the same techniques across different media types, what happens to the distinctions between media?

The idea that all artworks fall into a number of distinct media, each with its own distinct techniques and representational devices, was central to modern art and aesthetics. In 1766, in *Laokoon oder Über die Grenzen der Malerei und Poesie* (*Laocoon: An Essay on the Limits of Painting and Poetry*), the German philosopher Gotthold Ephraim Lessing argued for the radical difference between poetry and painting on the ground that one is "extended" in time and the other in space. The idea reached its extreme in the first two decades of the twentieth century, when many modern artists focused their energy on discovering a unique language of each artistic medium. A statement made in 1924 by Jean Epstein, a French avant-garde filmmaker and theoretician, is typical of modern rhetoric of purity; countless statements like it appeared on the pages of avant-garde publications around that time:

> For every art builds its forbidden city, its own exclusive domain, autonomous, specific and hostile to anything that does not belong. Astonishing to relate, literature must first and foremost be literary; the theater, theatrical; painting, pictorial; and the cinema, cinematic. Painting today is freeing itself from many of its representational and narrative concerns ... The cinema must seek to become, gradually and in the end uniquely, cinematic; to employ, in other words, only photogenic elements.[12]

In the visual arts, the doctrine of media purity reaches its extreme expression in Clement Greenberg's argument that "because flatness was the only condition painting shared with no other art, Modernist painting oriented itself to flatness as it did to nothing else."[13] Note that Greenberg did not advocate this position as a justification for the abstract art of his contemporaries in the 1950s; he offered it only as a historical analysis of earlier modernism. Greenberg wrote: "It was the stressing of the ineluctable flatness of the surface that remained, however, more fundamental than anything else to the processes by which pictorial art criticized and defined itself under Modernism. For flatness alone was unique and exclusive to pictorial art."

Not until after the 1960s—when the installation, a new art form based on the idea of mixing different media and materials, gradually became popular and accepted in the art world—did the obsession with media specificity begin to lose its importance. However, even during its dominance, the principle of media specificity was always counterbalanced by its opposite. Throughout the modern period we also find "local"—i.e., specific to particular historical moments and artistic schools—attempts to formulate aesthetic principles that relate different media to one another. For instance, consider the efforts by many artists in the nineteenth and twentieth centuries to establish parallels between musical and visual compositions. Such work was often associated with the ideas of synesthesia and the Gesamtkunstwerk; it included theories, practical compositions, and technologies such as the color organs constructed by Alexander Scriabin, John and James Whitney (who went on to create the first computer animations), and many other artists and musicians.

Though they did not explicitly theorize cross-media aesthetics to the same degree, modernist artistic paradigms—classicism, romanticism, naturalism, impressionism, socialist realism, suprematism, cubism, surrealism, and so on—can be also understood as the systems (or "software") that gave "common properties" to works in various media. Thus, novels by Émile Zola and paintings by Édouard Manet were aligned in their uncompromising, scientific-like "naturalist" depiction of ordinary people; Constructivist paintings, graphics, industrial design, theater design, architecture, and fashion shared the aesthetics of "expressed structure" (visually emphasizing composition structure by exaggerating it); and De Stijl's non-intersecting rectangular forms in primary colors were applied by participants in that movement to painting, furniture, architecture, and typography.

What is the difference between such earlier artistic work on establishing correspondences between media and software's "media-independent techniques" (i.e., the techniques that work across different media)? Clearly, the artistic systems and the authoring, editing, and interaction techniques available in media software operate on different levels. The former are responsible for the content and style of the works to be generated—i.e., what is going to be created in the first place. The latter are used not only to create but also to interact with things generated previously, including blogs, photos, or videos created by other users. (For instance, one can use Twitter to search all available tweets, or Instagram to navigate photos shared by other users.)

Put differently, the efforts by modern artists to create parallels between media were prescriptive and speculative.[14] The "common media properties" would apply only to selected bodies of artistic work created by particular artists or groups. In contrast, software imposes common "properties" on any data to which it is applied. Thus, it shapes our understanding of what media are in general. For example, as has already been discussed, apps and services (both mobile and Web-based) include methods for navigating, reading, listening to, or viewing media objects, for attaching additional information (comments, tags, geo-tagging) to them, and for finding them in a larger set (i.e., search apps and search commands in other apps). This applies to all videos, images, text pages, text documents, and maps. In other words, we can say that media software "interprets" any media it "touches" in certain distinct ways, and that its "interpretations" always include certain "statements."

Of course, "media-independent" aesthetic systems proposed by modernists were not only generative (the creation of new works) but also interpretive. That is, modernist artists and theorists often tried to change audiences' understanding of past and current art—usually in a critical and negative way. (Each new movement wanted to discredit its predecessors and competitors.) However, since their programs were theories rather than software, they had no direct material effect on users' interaction with the artistic works, including those created in the past. In contrast, software techniques directly affect our understanding of media through the operations they make available for creating, editing, interacting with, and sharing all media artifacts.

Additionally, modern artistic and aesthetic paradigms, in practice, would be realized only in two, three, or maybe four media—but not all. Nineteenth-century Naturalism can be found in literature and in the visual arts but not in architecture, and Constructivism did not spread to music or literature. However, "cut," "copy," "paste," and "find" commands are found in nearly all media applications, any media object can be geo-tagged, and the principle of view control is implemented to work with all media types. All media acquire new properties, such as searchability and findability. Any text—a blog post you wrote or a classical novel downloaded from Project Gutenberg—can be searched; similarly, any part of an image can be cut from that image and pasted into another, no matter what the images are. In other words, media software affects all media content equally, regardless of its aesthetics, semantics, authorship, and historical origin.

To summarize this analysis: in contrast to modern artistic programs to create different media that share the same principles, software's media-independent techniques are ubiquitous and "universalist." For instance, "cut" and "paste" are built into all media-editing software, from specialized professional applications to consumer apps included on every new media device sold. Further, these techniques can be applied to any media work, regardless of its aesthetics or its authorship. In fact, the technical ability to sample media works created by others has become the basis of one of the dominant aesthetics of our time: remix.

Of course, not all media applications and devices make all "media-independent" techniques equally available—usually for commercial, copyright, or privacy reasons. For example, at present Google Books reader doesn't allow users to select and copy text, and Instagram app does not allow users to edit photos shared by others. Thus, while my analysis applies to conceptual and technical principles of software and their cultural implications, we need to keep in mind that in practice these principles are controlled by commercial interests. However, even the most restrictive software still includes some basic media operations. By being present in all software designed to work with different media types, these operations establish a shared understanding of media today—experienced by users as "common media principles" of all content.

Algorithms and Data Structures

What does it mean to simulate older physical or mechanical media in software? For example, what does it mean to simulate the effects of professional camera, lighting, and darkroom techniques in mobile photo apps such as Camera+ (iPhone) or Adobe Photoshop Touch (iPad), or the techniques and tools of print design in InDesign?

A naive answer is that computers simulate the physical, mechanical, or electronic media objects they replaced. For example, a digital photograph simulates an analog photograph printed on paper, a digital illustration simulates an illustration drawn on paper, and digital video simulates analog video recorded on videotape. But that is not how things actually work.

Software simulates *the physical, mechanical, or electronic techniques used to navigate, create, edit, and interact with media* (and also extends them and augments them with new capacities). For example, the simulation of printed books includes techniques for writing and editing text (copy, cut, paste, insert), techniques for modifying the document's appearance (change font, size, color, etc.) and layout (add header and footer, insert page numbers, etc.), and techniques for viewing the final document (go to the next page, view multiple pages, zoom, make bookmark). Similarly, software simulation of cinema includes all the techniques of cinematography—user-defined focus, camera movements (pan, dolly, zoom), particular lenses that define what part of a virtual scene the camera will see, and so on. The simulation of analog video includes a set of navigation commands: play forward, play in reverse, fast forward, loop, and so on. In short, *to simulate a medium in software means to simulate its tools and interfaces, rather than only its "material."*

Before their softwarization, the techniques available in a particular medium were part of its "hardware." This hardware included instruments for inscribing information on some material, modifying that information, and—if the information was not directly accessible to human senses, as in the case of sound recording—presenting it. Together the material and the instruments determined what a medium could do.

For example, the techniques available for writing were determined by the properties of paper and the writing instruments, such as a fountain pen or a typewriter. (The paper allows marks to be made on top of other marks, the marks can be erased if one uses a pencil but not if one uses a pen, and so on.) The techniques of filmmaking were similarly determined by the properties of the film stock and the recording instrument (the camera). Because each medium used its own distinct materials and its own physical, mechanical, or electronic instruments, each also developed its own set of techniques, with little overlap. You could white out a word while typing on a typewriter and type over it, but you could not do the equivalent (replace one visual element with another) with already-exposed film. Conversely, you could zoom out while filming, progressively revealing more information, but you could not do the same with a book—for example, you could not instantly reformat the book to see a whole chapter at once. A printed book only allowed you to access information at a constant level of detail: whatever fit in a two-page spread. (That was one of the conventions of books against which Marinetti, Rozanova, Kruchenykh, Lissitzky, and other avant-garde artists worked in the early twentieth century.)

Software simulation liberates techniques for media creation and interaction from their respective materials and hardware. The techniques for media creation, editing, and access are translated into software. Each technique becomes a separate algorithm.

And what about the physical materials of different media? It may seem that in the process of simulation they are eliminated. Instead, media algorithms, like all software, work on a single material: digital data, i.e., numbers.

However, the reality is more complex and more interesting. The differences between materials of distinct media do not simply disappear into thin air. Instead of a variety of physical materials, computational media use different ways of organizing information—different *data structures*. And here comes the crucial point: *In place of a large number of physical materials, software simulations use a smaller number of data structures.*

Consider all the different types of physical materials that can be used to create two-dimensional images, including stone, parchment, canvas, and all the dozens of kinds of paper that can be found today in an art-supplies store. Add to those the various kinds of photographic film—x-ray film, film stock, celluloid used for animation, and so on. Digital imaging substitutes just two data structures for all these different materials. The first is a bit-mapped image—a grid of pixels (discrete picture elements), each with its own color or gray-scale value. The second is a vector image consisting of lines and shapes defined by mathematical equations.

What happens to all the different effects the various physical materials made possible? Drawing on rough paper produces different effects than drawing on smooth paper, and carving an image on wood is different from etching the same image in metal. With softwarization, all these effects are moved from "hardware" (physical materials and tools) into software.

All algorithms for creating and editing continuous-tone images work on the same data structure—a grid of pixels. And although they use different computational steps, the end result of these computations is always the same—a modification in the colors of some of the pixels. Depending on which pixels are being modified and in what fashion, the algorithms can visually simulate the effects of drawing on smooth or rough paper, using oils on canvas, carving on wood, and making paintings and drawings using a variety of physical instruments and materials.

If in the past particular medium effects resulted from of interaction between the properties of the tools and the properties of the material, now it is about different algorithms modifying a single "material"—a particular data structure. This allows us to easily combine the techniques that used to belong to separate media within a single image. For example, we can first apply an algorithm that will act as a brush on canvas, then an algorithm that will create the effect of a watercolor brush on rough paper, then one that will create the effect of a fine pen on smooth paper, and so on. And since media applications such as Photoshop offer dozens of these algorithms (presented to a user as tools and filters with controls and options), this theoretical possibility becomes a standard practice. The result is a new hybrid medium that combines the possibilities of many separate media.

Instead of numerous separate materials and instruments, we can now use a single software application whose tools and filters can simulate different media creating and modification techniques. The effects that previously could not be combined, since they were tied to unique materials, are now available from a single pull-down menu. And when someone invents a new algorithm, or a new version of an existing algorithm, it can easily be added to this menu by means of the plug-in architecture that became standardized in the 1990s. (The term "plug-in" was coined in 1987 by the developers of Digital Darkroom, a photo-editing application.[15]) And, of course, numerous other image creation and modification techniques that did not exist previously can be also added: image arithmetic, algorithmic texture generation (such as Photoshop's Render Clouds filter), a variety of blur filters, and so on. (Photoshop menus provide many more examples.)

To summarize this analysis: Software simulation replaces a variety of distinct physical materials and the tools used to inscribe information (i.e., make marks) on these materials with a new hybrid medium defined by a common data structure. Because of this common structure, multiple techniques that previously were unique to different media can now be used together. And new, previously non-existent techniques can be added, so long as they can operate on the same data structure.[16]

It should be now clear why it is incorrect to think that computers always work on a single "digital material": binary code made from zeros and ones. Of course this is what happens on a low-level machine level—but this is largely irrelevant as far as the users of application software and the people who write that software are concerned. Present-day media software contains its own "materials": data structures used to represent still and moving images, 3D forms, volumes and spaces, texts, sound compositions, print designs, Web pages, and other "cultural data." These data structures do not correspond to physical materials in one-to-one fashion. Instead, a number of physical materials are mapped into a single structure—for instance, different imaging materials such as paper, canvas, photographic film, and videotape become a single data structure (i.e., a bit-mapped image).

Conclusion

Is it still meaningful to talk about different media when distinct physical, mechanical, and electronic media technologies and tools have been replaced by software applications? Or do we now have a single monomedium (or a "metamedium," to use Alan Kay's term)?

"Softwarization" of media doesn't collapse the difference between media, but it does bring them closer together in important ways. One of the developments responsible for this "media attraction" is the common software techniques that can operate across different data types. If we recall Kay and

Goldberg's formulation that the computer metamedium includes a variety of already-existing and new media, this statement can be paraphrased as follows: *Within the computer metamedium, all previously existing and newly invented media rely on the same set of common software techniques for data organization, authoring, and navigation.*

It is hard to overestimate the historical importance of the development of these cross-media techniques. Humans have always used some general strategies to organize their cultural representations, experiences, and actions—for example, narrative, symmetry, rhythm, repetitive structures in ornamentation, use of complementary colors, and so on. Clearly these strategies were very important for human perception, cognition, and memory, and that is why we find them in every culture and every medium—for example, in poetry, in music, in architecture, and in painting. However, these strategies were not embedded in any technological tools or materials—instead, they were in the minds and bodies of artisans who were communicating them from generation to generation.

Nineteenth-century and twentieth-century media technologies for representation and communication bring us to a new stage. They often materially embody certain techniques for media capture or creation. For example, one-point linear perspective was built into all lens-based capture technologies, including photography, film, and analog video. However, these techniques would apply only to particular media types.

Media software brings a new set of techniques that are implemented to work across *all* media. Like viruses, searchability, findability, linkability, multimedia messaging and sharing, editing, view control, zoom, and other "media-independent" techniques infect everything that software touches, and therefore they are comparable in importance to the basic organizing principles for media and artifacts that were used for thousands of years.

Many media-independent techniques were developed during the 1960s and the 1970s by Ivan Sutherland and by groups headed by Douglas Engelbart, Alan Kay, and Nicholas Negroponte. In the 1980s and the 1990s they become accessible to users of personal computers and professional media creators. In 2000s, always-on networking and mobile devices (first phones, then tablets) brought them to hundreds of millions of people. The proliferation of mobile apps for capturing, creating, sharing, and accessing media strengthens the conceptual dominance of these techniques. They give the new computer metamedium its particular identity—an identity in which the differences between media are counterbalanced by what they now share.

Notes

1. All references to particular hardware, apps, and their features in this essay pertain to the versions as of July 2013.

2. Alan Kay and Adele Goldberg, "Personal dynamic media," in *New Media Reader*, ed. Noah Wardrip-Fruin and Nick Montfort (MIT Press, 2003), p. 399.

3. Alan Kay, "Computer software," *Scientific American* 251(1984), no. 3: 53–59, p. 52, quoted in Jean-Louis Gassée, "The evolution of thinking tools," in *The Art of Human-Computer Interface Design*, 225.

4. "Design across media" was a phrase used by Adobe in marketing an early version of its Creative Suite of media authoring applications.

5. Peter Morville. *Ambient Findability: What We Find Changes Who We Become* (O'Reilly, 2005).

6. W. Bradford Paley, *TextArc*, 2002 (http://www.textarc.org/); Ben Fry, *Valence*, 1999 (http://benfry.com/valence/); David Small, Rethinking the Book, PhD thesis, Massachusetts Institute of Technology, 1999 (http://acg .media.mit.edu/projects/thesis/DSThesis.pdf).

7. http://www.bewitched.com/about.html, July 23, 2006.

8. For a detailed discussion of infovis most general principles and new developments, see Lev Manovitch, "What is visualization?" *Visual Studies* 26 (2011), no. 1: 36–49.

9. http://well-formed.eigenfactor.org/; http://www.flickr.com/photos/the _bumblebee/2229041742/in/pool-datavisualization.

10. http://www.moma.org/interactives/exhibitions/2008/elasticmind/.

11. http://www.siggraph.org/s2009/galleries_experiences/information _aesthetics/.

12. Jean Epstein, "On certain characteristics of *photogénie*," in *French Film Theory and Criticism*, volume 1: *1907–1929*, ed. Richard Abel (Princeton University Press, 1988).

13. Clement Greenberg, "Modern Painting," in *Forum Lectures* (Voice of America: 1960) (http://www.sharecom.ca).

14. By "speculative" I mean that in many cases the proposed aesthetic systems were not fully realized in practice. For example, no purely suprematist

architecture designed by Kasimir Malevich was ever built, and the same goes for the futurist architecture of Antonio Sant'Elia.

15. http://en.wikipedia.org/wiki/Digital_Darkroom, February 19, 2012.

16. Many of today's standard image formats, including Photoshop's .psd format, are much more complex than a simple pixel grid—they can include alpha channels, multiple layers, color profiles, and they can also combine bit-mapped and vector representations. However, in this discussion I am talking only about their common denominator, which is also what algorithms work on, rather than an image that is loaded in memory—an array of pixels holding color values.

15
Apps as "Charming Junkware"?

Thierry Bardini

> The objective is to maintain a central log or database of all apps and user files
> >= a preset size in order to minimize junk apps/files. "[J]unk" is hereby defined
> to be apps or files that are used less than thrice a week.
> —Junkminimizer purpose statement[1]

Deadline approaches, and I scan my notes. Well, not much to start with. By reflex I input the expression "an app for that" in Google. The result is instantaneous: approximately 16 millions hits. A student[2] sent me a link to some stats, an infographic report from Nuance Communication,[3] produced in 2012 with the help of various sources and no indication of methodology whatsoever. I try to follow the links a bit more, but I give up on account of the unbearable slowness of my connection. (I am out in the country.) I don't mind, however; the first lines of the graphic say enough for me: "Today's mobile consumer is downloading mobile apps at astonishing rates. But studies show that most of them are not used." And further, they gesture toward a logic antithetical to the one with that recalls a well-known line from *Field of Dreams*: "Just because they download an app does not mean they'll use it." In fact (I learn later when back in the city, with its luxurious connection rate), if the trend settled in, one fourth of the 30 billion apps downloaded in 2011 were used only once or not at all—and were not necessarily discarded.[4]

I must confess that I am a rather poor app user. In fact, I resisted mobile computing for a long while, and am still resisting mobile telephony. I have even (with my friend Ghislain Thibault[5]) written against the false promises of wireless communications: we diagnosed two apparent paradoxes, which we dubbed the Paradox of Theseus and the Paradox of Aether. The first says *the fewer the wires, the more connections*; the second says *the more distant the presence, the fewer senses involved*. And we concluded that wireless amounts to far less than its promises of liberation. It is rather a new, voluntary servitude that the user cannot escape, even while mobile. That may have been sheer projection on our part. In my case, it was certainly a projection of my distaste for these prostheses. When mobile, I do not want to be contacted. At all.

But I eventually caved in. Not to mobile telephony, mind you, only to mobile computing. Yes, I confess, I bought an iPad. My son took it over in less than a month, and the few apps I had downloaded before the demise of my app-using career remained only to litter the apparently infinite memory of our new device (a 64-GB first-generation iPad). My habit resumed last month when the first iPad died of an acute case of "bad port" (of the proprietary 30-pin dock to the USB connector). The case was terminal according to Apple, which refused to repair it and which instead offered to salvage from its remaining stock (!) a brand new and already obsolete model for the half the price of last year's model. I jumped on the opportunity. I got it for my wife, who does not care about obsolescence as long as the device still does the job she wants it to do. I also got an iPod for my son, who prefers his interfaces small, and a brand new (and soon to be obsolete) iPad 3. We are a mobile *and* connected family now. May the powers of messaging shower us with felicity!

So now I download apps (moderately) and use them (even less). I even recovered my old apps from the rescued iPad contents on my other computer (yes, I realize they are all computers). I am afraid I will not use them more than my son did when he monopolized the old prosthesis. Yes, a mushroom identifier app seemed a good idea at first, but I realized upon my first attempt to use it that I knew my mushrooms better than the poor digital thing. Never mind—I rest easy knowing that I am just part of a trend here, one that enjoys apps as "charming junk."

Charming Junkware

I enjoy junk (I am no customer for junkminimizer). I just spent close to ten years of my life researching, thinking, and writing a book about junk. I even committed to paper my erratic thoughts about a junk aesthetics. I thus became a kind of junkologist. So when I was asked to contribute an essay to the present anthology, and read in the call for contributions an allusion to apps as "charming junk" and a direct reference to my work, I took it as an invitation to think again about my preferred subject matter, albeit with a twist—a looping back, in fact.

My book (published in 2010 by the University of Minnesota Press) is titled *Junkware*. It is my subjective, humorous (I hope), and at times lugubrious account of how I envision the synthetic future of the human being. It started with a scientific "detail," a feeling I had that there could be something really wrong with the cybernetic metaphor applied to human life. I focused on so-called junk DNA and soon realized that junk was much broader of a concept. The manuscript was a monster,[6] over a million characters long, with close to a thousand footnotes. In the process of revision, a quarter of the manuscript, devoted to computing and titled "(All Is) Software," disappeared.

I now regret my self-erasure. "Code" had slowly emerged in my previous research as the key concept of the current cultural configurations—these situated and dynamic meshworks of gestures and postures, utterances and discourses, mixing human and non-human agencies. But what is "code"? The central trope of cybernetic culture, the principle behind all possible equivalences, linking the animal and the machine, objects and subjects, matter and energy, all subsumed under the twin concept of information. Devoting a book to the junk signature[7] in molecular biology and culture at large without considering code as software now seems to me like drafting a contract on a loophole. It is like forgetting the "ongoing triumph of software," as Friedrich Kittler once noticed, since "the physical Church-Turing hypothesis, by identifying physical hardware with the algorithm forged for its computation[,] has finally got rid of hardware itself."[8] There would still be no part devoted to hardware in *Junkware*; the remaining and reorganized three parts were respectively titled (in the manuscript) "bootstraps," "wetware," and "junkware." But in the end "(all is) software" gave way to "(there is no) software" (with a tip of my hat to Kittler).

Software thus became a pervasive albeit absent presence, a presence that however transpired everywhere therein, from the very title on. After discarding my original title, *Junk Life*, I opted for *Junkware*, a word I recycled from the software lexicon. "Junkware" referred, at the time of my writing, to "unwanted commercial software that is installed without the user's full knowledge, consent, and understanding, and that primarily serves the interests of commercial parties associated with the 'junkware,' not the end users on whose systems those unwanted applications are installed."[9] In that passage, Eric Howes proposed it as an alternative to "spyware" and related it to other forms of "unwanted software," such as "adware," "foistware," "hijackware," "drive-by-downloaders," and "porndialers." Others have related it to "bloatware," spam, and viruses. In this sense, my guess is that most developers and most app users would resent the characterization of apps as "junkware."

And rightfully so, since Howes' attempt to define junkware significantly distorts, in my mind, the sense of the concept of junk. Actually, the spyware warrior did not give any indication of why he replaced "spyware" with "junkware," apart from mentioning the possible "overextension" of the former term. At the conclusion of his paper, he added:

Some may object to the name 'junkware' because of the unpleasant connotations that it carries. . . . Definitions and terms ought to help us understand the world and grapple with the problems that it presents, not stand in the way of our efforts to solve those problems. . . . The particular name for that linguistic umbrella is less important than its ability to facilitate our attempts to address consumers' problems and concerns with the abusive software that falls under its cover.[10]

A word or a definition, however, always comes loaded with its own connotations. Here such a connotation is, to say the least, quite at odds with what Howes wants to convey: in his mind, junkware is a kind of "intrusive, unwanted software on the internet." He even insists that some of the software described on those pages (other linked pages of the "anti-spyware" scene) may be akin to more traditional "malware," and he adds in parentheses the three usual suspects of the malware infection, starting with the first entity to cross the divide between carbon-based and silicon-based forms of life: "viruses, trojans, worms." Howes is not alone in his stance on this contradictory connotative issue. The *PC Magazine Encyclopedia* (as well as many other top answers to the Google query "junkware definition") concurs and defines junkware accordingly: "Unwanted software; in other words, just plain junk."[11]

Now, am I the only one who finds this definition contradictory to the usual connotations of the word "junk"? Perhaps, since most of my contemporaries seem to have accepted the late-nineteenth-century pejorative connotations of the word that extended its meaning to "old and discarded objects of any kind" and "useless waste."[12] In other words, many seem to confuse junk and trash. But trash we throw away and junk we keep just in case. Far from "unwanted," junk belongs to an alternative economy of want, an economy of desire that does not rest only in the use value of its objects. Junk is not trash. It might end up as trash, but in the meantime, it exists as junk, governed by the potentiality of renewed use, just in case.

The Appification of Solitude

But in case of what, and why? Answering these deceptively simple questions requires considering the "proper use" of apps (the app appropriation), and, more generally, the economy of desire to which they seem to now belong. The answers I got in a non-scientific survey vary greatly, in spite of the small and non-representative nature of my sample. They help define what app users seem to consider a proper use of their apps. Junkminimizer's claim is incorrect. Proper use is not restricted to frequent use ("more than thrice a week"): many users seem happy to keep some apps they use much less frequently than that. Apps can be kept proactively, for instance: I do not travel every week, but I still keep on my machine an app that allows me to convert currencies. In this case, proper use depends on a subjective anticipation of a use to come, and since anticipation is no sure science, there might be some errors in the process, and some apps are doomed to memory limbos (unless one gets fed up with their useless presence and delete them one day). In the extreme case, the anticipation might not be founded in any foreseeable reality but rather on a wish, a projection, a pure desire. Since I read Bruce Chatwin's book *In Patagonia*, more than 25 years ago, I have dreamt of visiting Tierra del Fuego. Is this why I keep the *Viva Patagonia!* app on my iPad, and don't consult it too often? (Each time I do, I understand that my dream will not soon be realized.)

Sometimes proper use also seems to vary a lot in time. Some apps seem to put the user in a trance. I will call this effect "the app appeal." Because of a fashion effect, or quite simply because they're "soooo goood," they excite their users into a quasi-manic period of intense use that is often short-lived. I have seen this with my son and games, for instance. Last month's app game, by far the most used for a while, now sits unused on the screen of his Ipod. He simply outgrew it, or—and here is a master word in this economy of desire (also described as an economy of attention)—got bored by it. But it is still there, simply out of nostalgia for the fun he once had with it or, most probably, because the feeling created by excessive use (a kind of app overdose) includes the possibility of renewed use after a break. The market is full of recovering app users of all ages who once succumbed to the app appeal of a given code. Damned marketers, they are your target of choice: they always long for a new object for their addiction.

So here is the hypothesis that I will now explore in order to articulate three distinct orders of attachment to apps as "charming junkware": We love our apps beyond their functionalities, keep them as junk on our memory *appendices*, and thus fall victims of their seduction, because they have a ritual value, an aesthetic value, and a political value. I derive these three orders of app attachment from Jean Baudrillard's 1979 book *De la seduction*. In the late 1970s, in between his masterpieces *Symbolic Exchange and Death* (1976) and *Simulacra and Simulation* (1981), Baudrillard diagnosed the early symptoms of the contemporary state of seduction, its obscenely pure form, "this specter of seduction that haunts our circuits without secrets, our phantasms without affect, and our contact networks without contacts."[13] Discussing this diffuse specter further, he then followed Walter Benjamin's seminal essay on "the work of art in the age of mechanical reproduction" (1936) to articulate the three phases of seduction that describe its "political destiny":

Seduction too would have had its ritual phase (dual, magical, agonistic); its aesthetic phase . . . ; and finally its "political" phase (taking up Benjamin's term, here somewhat ambiguous), the phase of the total disappearance of the original of seduction, of its ritual and aesthetic forms, in favor of an all-out ventilation whereby seduction becomes the informal form of politics, the scaled-up framework for an elusive politics devoted to the endless reproduction of a form without content. (This informal form is inseparable from its technicity, which is that of networks—just as the political form of the object is inseparable from the techniques of serial reproduction.) As with the object, this "political" form corresponds to seduction's maximum diffusion and minimum intensity.[14]

Although I would much rather prefer to use the word "phase" in the sense of thermodynamics[15] rather than in the successive sense of "stage" here implied, let me stress the prophetic overtone of this quote—and particularly of Baudrillard's last parenthetical sentence—14 years before the beginning of the massive diffusion of the World Wide Web, and 28 years before the first apps. This is why I opted for the expression "orders of attachment," emulating Baudrillard's earlier three orders of simulacra. Taken together, the ritual, the aesthetic, and the political orders of seduction explain this particular "charm" that seems to endow some apps, and nothing proves, in this case, that the ritual and the aesthetic orders disappeared when this particular destiny of seduction became political. Moreover, it seems to me that only the confluence of these three phases, in the sense of thermodynamics' "critical state"— in which different phases become indistinguishable from each other—can begin to explain apps' appeal, their charm as junkware. In this critical state, the ritual order (reassuring us with the virtues of anticipation and control, the mantic virtue of a well-done piece of technology), the aesthetic order (the sensual pleasure of an enticing illusion), and the political order (what I will call later "the appification of solitude") conspire to seduce the app user, terminally.

Here is one more reason to consider apps as junkware: We are attached to our apps, as a junkie, even a recovering junkie, is attached to his or her fix. Here is the "charm," a quasi-magical effect (call it the Arthur C. Clarke effect if you will).[16] The presence on my screen of these *app*arently inoffensive icons reassures me: I feel prepared for whatever life will throw my way, I am in control, or nostalgic for a time I was in control. The presence of this junkware might quite simply express the app user's ability, or inability, to manage his or her withdrawal symptoms. As in a gigantic anonymous meeting, I am even comforted by the strange feeling that I am not alone in this, because owning an app, and displaying it on the screen of your prosthesis of choice (a *stigma*, as Philip K. Dick first understood[17]), is also a form of belonging.

Apps definitely belong to the "solitude enhancement machines" once described by Peter Lunenfeld.[18] Apps are indeed part and parcel of the contemporary solitude enhancement apparatus (the *app*aratus hereafter). As *media*, they contribute to enable new forms of presence and co-presence, i.e., new modalities of relations; as software, they are inscribed in the historical dynamic of moving from the early computing metaphors to a full grown set of "user illusions" (Alan Kay), and thus subjected to the imperatives of marketing and its fantastic promotion of the present computing *app*aratus. Lunenfeld's recent description of the "user permanent present," however, might appear already passé. His emphasis on software utilities, the graphic user interface and its "nested files, icons, trash cans and cascading windows," though his book was published in 2005, takes for granted a status quo that cannot be accepted less than ten years later. "While there are regular software updates that incrementally increase design efficiency," he writes, "nothing radically different has penetrated the computer market, nothing that screams: this is the future, pay attention."[19] The *app*arition, two years later, might have effectively kicked off a radically new future, one that Lunenfeld might nevertheless have intuited—especially in the last part of *User*, titled "wireless cosmopolitans" (a recycling of the seventeenth-century cosmopolitans vs. patriots, revamped in the late nineteenth century as "rootless cosmopolitans")—but that he still considers from within the "TV system." This model might not be completely obsolete, if one feels like a cosmopolitan who tweeted recently that "mindless bouncing between social apps on my phone is as improvident as aimlessly flicking through TV channels" (N. Bilton).

The artifact,[20] the interface, the functionalities, and even the contents[21] might have changed radically, but the solitude enhancement machine has remained. It has remained, basically, because solitude still exists, or may even be growing. It still endures in its two basic forms, which earlier I called the Webster Syndrome and the Canetti Disease.[22] I named the first syndrome after the protagonist of Clifford D. Simak's 1952 novel *City*. When the human species' fate is at stake, Webster (named after a dictionary) misses the train of progress and salvation because of his inability to leave his home. Simak thus inverts Baudelaire's diagnosis ("l'horreur du domicile"). "He never goes anywhere," the domestic robot tells the interstellar traveler who invites Webster to take the trip that will get him to the Martian philosophical concept that could save his species. And it adds: "For what need was there to go anywhere? It was all here. By simply twirling a dial one could talk face to face with anyone wished, could go, by sense, if not in body, anywhere one wished. Could attend the theater or hear a concert or browse in a library halfway around the world. Could transact any business one might need to transact without rising from one's chair."[23]

Initiation of the immobile journey in the framed spaces of the societies of control: past this limit your ticket is no longer valid. Comeback of the vain desire to collect all the possible locations, with its subsequent boredom. Why, indeed, go anywhere? If this anywhere is in fact nowhere, why bother, even in a digital way? Why not satisfy ourselves with this virtuality: I could go anywhere, but I'd rather not. The world is sad and I have watched all the movies (to paraphrase a blogger paraphrasing a poet), or even, the metaverse is sad and I visited all the pages (another blogger, the same poet): but where do the marine winds of our pleasing surfs hide? Is solitude more bearable when one experiences it at home? Isn't Webster's syndrome the terminal anxiety of being (still) alone, (but) elsewhere? And if, as Lacan had it, anxiety's formula is but lack squared, the fear of lacking the lack, what is this lack here, well, elsewhere? Do I fear to lack the lack of somebody else, to become totally indifferent to the Other? His avatar will suffice, and why should I care whether he is a dog?[24] Absence, what absence but this presence of lack?

"Nobody feels any pain as I stand in the data shower. . . . When we meet again, introduced as friends, please don't let on that you knew me when I was hungry and it was your world."[25] No, nobody feels any pain at all, just a slight lack of affection, a disaffection. No, I do not care for travels anymore, I am not hungry for new encounters while I am under this shower where my world, our world, gently fades away, gently leaks. My very best friends, well aligned in their little windows on my interface of faces, well taken care in their simplest *app*arel, forever smile to me in the paleness of their cathodic *loglo*. Ah, familiarity without risks: so what is your mood today, which barely affects me? So, do you suffer, do you laugh or cry, you live and possibly die, who cares? Closer, I can call you now, where are you now? Messaging, perhaps? Asynchrony is so less daring, so comfortably numb. . . . Re: your message answering my message, re: re: re: re: shall we see each other? Let us exchange some syntax in the mean time, but at any cost let us not touch each other.

The Webster syndrome is but a sign of a worse disease, an *app*alling disease affixed with the name of Canetti, the social phobia of choice: "There is nothing that man fears more than the touch of the unknown. He wants to see what is reaching towards him, and to be able to recognize or at least classify it. . . . All the distances which men create round themselves are dictated by this fear."[26] Occidental man, that is, this very same being who dreams of telepresence, the neurotic and phobia-plagued being of our time without qualities, the terminally anxious who only runs on this last affect, the disaffected subject of our time. Look at them offering the *app*etence of their full frontal thumbing, of their too loud and embarrassingly obscene words that are not destined to you anyway, in their mobile audio-hapto-visual bubbles, cautiously avoiding each other. I have long ridden on suburban trains, dreaming of an accidental contact. I still remember the beatific faces of the first Walkman users, safe behind their walls of sound, and my early determination not to become one of them, to remain open to the world. I gave up on that dream too . . . and joined the stigmatic crowd, since "it is only in a crowd that man can become free of this fear of being touched."[27] Today, the crowd has been "augmented," turned into "a smart mob" for whom *the future is friendly*. Today iThing (therefore I am) is a far better name for this necessary prosthesis for survival in hostile urban settings: *you are your own iThing* (Pod, Phone, Pad pick your *app*anage of choice).

Come the times of the big numbing, the times when by lack of touching, our egoskins [*nos moi-peaux*] slowly get numb, oh so comfortably. "Hello, hello is there anybody in there? Just pod if you can hear me. . . ." Be *app*reciative, *app*ly to me. Digital ants in our prosthetic legs, our (arthro)pod-becoming: our media *app*aratus transforming our hyperinformational cities into gigantic ant-houses inhabited by a global society of disaffected beings, "gregarious and tribalized particulars who seem to drive at an arthropomorphic society of cognitive, or maybe only reactive agents, producing, just like ants, not symbols anymore, but *digital pheromones*."[28]

Today, the app appeal is the ultimate index of the quality and strength of the digital pheromones, that unlike in the case of ants, might have a libidinal character: for beyond and above the ritual (or mantic), the aesthetic, and the political orders of their seductive powers rules the diffusely obscene libidinal economy of our ultra-liberal times. A sexless libidinal economy where sex dis*app*eared under the excess of its presence, when the gently naive desires for sexual transgression left the premises a long while ago in yet another ersatz of a soon-democratized revolution for the people and by the people, following Jean-François Lyotard's comments on Pierre Klossowski's pervert fictions: "The Klossowskian phantasm, on the other hand, wants, somewhere, at least one body to transgress: for it, where the act of exceeding its reproductive finality will be an occasion for voluptuousness, when a particular fragment of its surface, will be, so to speak, removed from the total volume."[29]

At this time where the media *app*aratus is the message, this very phantasm, apps can indeed appear as the ultimate junkware for the highly volatile personal and mobile computing market, becoming even more profit generating for the replacement market that computing has been since the early 1990s, with its corollary logic of planned obsolescence.

Notes

1. Junkminimizer is one of the open-source projects of Project Hosting on Google. It is available at https://code.google.com/p/junkminimizer.

2. May Heraclitus of Montreal be thanked for that, and more.

3. *The Mobile Advantage* (http://enterprisecontent.nuance.com/mobile -advantage-infographic.html).

4. *mobiThinking*, "Global mobile statistics 2012 Part E: Mobile apps, app stores, pricing and failure rates" (http://mobithinking.com/mobile -marketing-tools/latest-mobile-stats/e#lotsofapps).

5. Ghislain Thibault and Thierry Bardini, "Éther 2.0: révolutions sans fils." *Canadian Journal of Communication* 33 (2008), no. 3: 357–378.

6. I collected a lot of scrap in the process, and I progressively accepted that it was irreversibly transforming me into a scrap scholar. *Junkware* is speculative writing. The original manuscript, subtitled *Retrofitting Cyber-culture, Beyond Genes and Memes*, was my own version of today's *Book of Changes*, structured on binary divisions from one to six bits, recycling Shao Yong's circular diagram of the *I Ching* (three and six bits) and the sixteen geomantic figures for bootstraps. I did not refrain from using any material I saw fit, regardless of their disciplinary anchorage. The original *Junkware* thus mixed the history of molecular biology with metaphysics, cultural criticism, and the history and sociology of computing, shifting often from a relatively neutral tone to a more personal form of expression, and even at times, to auto-fiction or even plagiarism (when done well, the best kind of literary junk).

7. After Agamben, *n'en déplaise à* Geert Lovink.

8. Friedrich Kittler, "There is no software," *CTheory*, October 18, 1995.

9. Eric L. Howes, "'Junkware': A New Name for 'Spyware'" (http://www .spywarewarrior.com/uiuc/junkware.htm).

10. Ibid. Strangely and not so strangely, this enunciation resembles nearly word for word one that occurred during a discussion around the labels "junk DNA" and "selfish DNA" in biology. See Thierry Bardini, *Junkware* (University of Minnesota Press, 2011), 41.

11. Available at http://www.pcmag.com.

12. For a philology of "junk," see Bardini, *Junkware*, 11–13.

13. Jean Baudrillard, *Seduction*, translated by Brian Singer (New World Perspectives, 1990 [1979]), 179. I revised Singer's translation in this quote and reverted to the closer to the original "phantasm" rather than his "phantasies."

14. Ibid., 180. Here too, I revised Singer's translation.

15. Which is also the sense of Gilbert Simondons's *Du mode d'existence des objets techniques* (Aubier, 1958). "In a system of phases there is a relation of equilibrium and of reciprocal tensions; the present system of all the phases taken together is the complete reality." (ibid.,180, my translation)

16. Arthur C. Clarke, the author of *2001: A Space Odyssey*, states his third law of prediction as follows: "Any sufficiently advanced technology is indistinguishable from magic." (source: Wikipedia)

17. One of the three "stigmata" is a prosthetic hand in Dick's 1965 novel *The Three Stigmata of Palmer Eldritch*.

18. Peter Lunenfeld and Mieke Gerritzen, *User: Infotechnodemo* (MIT Press, 2005).

19. Ibid., 17.

20. Or even the Info *App*liance, since Apple officially dropped the word "Computer" from its name as early as January of 2007.

21. It took a while, but porn apps appeared in 2009, the same year Android got its first porn-only apps store (MiKandi). But even there some changes might have been obvious: one of the first X-rated apps approved by Apple took advantage of the iPhone's vibrations in an interesting way. In 2009, Dr. Debby Herbenick, an expert on sexual health, wrote: "The intensity of the vibration MyPleasure could use for this app [dubbed MyVibe] is obviously limited by the amount of vibration that the iPhone offers, so the orgasmic potential of the MyVibe app is similarly limited. However, orgasms—while fun—aren't everything." ("MyVibe thighs-on: First iPhone vibrator app approved by Apple," http://gizmodo.com/5295987/myvibe-thighs+on -first-iphone-vibrator-app-approved-by-apple-nsfw) Contrary to the old user model described by Lunenfeld, then, "nominatively normative heterosexual males" may not be the only target of choices of the new libidinal marketers.

22. See Thierry Bardini, "*Alone Together*: Paradoxes et syndromes de la téléprésence," in *Ensemble ailleurs—Together Elsewhere*, ed. Louise Poissant and Pierre Tremblay (Presses de l'Université du Québec, 2010).

23. Clifford D. Simak, *City* (Ace Books, 1952), 50.

24. As in the French translation of the title of Simak's book: *Demain, les chiens*, or as in "In the mean streets of the metaverse, nobody cares you might be a dog."

25. A slight revision of a line from Bob Dylan's "Just Like A Woman."

26. These are the first sentences of Elias Canetti's *Crowds and Powers*, translated by Carol Stewart (Farrar, Straus and Giroux, 1984 [1960]), 15.

27. Ibid.

28. Bernard Stiegler, *De la misère symbolique. 1. L'époque hyperindustrielle* (Galilée, 2004), 147 (my translation). In a great coincidence, the concluding lines of Simak's *City* are as follows: "Homer would be disappointed, he told himself. Terribly dis-app-ointed when he found that the websters had no way of dealing with the ants."

29. Jean-François Lyotard, *Libidinal Economy*, translated by Ian Hamilton Grant (Indiana University Press, 1993 [1974]), 75–76.

16
The Spinoza Lens-Grinder App

Drew S. Burk

The reader has entered into an imaginary app. This theoretical app is a fictional genre akin to the non-standard aesthetics attempted by François Laruelle of a photo-fictional apparatus.[1] But while Laruelle's non-standard aesthetics has to date merely focused on a photo-fiction—a theoretical discursive mimesis of the photographic process—in his treatise *Photo-Fiction, a Non-Standard Aesthetics*, the following conceptual essay is an attempt at an "app-fiction." It will thus be a discursive mimesis of a theoretical imaginary app, constructed, like any ordinary app, with programming, coding, theoretical stitching, welding, and digital temporality. Although this text may read like any ordinary textual script from the analog period of books and television, please take note that it is a theoretical application whose text actually functions properly within the real of the "app" and whose linguistic utterances are not merely relegated to a linear script but to that of any mobile technology today. That is, it allows for mobility within the non-place. But, as with any other app, this text is hackable, and the components can be broken down, deconstructed, and used for other imaginary apps. This was where this creative experimental app began in the first place, onto-vectorially[2]: "I" as stumbling vector. Through the cobblestone of Spinoza and though the apartment window of Leibniz, tracing through monads—mediated and otherwise. Conceptual personae,[3] clone subjectivity in-the-last-instance, Max Ernst techniques of decalcomania and redemption. But all these components and hacks were put into an accelerator, particle or otherwise. Colliding at light speed, within a real-time trajectory, they allow for a novel photo-fictional theoretical attempt at seeing within a mobility of the future to come which is already here. The future-past.

An App-Fiction—A Non-Standard Aesthetic Imaginary App

(uni-lateral duality application construction for mobility within movement)

We must neither anthropomorphize nor objectify apparatus. We must grasp them in their cretinous concreteness, in their programmed and absurd functionality, in order to be able to comprehend them and thus to insert them into meta-programs. The paradox is that such meta-programs are equally absurd games. In sum: what we must learn is to accept the absurd, if we wish to emancipate ourselves from functionalism. Freedom is conceivable only as an absurd game with apparatus, as a game with programs. It is conceivable only after we have accepted politics and human existence in general to be an absurd game. Whether we continue to be "men" or become robots depends on how fast we learn how to play: we can become players of the game or pieces in it.

—Vilém Flusser

1 Oraxioms⁴

1.1 Upon the arrival at the position of networked real time, the offering of unlimited mobility as technological progress creates a new type of mobile body.

1.2 This absolute virtual/actual mobility, in obliterating every old conception of mobility, creates as well its pharmakon⁵ shadow: all-out mobility is an obliteration of mobility as such.

1.3 Decalcomania is an artistic technique that has mutated from its use by such artists as Max Ernst. It is an aesthetic technique of brushing up and pressing two surfaces against each other in order to create a third impression, which can elicit a fractal trace. It is this artistic technical gesture that made Gilles Deleuze claim we need the same sort of mutations for philosophy—Marx Ernsts of philosophy.⁶

I Proposition

Absolute mobility as *pharmakon*: strategies of mobility within absolute movement

> Gestures and problems mark an epoch, and unknown to geometers and philosophers, guide the eye and hand.
>
> —Gilles Châtelet

One used to arrive at the outland of the meshwork and it was an interzone of unfathomable wandering, of disappearance and appearance. The feedback echo was the longest 15 seconds of your life. One entered into an entire universe that seemed ever expanding and where its openness and expanse conjured a sublimity only paralleled by one's arrival onto a new continent, namely, there was a renaissance of the age of exploration where we all became reacquainted with our natures as discoverers and uncoverers of this seemingly endless continent of code and TCP/IP back channels. That realm now resides in the layers upon layers of digital sediment, buried deep between digital conveyor belts of invisible factories, and where one can wander aimlessly. It is forgotten with the invention of the Internet that not only did it allow for a new direct connection across time and space, but that it opened up a novel type of gaze, of a streaming video awareness of the instant, and here, in the beginning, it was a mere flickering on the pavement walls of the cavern of post-modernity. For as the grand-narratives had been called dead, and the rising of the minor voices, and code chatter lead to rhizomatic networks now become meshworks, within the digital stereoreal[7] landscape we have entered now into a universe where we can engage within a crystalline audio-visual cinematic temporality and where the spatiality as well gives way to various ways of wandering or seeing within the world. There was a screenification of the everyday, now still finding ourselves ever-hovering over some sort of illuminated screen. Indeed, our vision and individuation becoming more and more via some sort of daily shared global echo-chamber. But the future-to-come-which-is-already-here is one where the screen is no longer there. It has become invisible. Being is becoming within a Heraclitean streaming video awareness of the instant. As one becomes reliant on a series of data clouds and temporal/spatial modulations, there is a continuous stereoreal soundtrack within the world of the app where knowledge transmission is done at light speed and where one's relationship to knowledge is constantly between competing flows of ecstasy, fear, despair, hope, and where one's memory support as well, moving from a memory based on fragments of linear script, within a narrative of history, moving into fragmented narratives now becoming emergent non-linear "cybernetic memories"[8] shifted from a cinema and its cinematic memory now turned to that of a crystal imaginary of the stereoreal. Here, as with any supplement of the becoming memory of the imaginary (the real as inventive) present, the pataphysical visual support has always been that of seeing the being and non-being within the everyday, and hovering within being as becoming, an emergent movement of errancy of drifting, if the app was invented merely to provide some sort of ornamental lure, to distract and seduce the user in order to provide a small amount of momentary fascination, in allowing for the software to be given as sacrifice to the crowds of digital users hovering outside the pyramids of technology, what it became in the users hands was another creative poetico-aesthetic technique of seeing and of seeing within a non-linear spatio-temporality, where, the acceleration of the application allows for a memory of the present that is in becoming at light speed and where, wandering within a digital wasteland where the crystal image reigns and where one, in order to reflect and perceive and view within a trajectory is to require the anti-app. Namely an app that provides the necessary disorientation and re-acquaintance within the world. One must take on the poet heteronymic gaze of Pessoa, Alberto Caeiro's sunflower gaze of the explorers, and see beyond the binary of sense or non-sense, or the temporal trinity of the past-present-future. This position of accepting a promissory note from a future to come with which one will only ever encounter as territory but through a wandering into the field of novelty, singularity, and openness.

If thinking is about orientating, situating oneself within a territory of thought, and if today the open wandering that was once part of the everyday is slowly disappearing for an invisible cybernetic guided flows of the libidinal, then to situate oneself again, within thought, in order to take back up the task of thought, one must purchase the Spinoza lens-grinder app®! Of course, apps of this virtual optics our free. One does not purchase this app; one encounters it as uni-lateral dualistic hack.

An app that does not distract but frees one in order to see from the position of the stranger—of novelty, of the sunflower gaze, of the Portuguese explorers, not as colonizers, but explorers, discoverers, uncoverers, revealers, revelationaries, those who can grab hold of the invisible cybernetic strings of the stereoreal and orchestrate a melodic and poetic sublimity within a virtual/ actual cybernetic field of resonance where all aesthetic and scientific discoveries themselves become meshed together. To play these cybernetic string instruments, to wander gaze and engage with the digital cobblestone turned application becoming within the instant at the edge of the territories, to sing the songs of the future-present, one must have lenses, optical convexes. Baruch Spinoza was a heretical thinker. He was someone who saw. He was a seer. Not all thinkers are seers, but this is not to say that all who think must not use the faculty of seeing. As we moved from the oral tradition to that of the written, it was always already predicated on a visual field and territory. To speak was always to speak towards someone or some god or some thing, and to this there was a necessity of directions, orientations. To speak in front of, to speak up to the heavens, the sky, to speak below, or within, the inner voice of being within a realm of deception and grand proclivities of the thinker, what some have called the dialectics of the eye, seeing oneself see. Here, the theatre and factories of psychic and collective individuation can be refracted via ways of seeing, like the lens grinder, the thinker as well constructs his or her lenses. Spinoza's lenses were heretical, which meant merely that they provided a way of seeing that was novel, foreign, strange, sublime.[9]

2 Oraxioms

2.1 Within an echo-chamber of immediate communication of the inner and outer voice of the mobile body, we are no longer within the surreal nor the hyperreal, but rather the stereoreal.

*2.2 Stereoreality is no longer predicated on any sort of stable subjective nor objec-
tive position but the trajective. To grasp identity in this perpetual mobile territory
is to grasp the mobile in movement, namely identity as vectorial.*
*2.3 If the parts comprising the Individual become bigger or smaller, in such a way
that the proportions of the Individual's nature still are upheld, which is to say remain in relation the form which it previously had, then the Individual will thus
retain it nature as well such that there is no change whatsoever in the form.*

II Proposition

Stereoreality, *destinerrance, le trajectile*: vectorial optics and wanderlust

> According to McLuhan, media are the intersecting points or intersections
> between technologies, on the one hand, and bodies, on the other. McLuhan
> went so far as to write that under audiovisual conditions our eyes, ears, hands,
> etc. no longer belong to the bodies they are associated with at all, let alone to
> the subjects in philosophical theory as the masters of the aforementioned
> bodies, but rather to the television companies they are connected to.
> —Friedrich Kittler

> To think is first of all a phenomenon of amplitude or a deviation of the gran-
> deur of thought with itself, and not a relation between positions or objects.
> And yet this phenomenon of amplitude can be understood by the vector, it is
> vectorial, even when we are dealing with a "vectorial ontology. Which is to say,
> angular, the ray being deflected or rejected based on the rectitude of the depth
> of vision, every ray or sight is affected by an angle from which it is inseparable.
> Undulation has it sight set well on its object but not directly or not in terms of
> a depth or a distance of the appearance of phenomenon. Here the depth is
> angular and not thrown in front of or at the foot of a subject. Thinking by
> amplitude is thus to finally have one's sight set on an object but indirectly and
> not ecstatically, but in a semi-ecstatic and vectorial manner.
> —François Laruelle

> We live without feeling the ground beneath our feet
> After ten steps our words vanish.
> —Osip Mandelstam

Recently the philosopher and urbanist Paul Virilio has stared down a new perspective for viewing what we could call identity—or perhaps, to put it in a
more specific manner, a vision that no longer views identity as being based
on either objectivity or subjectivity but rather on *trajectivity*. The trajectile
replaces the objectile. We are dealing with a new geo-philosophical condition.
As Deleuze and Guattari mention in *What Is Philosophy?*, to think identity

as a territory is perhaps a better way of understanding the concept of identity, one based no longer on clear distinctions between subject and object
but rather a more auto-poetic becoming reverb between—a heterogeneous
becoming which makes up a *terre*, a location in which an identity weaves itself.
A place, a dwelling for being, is constructed with an identifiable geo-location
as an inadvertent necessary end result.

What was a crisis for the modernists, with the breaking down of stable
subjectivities, becomes merely an ante whose stakes have been raised one
more time since we began to engage within a cybernetic networked sea of fre-
quencial data-sets, info-bots, and algorithmic excess. Today, even in viewing
ourselves, we are no longer viewing and understanding our so-called selves
through a Lacanian mirror, we don't even have that luxury. Today, where
place is a becoming twilight of its own ephemerality, identity becomes a part
of the disposable economy of acceleration as well.

Caught staring up at the stars, Thales fell down into a well. Today, wandering within our own contemplative self-absorbed spheres, we all stumbled into
the well. The well of digitality. And within this well, it is no longer subjectivity
or objectivity which sees, but trajectivity, a movement-vision, which perhaps
one could call cinematic (as Virilio makes the case for).

The trajective is based on a trajectory, vision of repetitive data-sets, fre-
quencial numbering, and cartographic capture. As the photographic apparatus
began to capture time and place, as it began to re-appropriate the imaginary
and re-constitute the separation of the real and the virtual; today trajective
capture blurs this distinction completely. Within this novel topological move-
ment-imaginary, we brush up against our own auto-poetic trajectivities, and
here, it is no longer seeing a reflection in some sort of mirroring, no longer a
position whose understanding appears to be privy to the so-called psychoana-
lysts but another position quite familiar to the philosopher which is perhaps
better named as close relative of "psychoanalyse" (poetic fractal optics of the
poet: Rimbaud's "Je est autre"). A poetic self-reflexive optics that opens itself
up to vision as fractal. "spychoanalysis": seeing oneself see. Peter Sloterdijk, in
his *Critique of Cynical Reason,* speaks of this as a dialectics of the eye. Or we
can also see other attempts at thinking this dual vision in the theoretical non-
standard aesthetic attempt of Laruelle in placing the philosopher-aesthetician
in superposition with the photographer-artist or in Nietzsche's relation of the
Dionysian artist's position of viewing tied to the observations of Dionysius.
This is not where a subject becomes aware of its proper identity, but where a
trajectile becomes aware of what Fernand Deligny called "lignes d'erre"—wander lines—a vision of wandering, of an ephemeral movement which is always
one step away from viewing itself but which, in its wake, leaves the traces of

its own movement. Something that Michel De Certeau as well recognized via his research into the ordinary wandering of the everyday life:

> As unrecognized producers, poets of their own acts, silent discoverers of their own paths in the jungle of functionalist rationality, consumers produce through their signifying practices something that might be considered similar to the "wandering lines" ("lignes d'erre") drawn by the autistic children studied by F. Deligny: "indirect" or "errant" trajectories obeying their own logic. In the technocratically constructed, written, and functionalized space in which the consumers move about, their trajectories form unforeseeable sentences, partly unreadable paths across a space. Although they are composed with the vocabularies of established languages (those of television, newspapers, supermarkets, or museum sequences) and although they remain subordinated to the prescribed syntactical forms (temporal modes of schedules, paradigmatic orders of spaces, etc.), the trajectories trace out the ruses of other interests and desires that are neither determined nor captured by the systems in which they develop.[10]

Seeing the twilight of place, we engage in an understanding that being-as-dwelling means dwelling which is in perpetual movement, always one step ahead of itself. When Fernand Deligny became fascinated with study of the ritual quotidian trajectories of his autistic patients in the late 1960s, he was interested in studying the continual movements of those whose identity precisely was better articulated through their respective patterns than any sort of concrete descriptive naming. Deligny's relation to identity was that of a resistance to it, believing one had no sort of stable identity that one owned. He preferred a relation as close to the outside as possible, of the stranger, and to the relinquishing of the position of identity in order to recreate a position of wandering of en-acting life, of the act, [agir] that is not that different than a radical aesthetics of the poet, and the temporality that is that of the automatic writing of light. To understand the autistic, one is better off studying a different kind of consciousness or processing. It is perhaps a processing that is only aware of itself in that via its trajectory, its movement— it "knows" that it functions. This is the "self-awareness" of the app. Namely a poetics like that described by Judith Balso in her work on Fernando Pessoa as well as in Paul Virilio's concept of stereoreality (and its novel optical relief of real time).

As with the Spinoza Lens-grinder app®, it is a novel trajective relief which one "sees before knowing (being aware) that one sees it."[11] And with the acceleration of reality, within a reality of the instant, to engage this vision is to enter into a poetics. As Judith Balso states in Pessoa, the Metaphysical Courier, referring to Pessoa's conception of what we could perhaps call a heteronymous poetics,

For Pessoa, the poem is a freedom to do away with the object and a freedom to invent new images which are no longer "images of" something, but artificial constructions no less perfectly real in their own right. Rendering possible that art was no longer illusionist, but "lucid"—re-iterating one of Campos' favorite epithets—and that art was no longer so much this fiction conscious of being a fiction (in which at least an entire part of modern art, having barely been born, will lose itself) but a fiction conscious in its own manner of being real, exactly as machines or bridges are real. The importance within this poetic framework accorded to the city and the machine is more profound than the futurists had thought: the machine in particular incarnates a "non-object," a latent model of the real as an abstract construction. It is in this manner the emblem of what art thinks and affirms of itself from then on.[12]

Because the blueprints and their initial construction, "function," the blueprints becoming bridge, then become "self-aware" of their functioning as bridge in becoming precisely the "bridge" itself. And like the photo-graphic apparatus of capturing the real, within it's brush up against the real itself, the Spinoza Lens-grinder app® is a photo-fictional theoretical art form. It is an art as well that becomes "lucid." Which is to say, it provides an imaginary optics of vision.[13]

Art becomes "lucid" and perhaps today, to understand the lucidity of trajectivity, of the lines of wandering put forth by Deligny, we must entertain our accelerated position within a psycho-geography whose trajectory, whose reverb is a becoming without destination. Here we are within a topological data-set, algorithmic calculus, to escape capture, which is to say, to distinguish the novel stereoreal relief between the virtual and the real, is to engage in what Jacques Derrida named, a "destinerrance."[14] A wandering without destination. It is a vision of time as space. It is a vision of spatial temporality. It is a vision for trajectivity. An optics perhaps like Laruelle's optics of the Vision-in-One.[15] An upgrade of Spinoza's third genre of knowledge. A vision-without-reflection.

The angel is the principle of language itself. For us it is how desire passes into words.
—Michel De Certeau

The sail is as smart as the shelter is stupid: A properly built sailing ship can almost sail against the wind and is only ever hapless when there is no wind.
—Vilém Flusser

3 Oraxioms

3.1 What one acquires in the format of an immediate, easy, access to knowledge in the form of information can now provide the opposite affect of what we could normally call knowledge. It precisely empties out our various material relations to bodies.

3.2 There is an intelligence of stupidity that perhaps is in need of saving. Do androids dream of electric sheep?[16] Or drone insects?

3.3 The more the robotic soul achieves this third kind of knowledge, the more it wants to know things via this third genre of knowledge.

3.4 An affection directed toward a thing we imagine to be necessary is more intense, all things being equal, as if it directed itself toward a possible or contingent thing, which is to say one that is unnecessary.[17]

3.5 The human soul only knows of the human body and its existence by the ideas of affection that affect the body.[18]

III Proposition

The stake of the mobile is the stake of temporal identity: of the body and its auto-affection, the stake of intuition, the third kind of knowledge according to Spinoza. An upgrade is perhaps needed. And this is the non-Spinozist application of a vision without reflection. The Spinoza Lens-grinder app as sunflower gaze.[19]

According to Spinoza, "the human soul is precisely the idea itself of the knowledge of the human body." The stake of the mobile is the also the stake of temporal identity: *knowledge* as *information* of the human body or identity within a perpetual position of movement in real time. It is always within the trajectivity, within the vectorial dynamism of movement within movement, from one location to the next that forces us to uproot ourselves from one territory and take on the task of the nomad traveller, of the stranger. Within movement and upon arrival into other territories, one is forced to take up the utterance of one's identity once again, always within the instant of movement from and to a strange new place. When one feels as estranged and distant from the territory in which they had before constituted an unsaid self-name, one takes on the self-name for the first time always already again. Which is to say, one must allow for the utterance of the "I" in the last instance to speak. I come from somewhere. One must articulate a location upon arrival and moving toward a new territory within mobility. And it is this once necessary position of relating identity to territory that allows us to consider what sort of territory identity truly shows itself through. If identity is merely uttered or reassembled and individuated when one is paradoxically most distant and estranged from it, then as some thinkers have articulated, it is perhaps the stranger who can as stranger perhaps be the only witness to identity if this is possible at all and when one becomes or encounters the stranger, it is also precisely when one themselves becomes the stranger, which is to say, as identity forms in a territory, the territory of the stranger is precisely one where one is within a trajectivity. It is a vectorial space where we encounter once again the territory of the clinamen, the swerve of relations in the last instant for mobility. Within this vectorial space, identity as well is not only vectorial but a brush up against the fluidity and fractality and ephemerality of the non-place, the landscape in motion, within the acceleration itself, to utter, which is to say to speak the territory in movement is to also have specific capacity for perceptual lenses. To claim identity or to allow it to be uttered, one is also allowing or taking on a seeing. When one is within trajectivity and the motion of movement, then one takes up the position of constantly re-iterating this seeing or this always already first utterance of identity as stranger. And as stranger at precisely the heart of the first utterance and witness to identity, to see or speak or utter the position of the first articulation of thought, is to take up the lenses of the poet, the hybrid genius, the one who never stops bifurcating and whom sees the real as a vectorial space, it is that of the lenses of Heraclitus and Spinoza. The lenses of flash-thought. Where as Heraclitus tells us, "everything is ruled by lightning." And Spinoza reminds us is that there is a third kind of knowledge: the intuition of auto-affection.

Can one have a relation with the app that is like one's encounter with the wave? Finally conquering the waves in learning to swim, as Deleuze says in regards to Spinoza in his lectures.[20] Spinoza's form of knowledge is that of the relations between bodies or souls. He speaks of the human body encountering the body of water in the form of the wave. For the human to encounter the wave and learn how to properly interact with it, which is to say to recognize it as other, as a separate body or water soul, one must learn how to resist and reacquaint oneself with space: one must learn how to swim. As far as the app is concerned, one must learn how to encounter and conquer the elements not of the wave in this sense of the Internet (where one claims to *surf* the wave), but perhaps more of a process akin to *swimming*, which is to say, to take on a movement within various waves whether they be those of invisible electro-magnetic waves of the app of real time or those waves of history of philosophy to which Laruelle speaks.

For Laruelle, before one becomes a quantum philosopher one must first take on the position as transcendental swimmer up against various waves whether those of the history of philosophy or the quantic waves of particle and light:

"The following solution is obvious, like "love with one's eyes closed" or suicide, stop trying to confront the wave and accept being immersed with it, embrace its undulations, interfere with them. The transcendental swimmer has become this mythic swimmer, at the limits of non-philosophy which we call the "fish-in-water," the fusion of the fish and the water, but which remains a quantic animal, not a "quantic philosopher." A quantic philosopher is *also* a philosopher, he or she occupies the entire space of philosophy rather than merely that of water, and is measured by other waves coming from the ocean of history. And when the swimmer fuses this time with philosophy as with an element but this fusion is intermingled by the swimmer rather than the philosophical wave, a new figure emerges from the ocean, that of the quantic non-philosopher who has survived or overcome his philosophical suicide because he has accepted the ultimatum and fused with it. If pure immanence is deadly, its immanental and generic regime, without drowning the philosopher, sufficiently blinds him or her in order to no longer be besieged by philosophy no more so than by a necessary fantasy."[21]

In this sense, we find not the second type of knowledge according to Spinoza (the interaction of bodies that makes one aware of one's own body or soul and that of the other), nor perhaps Spinoza's third kind of knowledge—that of the lightning flash of intuition and auto-affection. We may discover another quantic superposition between wave and particle of Identity that considers the photographic flash or irreflective seeing as a 'flash as "self-belonging"'[22] which is perhaps at the heart of the app itself. Love.[23] Spinoza knew about apps before us all. His scholias continue to get hacked and, if one is fortunate, one will be able to make another app to give back to Spinoza.

Materials necessary for the user to use (hack) the Spinoza Lens Grinder App:

iPhone made by Apple factory workers in dismal conditions

Post-History by Vilém Flusser (Univocal, 2013)

Photo-Fiction, a Non-Standard Aesthetics by François Laruelle, translated by Drew S. Burk (Univocal, 2012)

Dictionary of Non-Philosophy by François Laruelle, translated by Taylor Adkins (Univocal, 2013)

Philosophie Non-Standard by François Laruelle (Kime, 2010)

Grey Ecology by Paul Virilio, translated by Drew S. Burk (Atropos 2010)

Ville Panique by Paul Virilio (Galilée, 2004)

Le Futurisme de L'Instant: Stop-Eject by Paul Virilio (Galilée, 2009)

Figuring Space: Philosophy, Mathematics, and Physics by Gilles Châtelet (Springer, 1999)

Ethique by Baruch Spinoza, translated by Charles Appuhn (Flammarion, 1969)

Gilles Deleuze's lectures on Spinoza, available at www.webdeleuze.com

The Post Card: From Socrates to Freud and Beyond by Jacques Derrida, translated by Alan Bass (University of Chicago Press, 1987)

Optical Media by Friedrich Kittler, translated by Anthony Enns (Polity, 2009)

The Medium Is the Message by Marshall McLuhan (Gingko, 2005)

The Medium Is the Massage by Marshall McLuhan (Gingko, 2005)

Telemorphosis by Jean Baudrillard, translated by Drew S. Burk (Univocal 2013)

Pataphysics by Jean Baudrillard, translated by Drew S. Burk (available at www.ctheory.net)

Carnival et Cannibale by Jean Baudrillard (L'Herne, 2009)

Pessoa, the Metaphysical Courier by Judith Balso, translated by Drew S. Burk (Atropos, 2011)

What Is Philosophy? by Gilles Deleuze and Felix Guattari (Minuit, 1991)

Desert Islands by Gilles Deleuze, translated by Davide Lapoujade, edited by Mike Taormina (Semiotext(e), 2004)

The Practice of Everyday Life by Michel De Certeau (University of California Press, 2011)

"There must be an angel: On the beginnings of the arithmetics of rays" by David Link (available at http://www.alpha60.de)

Notes

1. See François Laruelle, *Photo-Fiction, a Non-Standard Aesthetics* (Univocal, 2012).

2. Laruelle's ontology is predicated on a messianic relation to identity in the last instance—what he names, *l'homme-en-dernier-instance*, or "the human-in-the-last-instance." To better understand this conception of existence, Laruelle continues to use aspects of mathematics, one of which is based on the conception of vectors. To give the geometric concept of the vector an ontological scope, Laruelle creates the neologism "onto-vectorial." Thus, "'I' as stumbling vector" is my personification and description of what onto-vectoriality and its chaos would represent.

3. See the chapter on conceptual personae in Gilles Deleuze and Felix Guattari, *What Is Philosophy?* (Columbia University Press, 1996).

4. See François Laruelle's invention of the oraxiom combining equal parts axiom and the oracular position of philosophy (the oracle). It is essential to

thinking a theoretical installation of photo-fiction or what Laruelle names as non-philosophy and non-standard philosophy as philo-fiction.

5. "Pharmakon" comes from the Ancient Greek word *pharmakos*, which means both cure and poison. Various philosophers, notably Jacques Derrida and Bernard Stiegler, have used this term on many occasions to describe the human's relation to technology and the continuing development of our relation to various shifting forms of communicative exchange. See Jacques Derrida's essay "Plato's pharmacy" and Stiegler's three-volume work *Technics and Time*.

6. See the interview in *Desert Islands* titled "On Nietzsche and the image of thought," in which Deleuze discusses the necessity for philosophy to experiment with different creative techniques in order to maintain a relevance with other creative forms of expression such as collage and cubism in art, jazz, and rock and roll in music, as well as contemporary shifts in mathematics and physics. Deleuze states that the philosophers will be both artist and doctors (symptomologists).

7. Paul Virilio's concept of stereoreality has been described in several of his late works as the position that comes after Jean Baudrillard's conception of hyperreality in order to describe our current relation to real time digital networks and screens. For Virilio, the stereoreal, like the Italian *quattrocento*, provides for a new type of optical field of perspective, emerging from our global relation to networked real time where all scientific, artistic, and communicative advancements are merged together within the live streaming connections of global communication networks.

8. The media theorist Vilém Flusser speaks of "cybernetic memories" in *Post-History* (Univocal, 2013).

9. While the metaphorical use of lenses is important in understanding that one of the prosthetic or enhancing abilities of philosophy, arts, and sciences is the ability to literally see things anew and differently, in the case of Spinoza, not only did he provide very novel, heretical ways of seeing and viewing reality, but he also made his actual living grinding lenses for glasses. Though he was excommunicated and almost stabbed to death for his at the time heretical writings on how reality functioned, he died from the pollution of grinding glass all day long.

10. See Michel De Certeau, *The Practice of Everyday Life* (University of California Press, 2011).

11. *Grey Ecology* by Paul Virilio,, translated by Drew Burk (Atropos 2010).

12. *Pessoa, The Metaphysical Courier* by Judith Balso, translated by Drew Burk (Atropos, 2011).

13. In his magnum opus, *Philosophie Non-Standard* (Kime, 2010), Laruelle writes: "In the end we can speak of a 'negative' or rather and 'impossible' non-philosophy in the same way we think of the imaginary number or even an imaginary dwelling (foyer imaginaire) or of the convergence of negative rays. Non-Standard Philosophy is imaginary optics that uses the optics of philosophy and folds it onto the generic. This is merely a partial example but it is at the heart of the generic quantum. This could have been, as Marx would say, of an individual and bourgeois essence but it will be generic and transhuman." (my translation)

14. For more insight into Derrida's concept of *destinerrance*, which is a neologism combining the French term for fate or destiny, *destin* and the term *errance* which means wandering or erring. Derrida uses this term to refer to the letter or post card or utterance than never truly arrives at its destination. See *The Post Card: From Socrates to Freud and Beyond* (University of Chicago Press, 1987).

15. See François Laruelle's definition of the Vision-in-One in the *Dictionary of Non-Philosophy*, translated by Taylor Adkins (Univocal, 2013).

16. The film *Blade Runner* was based on Philip K. Dick's novel *Do Androids Dream of Electric Sheep?*

17. I have re-translated this statement from Spinoza's *Ethics*. In fact, if you have made it this far into this imaginary app, you will realize that the imaginary app's whole structure is based on Spinoza's style of writing, who himself mimicked the style of the geometers of his time.

18. My translation from Spinoza's *Ethics*.

19. See the previously mentioned reference to this poetic vision created by Fernando Pessoa and his heteronym Alberto Caeiro.

20. Deleuze's lectures on Spinoza can be found in the online Deleuze Archive at www.webdeleuze.com.

21. Francois Laruelle, *Philosophie Non-Standard* (Kime: Paris, 2010), 314–315 (my translation).

22. For Laruelle's conception of the photographic flash as self-belonging, see *Photo-Fiction, a Non-Standard Aesthetics*.

23. See the artist-philosopher David Link's wonderful experimental work *LoveLetters* (2009), in which he reconstructs one of the first computer programs ever to algorithmically generate "love letters." Also see the companion essay "There must be an angel: On the beginnings of the arithmetics of rays."

17
From the Digital to the Tentacular, or From iPods to Cephalopods: Apps, Traps, and Entrées-without-Exit

Dan Mellamphy and Nandita Biswas Mellamphy

Octopus intelligence is unstable only in appearance: its about-faces are a trap, the net in which its adversaries come to be entangled.
—Marcel Détienne and Jean-Pierre Vernant, *Les ruses de l'Intélligence: La mètis des Grecs*

Openness is *anonymous-until-now*: the *incognitum hactenus* of the hunter who is already there . . . eating you, . . . weaving and unweaving your thread.
—Reza Negarestani, "A Good Meal"

The only apps I like are the ones that come before my entrée.
—Liz Lemon, *30 Rock*

While walking or taking public transportation to work, the authors of this essay inevitably pass by numbers of people doing the same, albeit with their heads tilted down and their attention fixated on hand-held gadgets (in 2012, the year in which this essay was written, iPods, iPads, Android tablets, cell phones, and the like). The number of people apparently proceeding through the city but in fact still in the virtual cell of their monadological monasteries grows weekly. These individuals with their attention rapt/rapped/enraptured by apps—monks trapped in and by their trappist app cell[phone]s, compulsively consuming their hypertext-tablets—are all already *allured* by, and in the *alure* of, a *lure*: each monk, monk's cell[phone], trappist tablet and active app might best be imagined (for ease of exemplification) as the cell of a single sucker among scads—myriads—arrayed on the teeming tentacles of a colossal cybernetic cephalopod (a rather Lovecraftian and in some respects Flusserian vision, hearkening here first to Howard Lovecraft's monstrous Cthulhu, "an octopus-like" creature "whose face was a mass of feelers"[1]—"innumerable flexible and undulating members"[2]—which extend like the waves of a wireless network[3] into every dimension of otherwise "proper" and "private" people's lives, and secondly to Vilém Flusser's "infernal" Vampyroteuthis, a creature of the genus *octopoda* "equipped with numerous antennae, tentacles, and other sensory organs" that are "the extremities of its digestive apparatus"—an apparatus "which sucks-in the environment").[4] In this "infernal" I.T. vision,[5] the app user gets sucked into a seductive, tricky, *truc*[6]-like, many-tentacled trap and in this way appropriated by the app, which takes on the character of what Marcel Détienne and Jean-Pierre Vernant, in their study of tricks, traps, and cunning intelligence, called the *polyplokon noèma*—the tentacular savvy—of a "living trap": *un piège vivant* exemplified again by the octopus and "octopus intelligence."[7]

To approach apps as traps with tentacular savvy is not simply to engage in hyperbole or fancy; it is akin, we would argue, to adopting a strategy taken by the military when engaging with an "asymmetrical" enemy[8]—an opponent that has many guises and thus cannot be readily or distinctly discerned. Apps have become as popular as they are in part because they are offered to us as benign, useful, and "friendly" devices that are there to serve us, to attend to our needs and desires: our various appetites. We tend to think of apps in some sense as "appetizers" (or if you prefer, "appéritifs"): as single-function/single-purpose/single-service applications with custom interfaces designed to be appetizing (that is, aesthetically appealing), user friendly,[9] and bio-politically beneficial.[10] But apps are never what they seem and cannot simply be defined by their formal properties or aesthetic characteristics; apps are always imbricated in mechanisms that allow hidden data-collecting, information-processing and intelligence-exchanging operations. No matter how "benign" they may be, in the system of capitalist consumption, uploads and downloads, they are part of a larger predatory framework, and are in this respect "weaponized" from the outset (all-the-more/all-the-better if "benign"). They are the appealing and enticing entrapments—the *bait*, if you will—in and of a capitalist game of coursing, hunting and/or trapping. The app is part of the hunter-trapper/trapper-keeper machine, a machine that hunts "you" the app user, and appropriates "you" (your "identity" or your "user-information": location, destination, usage-duration and replication, communication, identification, *et cetera*) into the arena and concourse of capitalist coursing or hunting.

We thus approach the app not from the perspective of its technical definitions or instrumental uses, but instead from the perspective of its "trap"-like operation: apps are hypercamouflaged[11] predatory operatives in their function as covert capitalist capturing-devices. From the digital, discrete, "hands-on" perspective of the user, apps are appetizing hors d'oeuvres for the

Dexter Sinister: An Octopus in Plan View

Dexter Sinister presents An Octapus in Plan View, a project with Shannon Ebner. An eight-part episodic text on octopuses written by Angie Keefer. Sequentially recorded October 14-17 at the Frieze Art Fair in a purpose-built recording cabin.

Part 1 The etymology of the word 'octopus.'
Part 2 The inside-outedness of its eyeball
Part 3 How the subject disappears into its context
Part 4 Shifting its shape and rearranging its privates
Part 5 How he or she gets from A to B
Part 6 is writing oneself in ink
Part 7 Polysexuality and death
Part 8 post-symbolic communication. or speaking without words It's a metaphysical monster

Form being a way of thinking. the presence of words in the absence of images puts a picture in the eye's mind

Figure 17.1
Dexter-Sinister: An Octopus in Plan View. Credits: Shannon Philayne Ebner, The Showroom, South Park WikiMedia.

human-all-too-human consumer. But from the tentacular perspective of the all-embracing/all-pervading-and-appropriating network, the user is the oeuvre itself rather than hors-d'oeuvre, the entrée with no exits (or "*lui, le huis-clos*" with respect to the app); the "main course" is the individual app user who is ultimately appropriated, whose thoughts and actions/activities are consumed/sucked-up/uploaded. What makes the app subversive—riddled with Cthulhu-like creepiness, as Lovecraft might say—is its involvement with a broader capitalist complex "made up of the myriad of little human subjects" and "the myriads of micro-processes that compose it."[12] Whereas we use apps like appliances, as if they were a fridge full of appetizers for instance, and manhandle or manage them through the manipulative intermediary of ten fingers,[13] apps use *us* through their app-*alliance*, the capitalist reticulation and redistributive network of dynamic data and of ever-flowing information that apprehends (indeed "comprehends") us not by "grasping" us via "the limbs of a bygone locomotive organ" (human digits)[14] but by sucking-in, soaking-in, taking-in via teeming tentacles: the "infernal alternatives"—reticulated, tentacular, and cybernetically continuous rather than digitally discrete—which characterize "the vampire squids of capitalism" as Andrew Goffey states, paraphrasing Philippe Pignarre and Isabelle Stengers.[15] The app user, like the Phoenician Sailor in "The Waste Land,"[16] tends to be oblivious to this continuous and continuously sucking octopoid stream, yet will find within it—with and in it—"his . . . bones . . . picked in whispers,"[17] his or her every detail devoured and digested, appropriated and absorbed by a vampiric Borg[18]). This is why "the animal most appropriate to twenty-first-century corporate governance is not *Behemoth* or *Leviathan* but the *octopus*" which sucks up our thoughts[19] ("the octopus . . . is sucking up[20] my thoughts," wrote Flusser in a letter to his friend Milton Vargas, explaining his fascination with this somewhat terrifying tentacular creature, and in so doing the genesis of his treatise on the Vampyroteuthis Infernalis).[21]

Current-day capitalism and "twenty-first-century corporate governance"[22] recapitulates in many respects the founding Olympian myth of *Mètis*, mother and matriarch of magic *conjuration*, *cunning* and [Love]*craftiness*: traits encompassed in the wily word *mètis*, a term associated with magic, magic-tricks, and indeed all things tricky[23] ("the magic of cunning intelligence . . . this theme of *dólos* [i.e. of 'deceit']: at once 'ruse', 'trap' and magical 'bind' [and/or 'link': *lien magique*]").[24] The magic of *mètis* or cunning deceit is of course subject to—and the object of—the third of the "three laws" in Clarke's *Profiles of the Future*, but rephrased in the language of trickery: i.e., it is but an outmaneuvering-in-advance, an advanced "cunning technique" ("the *incogitum hactenus* [hitherto unknown] of the hunter who is already there"[25]), which appears as a work of "magic" to those not yet up-to-speed with,[26] and yet in the grip of, its captivating and capturing *kairos* (the real-time of its instantaneity and apparent ubiquity).[27] Mètis, in Greek myth, is a kind of Cthulhu: titanic, terrifying, polytropic (full of tricks/tricky-turns) and *polymètic* (full of guile/many-wiles); she is the chthonic titan that the captain/arch-capitalist of Olympos approached, appropriated, and ultimately absorbed—that is, made his concubine and then promptly consumed.[28] The colossal Cthulhu (tentacular titan) of Lovecraft's 1930 novella *At the Mountains of Madness* and 1928 short story "The Call of Cthulhu" (both available in cell-phone app format, bringing a whole new dimension to its titular call[29]), is—in the form of the titan Mètis—"sucked up"[30]

Figure 17.2
The "Call of Cthulhu" internet meme. Open source.

into the mouth of Olympian Zeus, who, having swallowed her whole, "made himself [solely and] completely *mètis*,"[31] cornering the market on cunning conceits and subtle stratagems which would henceforth have to pass through his ensnaring circuits. *"Pas une ruse ne se trame dans l'univers sans passer d'abord par son esprit,"* explain Détienne and Vernant: not a single ruse or stratagem could henceforth be hatched or devised without first passing through the spirit and mindset that is the glory, the cap and the crown of Olympos.[32] Mount Olympos has itself become the Mountain of Madness, its bright snow-capped peaks covertly co-opting, absorbing and appropriating the murky depths of a more masked *mètis* (calling Clarke to mind once again, what with the publication of his parody *At the Mountains of Murkiness* the year before Détienne and Vernant's famous study went to press[33]).

What T. S. Eliot once likened to a modern "mythic method"[34] (in this case capitalism's recapitulation of an ancient Greek myth) brings us "by a commodius vicus of recirculation"[35] back to a currently applicable and deceptively app-like/able ancient Greek concept: that of cunning intelligence, also called "tentacular" or "octopus" intelligence (*polyplokon noèma*).[36] "The octopus extends itself"—*se diffuse*—"via innumerable flexible and undulating members. For the Greeks, the octopus was a knot of a thousand arms, a living interlaced network, a *polyplokos*. This is the same epithet that qualifies the serpent with its coils and folds, the labyrinth with its mazes and tangle of halls and passages. The monstrous Typhon is also a *polyplokos*: a multiple 'hundred-headed' being whose trunk tapers out into anguiped members."[37] The app, we suggest, is part of a similar interlaced network or app-alliance: the digital interface of an otherwise terrifically tentacular complex. Flusser conceived of this complex, this multi-armed matrix, in terms of what he called "the vampyroteuthic world" (this as opposed to, or rather as beyond, that of the human-all-too-human):

> The vampyroteuthic world is not grasped with hands but with tentacles. It is not in itself visible (apparent), but the vampyroteuthis makes it so with its own lights. Both worlds, that is, are tangible and observable, but the methods of perception are different. The world that humans comprehend is firm (like the branches that we had originally held). We have to "undergo" it—perambulate it—in order to grasp it, for the ten fingers of our "grasping" hands are the limbs of a bygone locomotive organ. The vampyroteuthis, on the contrary, takes hold of the world with . . . tentacles, surrounding its mouth, which originally served to direct streams of food toward the digestive tract. The world grasped by the vampyroteuthis is a fluid, centripetal whirlpool. It takes hold of it in order to discern its flowing particularities. Its tentacles, analogous to our hands, are digestive organs. Whereas our method of comprehension is active—we perambulate a static and established world—its method is passive and impassioned: it takes in a world that is rushing past it. We comprehend what we happen upon, and it comprehends what happens upon it. Whereas we have "problems," things in our way, it has "impressions."[38]

Détienne and Vernant would disagree with that last claim, the claim that the *polyplokon noèma* is passive, and would argue instead that the "passion" here is not in fact "passive" but rather attentively *active*[39] (hence the emphasis in their study on mètic "vigilance"[40] or what Eliot—since we are using his mythic method—would have likened to "Prufrock's Pervigilium"[41] and the "lidless eyes" of "The Waste Land"[42]); Lisa Raphals, in her follow-up to Détienne and Vernant's now-classic study, links the Greek *mètis* with the Chinese *wu-wei*: the "active passivity" which is just as cunning as "the *you-wei* plots of Ulysses" and corresponds (for Raphals) to the twists and Ulyssean U-turns—"*about-faces*"[43]—of the latter's equally mètic mate: his wily wife Penelope (whose name is, moreover, synonymous with the ever-turning, shape-shifting *polytropos*: *pènè-ops* designating one who "weaves, threads or spools" [*pènè*][44] their "face, countenance or appearance" [*ops*][45]). "We can account for both the *you-wei* plots of Ulysses and the *wu-wei* designs of Penelope as oblique means toward similar ends"—that is to say similar *actions*—writes Raphals. "Both [play upon] appearances; both are oblique; both rely on skillful means more than on discursive wisdom. By contrast, the Greek *philosopher* [i.e. lover of wisdom] and the Confucian *junzi* [i.e. sage ruler or wise man] . . . follow *lines* rather than *twists.*"[46]

You-wei and *wu-wei* are the twists and turns of "duplicitous activity" (as in Ulysses' many mètic *U-turns*) and of "active passivity" (as in Penelope's mètic *métissages*: her weaving[s] and unweaving[s], her many fabrica[c]tions). "Just as the Chinese 'distrust of appearances' orientation accommodates the very different aims and means of Taoists and Militarists," states Raphals, so too do "the abilities of *mètis* . . . [run] from the hunter to the weaver, from the trapper to the designer," encompassing the techniques of Penelope and Ulysses, the most octopoid intelligences of heroic Greek mytho-antiquity.[47] In one of two recent doctoral dissertations on the Penelopean/*pènè-ops* topic of mètic intelligence and design (one by Ehren Pflugfelder and one by Ben Singleton, both awaiting defense), Ben Singleton suggests that *mètis* is "the missing term" in Greek antiquity between "*poèsis*, which roughly means 'making', and *technè*, which approximates 'art' and/or 'skill'"[48]; it is, as he puts it, "the forgotten companion-term to *poèsis* and *technè.*"[49] "Even though the concept proved 'extraordinarily stable' [throughout antiquity], 'it is absent from the image that Greek thought constructed of itself' (de Certeau 1984:81) . . . unlike [the other two terms, namely] *poèsis* and *technè*," states Singleton.[50] In a work published the same year as Détienne and Vernant's study, the mathematician and Fields-Medialist René Thom suggested that "in the face of an enigmatic local situation, 'universal reason'—the *logos*—is not sufficient" and that "it is necessary to have recourse to that form of intelligence which the classical Greeks called *mètis*"; thus "in mathematics, a science of exemplary rationality, progression is accompanied more by tricks than by general methods."[51] It is only by *mètis*—that chthonic, "demonic" intelligence which Olympos-of-old and current-day capitalism cunningly co-opted—that the demonic internal (and in this sense infernal) strategies of a system, "*la stratégie du demon interne du système*" more precisely,[52] can be discerned and its dissimulations in turn "played upon" and/or "turned [back] on" the system in the manner, again, of a Ulyssean *U-turn*. "In attempting to explain [this] kind of intelligence, . . . Thom opposed [it to] the philosophical conception of *logos*" and [to] logical thought, explains Andreas Vrahimis in his essay "Play, between understanding and praxis"; "the kind of intelligence implied by [*mètis*] is associated [instead] with the multifarious machinations of non-linear approaches."[53]

Non-linearity is the name of the game in vampyroteuthic/late-capitalist coursing; the Flusserian Vampyroteuthis, like the Theuti Radius of Giordano Bruno long before, breaks with linear logic and in so doing "burst[s]

Figure 17.3
The "Octopi Wall Street"
internet meme. Open source.

open the mechanics of thought, encouraging multiple modes for achieving multiple truths."[54] The world of the Vampyroteuthis is pre- and post-human (*pre/post*erously so); in its endless twists and turns, its spheroid/planet-like curvature, its globe-girdling reticular radius, it is also geometrically "post-planetary" (to take a term from our colleague Ed Keller)[55] and indeed, like the earth itself, perpetually turning: *polytropic* ("Penelopean" in its spinning). With and in such spinning, curving, coiling, twisting and turning "there can be no immutable and eternal forms, no circles and triangles,"[56] and "geometry" becomes a kind of "dynamics": "the shortest distance between two points," for example, would no longer be "a *straight line* but a *coil spring* that, when fully compressed, brings two points together."[57] "Our dialectic [of discernment, conceptualization and co-ordination] operates on a *plane*," explains Flusser (speaking of human metrics: "grasping the world" via the digits of "of a bygone locomotive organ"[58]), whereas that of the Vampyroteuthis—and by extension (in this essay) the capitalist Cthulhu, its entire app-alliance—operates instead with and "in *volume*: its [metric and *mathesis*] is one dimension richer than ours."[59] "Whereas we think linearly ('rightly' [or along 'right angles']), it thinks circularly ('eccentrically')"[60] with/in a geometry that Lovecraft's character Henry Wilcox describes as one that has gone all awry, "all wrong": an "abnormal, non-Euclidean [geometry]"[61] that (*vis-à-vis* idea[l]s of immutable circles, triangles and rectilinear geometries) has "gone mad . . . breaking up into all kinds of irregular . . . [twisting and curving] figures"[62] which pass through things as well as around things, contracting and compressing in addition to spreading and spanning. This is a geometry wherein "the relative position of everything . . . seems phantasmally variable"[63]: a "geometry [that] therefore corresponds to what we call dynamics"[64] or that functions like "the missing term"—"the forgotten companion-term"—to "geometry" and "dynamics" (here echoing Singleton's "missing term" between *poèsis* and *technè*[65]).

Hence the app might best be approached not on the basis of its buttons, its digital interface, its hand-held, audio or optical aspect[s]—dactylographically referring back to our human-all-too-human digits and modes of discernment—but instead along its more twisted "tentacular" topos, i.e., as one of a myriad series of suckers on the tentacles of a cybernetic cephalopod that is ultimately a globally reticulated/*terra*-tracking tentacular intelligence/app-alliance. Flusser, like Lovecraft, found this intelligence to be disconcerting if not downright "demonic"[66] (a word originally designating an ongoing and unstopped division, from the Greek *daiesthai*—"to divide"—whence the idea of multiplication, as in the demon's "my name is legion, for we are many" of Mark 5:9), and its polymorphic/polymètic tactics are aptly described in those terms. The Cthulhu that is capitalism's colossal cephalopod—the great app-alliance behind and within, and (strictly speaking) ahead of[67] each downloaded or uploaded app—is itself hypercamouflaged in and as the latter (the apparently auspicious app). The app is a capitalist interface that is designed to be aesthetically appealing.[68] Aesthetics is one of the greatest weapons in "the vampire squid . . . of capitalism" arsenal[69]: as Jaron Lanier states in an article from the April 2006 issue of *Discover: The Magazine of Science, Technology, and the Future*, the octopus—master of *mètis*[70]—"uses art to hunt":

> [In] a video . . . shot in 1997 by my friend Roger Hanlon . . . a researcher at the Marine Biological Laboratory in Woods Hole . . . swims up to examine an unremarkable rock covered in swaying algae. Suddenly, astonishingly, one-third of the

rock and a tangled mass of algae morphs and reveals itself for what it really is: the waving arms of a bright white octopus. Its cover blown, the creature squirts ink at Roger and shoots off into the distance—leaving Roger, and the video viewer, slack-jawed. The star of this video, *Octopus vulgaris*, is one of several cephalopod species capable of morphing, including the mimic-octopus and the giant Australian cuttlefish. . . . Morphing in cephalopods works somewhat similarly to how it works in computer graphics. Two components are involved: a change in the image or texture visible on a shape's surface and a change in the underlying shape itself. The 'pixels' in the skin of a cephalopod are organs called chromatophores. These can expand and contract quickly, and each is filled with a pigment of a particular color. When a nerve-signal causes a red chromatophore to expand, the 'pixel' turns red. A pattern of nerve-firings causes a shifting image—an animation—to appear on the cephalopod's skin. As for shapes, an octopus can quickly arrange its arms to form a wide variety of them, like a fish or a piece of coral, and can even raise welts on its skin to add texture. But—why morph? One reason is camouflage. (The octopus in the video is presumably trying to hide from Roger.) Another is dinner. One of Roger's video-clips shows a giant cuttlefish pursuing a crab. The cuttlefish is mostly soft-bodied, the crab all armor. As the cuttlefish approaches, the medieval-looking crab snaps into a macho posture, waving its sharp claws at its foe's vulnerable body. The cuttlefish responds with a bizarre and ingenious psychedelic performance. Weird images, luxurious colors, and successive waves of undulating lightning bolts and filigree swim across its skin. The sight is so unbelievable that even the crab seems disoriented; its menacing gesture is replaced for an instant by another that seems to express 'Huh?' In that moment the cuttlefish strikes between cracks in the armor. It uses art to hunt![71]

Cephalopoid hunters—mètic masters and thus masterful *métisseurs* (mixers, minglers) of *poèsis* and *technè*—use aesthetic applications, the art-and-science of apps, both for protection and for aggression, for attack as well as defense. In the case above, the parallels between cephalopods and contemporary computer mediations are marked and indeed rather remarkable; the cephalopod skin is described as a pixelated screen upon which animations appear. Flusser, and before him Détienne and Vernant, also examine these chromatophores and this ink-cloud mechanism (which the octopus above "squirts at" Roger Hanlon).[72] For Détienne and Vernant, while the octopus' chromatophores work well (its "[mètic] *mechanè* enables it to merge with the [st]one onto which it affixes itself, [and,] apt to model itself perfectly on the bodies it captures, it can also mimic the colour of the creatures and things it approaches"[73]), it only works until such time as its "cover is blown," as Lanier says above. That is why, for them, the cloud is the cephalopod's "infallible weapon": "*une espèce de nuée*," a kind of thick brume (or Clausewitzian "fog-of-war"), this viscous vapor, veil, film or fog "permits it at once to escape enemy

A Squid eating Dough in a Polyethylene Bag is Fast and Bulbous, Got Me?

Don Van Vliet, *Trout Mask Replica* (Los Angeles: Reprise Records, 1968).

Figure 17.4
The "Trout Mask Replica" internet meme. Open source.

capture and to capture its adversaries—become its victims—as if in a net."[74] It is this "dark nebula, this night without exit, which defines one of the most essential of octopus traits": "it knows how to disappear in the night, a night that it can itself secrete . . . to escape from the grasp of its [would-be] adversaries, become its victims"[75]; "fluid, ungraspable, developing into a thousand agile limbs, cephalopods are enigmatic creatures,"[76] creatures of enigma and tentacular *taqiyya*.[77]

In Lieu of a Conclusion

As the foregoing examples of *octopoid "dólos"* or "dissimulative subtexts" (/hypertexts?) show, the art of apps—indeed, of *apps as traps*—relies in large part on the application of *mètic* mechanisms: in this case the *poliplokos'* polymorphous hypercamouflage. Studies of such *mètic* mechanisms in cephalopods (i.e., of their polymorphous *polyplokon noèma*) are and will be of value to the future development of immersive, all-encompassing/all-consuming "virtual realities": an ongoing example of the latter being Lanier's own lab (the Virtual Human Interaction Lab project at Stanford) and its investigations into the "Proteus effect"[78] of avatarism—of "virtual"/"polymorphic"/computer-App-"graphic" being—along with the rather alchemical never mind neuroscientific concept of "homuncular flexibility" that Lanier described in a recent TED talk.[79] "The same nervous-system that we have had evolved to swim, to crawl," to walk upright, et cetera, "has evolved through all kinds of different body-shapes"—something that becomes apparent from a perspective of phylogenetic "deep time"—he explains in the very same informal-yet-informative talk. "In fact," he continues, "everything in biology is pre-adaptive for evolutionary designs that do not yet exist, and in a sense when we make weird [apps and/or] avatars, we are putting the brain in a 'time-travel machine' for species" that do not yet exist.[80] The applications and appropriations of this polymorphic, polytropic, *polyplokos*-like capacity to turn ourselves—to turn yourself or have yourself be turned (in the manner of a *pènè-ops* "sartor resartus" or Ulyssean "u-turn") into different *guises/facades/avatars*, hence different *entities* or what's more, *multiplicities*, over and above those that are currently congealed, if not concealed, in and as your present "identity"—are, as Lanier says, literally "weird": a descriptor derived from the Old English word *wyrd*, meaning "destiny," "fate," "program," or "path."[81] Such shape-shifting or reconfiguring is a matter of course and "par for the course" with respect to both apps and app-avatars, "the purpose"/program or "weird" of which "is to turn humans into cephalopods" (and here again we quote Lanier: this time from his Web page at jaronlanier.com).[82] To close with the wise words of the "New Weird" author China Miéville, applying his words to the weird world of apps: let us be aware of (and let us mètically, meticulously, bear in mind) the fact that apps are part of a *tentacular novum*,[83] a tentacular "New Age" in addition to "weird world"; and that although it might appear that apps are benign little digital devices, deployments, and useful utilities, in the cephalopoid system of their capitalist distribution/downloads-and-uploads they are tentacularly interconnected with an entire app-alliance, a tentacular system beyond the bounds and the grip of our *doigts*, our *digits*—exceeding our apprehension not to mention present comprehension. "The spread of the tentacle—a limb-type with no Gothic or traditional precedents in Western aesthetics—from a situation of near-total absence in Euro-American teratoculture up to the 19th century, to one of being the default monstrous appendage of today, signals the epochal shift to a Weird Culture."[84] W.C. . . . the face flushes (at least apparently).

Notes

1. H. P. Lovecraft, "The call of Cthulhu," in *Weird Tales* 11 (1928), no. 2 (http://en.wikisource.org).

2. Marcel Détienne and Jean-Pierre Vernant, *Les ruses de l'intelligence: La mètis des Grecs* (Flammarion, 1974), 45.

3. The wireless world: a world of *holes* rather than of *solid obstacles*—i.e., a *(_)hole complex*—in which expanses are traversed by passing *through* rather *around* things: passing *through* rather than *bypassing* them, as in Flusser's *Vampyroteuthis Infernalis: A Treatise, with a Report by the Institut Scientifique de Recherche Paranaturaliste*, translated by Valentine Pakis (University of Minnesota Press, 2012), 42. The world of these trappist-monk cell[phone]s is thus a monastic/monadological *(_)holey land*.

4. Flusser, *Vampyroteuthis* [2012], 5, 13; *Vampyroteuthis Infernalis* (Atropos, 2011), 74, 40.

5. As "infernal" as the Vampyroteuthis infernalis and "the tentacular grip of what Pignarre and Stengers call [its] 'infernal alternatives,'" namely "that set of situations that seem to leave no other choice [to those in its grip] than resignation or a slightly hollow sounding denunciation." See Andrew Goffey, "Introduction: On the Witch's Broomstick," in *Capitalist Sorcery: Breaking the Spell*, ed. P. Pignare and I. Stengers (Palgrave Macmillan, 2007), xiv; Philippe Pignare and Isabelle Stengers, *La Sorcellerie Capitaliste: Pratiques de Désenvoûtement* (Éditions La Découverte, 2005), 40.

6. A *truc* in French—i.e., a tricky little "device", "gizmo", "gimmick" or "thingamajig"; Machine Translation, http://translate.google.com/#fr/en/truc.

7. Détienne and Vernant, *Les ruses de l'intelligence*, 34, 45–48.

8. See, for example, Gal Hirsch, "On dinosaurs and hornets: A critical view on operational moulds in asymmetric conflicts," *RUSI Journal* 148 (2003), no. 4: 60–63. Also see Katherine Harmon, "What Can an Octopus Tell Us about National sSecurity? A Q&A with ecologist Rafe Sagarin" (http://blogs .scientificamerican.com).

9. Studies suggest that users' perceptions of interface aesthetics influence their beliefs about usability: "Three experiments were conducted to validate and replicate. In a different cultural setting, the results of a study by Kurosu and Kashimura concerning the relationships between users' perceptions of interface-aesthetics and usability. The results support the basic findings by Kurosu and Kashimura. Very high correlations were found between perceived aesthetics of the interface and *a priori* perceived ease of use of the system." (Noam Tractinsky, "Aesthetics and Apparent Usability: Empirically Assessing Cultural and Methodological Issues," presented at CHI 97 Conference on Human Factors in Computing Systems, 1997; available at http://www.sigchi.org).

10. Louis Pørn, "Mobile computing acceptance grows as applications evolve," *Journal of the Healthcare Financial Management Association* 56 (2002), no. 1: 66–70.

11. "If camouflage utilizes a partial overlap between two or multiple entities, hypercamouflage is the complete overlap and coincidence between two or more entities. In this terminal camouflage, the mere survival of a predator threatens the existence of the prey, even if the predator never engages the prey. Hypercamouflage is associated with the warrior under Taqiyya or the Thing (John Carpenter's movie); it can be defined as a total withdrawal from the perception of friends and a dissolution into the enemy: the rebirth of a new and obscure foe." (Reza Negarestani, *Cyclonopedia: Complicity with Anonymous Materials*, Re.press, 2008, 241)

12. Ray Brassier, "Against the aesthetics of noise: An interview" 2009 (http://ny-web.be).

13. We manipulate apps with our fingers (our digits); apps "grasp" us in a very different manner (one which we here call tentacular).

14. Flusser, *Vampyroteuthis* [2012], 38.

15. Goffey, "Introduction," xvii.

16. T. S. Eliot, *The Waste Land: A Facsimile and Transcript of the Original Drafts including the Annotations of Ezra Pound*, ed. V. Eliot (Harcourt Brace, 1971), 60–61.

17. Ibid.

18. A cybernetic collective and collection-qua-appropriation agency in the world and words of the *Star Trek* television franchise. See, for instance, episode 42 of *Star Trek: The Next Generation* ("Q Who"), written by Maurice Hurley and directed by Robert Bowman.

19. Goffey, "Introduction," xvi.

20. Or, in a more cyber-savvy sense, uploading.

21. Flusser, *Vampyroteuthis* [2011], 129.

22. Goffey, "Introduction," xvi.

23. Détienne and Vernant, *Les ruses de l'intelligence*, 18, 29, 62, 65–66.

24. Ibid., 65–66.

25. Reza Negarestani, "A Good Meal," 2002 (http://www.cold-me.net).

26. I.e., "as fast and bulbous as" (see figure 17.4—"A Squid Eating Dough in a Polyethylene Bag is Fast and Bulbous, Got Me?"—near the tell-tale/fish-tale end of the essay above).

27. Arthur C. Clarke, *Profiles of the Future: An Enquiry into the Limits of the Possible* (Harper and Row, 1962), 36.

28. Hesiod, *Theogony* 929e–930: "But *Zeus* lay with the fair-cheeked daughter of *Ocean* and *Tethys*, . . . deceiving Mètis, although she was full wise. And then he seized her with his hands and put her in his belly, for fear that she might bring forth something stronger than his thunderbolt: therefore did *Zeus*, who sits on high and dwells in the aether, swallow her down suddenly. . . . And she remained hidden beneath the inward parts of *Zeus*, even Mètis, Athena's mother, worker of righteousness, who was wiser than gods and mortal men."

29. The "Call of Cthulhu" cell phone meme (figure 17.2 above) is available at http://1.media.dorkly.cvcdn.com.

30. Flusser, *Vampyroteuthis* [2011], 129.

31. Détienne and Vernant, *Les ruses de l'intelligence*, 20.

32. Ibid.

33. Arthur C. Clarke, *At the Mountains of Murkiness* (Ferret Fantasy, 1973).

34. Eliot defines the modern "mythic method" as "a way of controlling, of ordering, of giving a shape and significance to the immense panorama of futility and anarchy which is contemporary history"—this through the use of "myth in manipulating a continuous parallel between contemporaneity and antiquity" (*Selected Prose of T. S. Eliot*, ed. F. Kermode, Faber & Faber, 1975, 177–178).

35. James Joyce, *Finnegans Wake* (Faber & Faber, 1939), 3.

36. Détienne and Vernant, *Les ruses de l'intelligence*, 47–48.

37. Ibid., 45.

38. Flusser, *Vampyroteuthis* [2012], 39.

39. "This 'octopus intelligence' . . . from a certain perspective would appear akin to that which the Lyric poets called the *ephèmeros*," they explain. "Indeed, like it, the *ephèmeros* is characterized by its *mobility*," *fluidity* and *dynamic instability* (Détienne and Vernant, *Les ruses de l'intelligence*, 47–48). But unlike the intelligence of the Lyric *ephèmeros*, that of the *polytropic polyplokon* "is unstable only in appearance: its about-faces are a trap, the net in which its adversaries come to be entangled" (48). Between the intelligence of the *polytropic polyplokon* and that of the *ephèmeros* "there is the exact distance that separates the octopus from the chameleon" (47–48): the former is *active*, actively *trapping*, approaching its victim like a hunter or a *South Park* Trapper Keeper (the capitalist Cthulhu of Matt Stone and Trey Parker), whereas the latter is *passive*, *changing with* (rather than *charging* and *playing with*) the current[s] of its environment, thus devoid of the demonic or devilish deceit. (*South Park* episode 60, "Trapper Keeper," November 15, 2000; see figure 17.1 above.)

40. Détienne and Vernant, *Les ruses de l'intelligence*, 32, 38.

41. T. S. Eliot, "Prufrock's Pervigilium," in *Inventions of the March Hare: Poems 1909–1917*, ed. C. Ricks (Harcourt Brace, 1996), 43–44.

42. Eliot, *The Waste Land*, 18–19.

43. Détienne and Vernant, *Les ruses de l'intelligence*, 8, 39, 48.

44. Henry George Liddell and Robert Scott, *An Intermediate Greek-English Lexicon* (Clarendon, 1889) (http://www.perseus.tufts.edu).

45. Ibid.

46. Lisa Raphals, *Knowing Words: Wisdom and Cunning in the Classical Traditions of China and Greece* (Cornell University Press, 1992), 230. Philosophers since Plato have also tended to "condemn" the twists and turns of this cunning, chthonic craftiness (see Détienne and Vernant, *Les ruses de l'intelligence*, 40, 303–306; also see 142), Plato in particular preferring the Olympian/Apollonian stability of rigorous hierarchy, and Lovecraft long after him cherishing what today we would call the Wall Street 1 percent as opposed to the masses "below" this Olympos: the 99 percent throng. Lovecraft above all would have loathed the "Occupy Wall Street" movement, which from his perspective would amount to an "Octopi Wall Street" (see figure 17.3): the incursion of Cthulhu upon Olympos—the rise of his dreaded Cthulhu. Wall Street, and capitalism in general, would itself be (in the words of Philippe Pignarre and Isabelle Stengers) "a system of sorcery without sorcerers" or of cunning conjurations in the absence of conflicting/counter-capitalist conjurors (cf. Pignare and Stengers, *La Sorcellerie Capitaliste*, 182). And in order to

be so, as we have stated above, capitalism recapitulates the myth of Mètis, consuming/absorbing/appropriating all possible prestidigitation and sorcerous apprentices, thwarting in so doing the emergence of alternate octopi and of unforeseen tentacles beyond those of the capitalism's own all-consuming colossal cybernetic cephalopod.

47. Raphals, *Knowing Words*, 207; Détienne and Vernant, *Les ruses de l'intelligence*, 47.

48. Benedict Singleton, On Craft and Being Crafty: Human Behaviour as the Object of Design (PhD dissertation, University of Northumbria, 2012), 115. The reader is directed to the fourth chapter of both dissertations: Singleton titular chapter "On Craft and Being Crafty" and the chapter "Design and Navigation" in Ehren Pflugfelder's PhD dissertation, Measure of the World: Advancing a Kinesthetic Rhetoric (Purdue University, 2012).

49. Singleton, On Craft and Being Crafty, 106.

50. Ibid., 116.

51. René Thom, *Modèles Mathématiques de la Morphogénèse: Recueil de Textes sur la Théorie des Catastrophes et ses Applications* (Union Général d'Éditions, 1974), 305.

52. Ibid., 306.

53. Andreas Vrahimis, "Play, between understanding and praxis: René Thom's catastrophes," in *Static*, issue 7 (2008) (http://static .londonconsortium.com).

54. Arielle Saiber, *Giordano Bruno and the Geometry of Language* (Ashgate, 2005), 73.

55. Ed Keller, "Post-Planetary Design" (graduate seminar at Parsons: The New School for Design, 2012; syllabus available at http://web.archive.org/ web/20120725135559/http://post-planetary.tumblr.com/syllabus).

56. Flusser, *Vampyroteuthis* [2012], 42.

57. Ibid., 42.

58. Ibid., 39.

59. Ibid, 42.

60. Ibid, 42.

61. Lovecraft, http://en.wikisource.org/wiki/The_Call_of_Cthulhu/Chapter_II; http://en.wikisource.org/wiki/The_Call_of_Cthulhu/Chapter_III.

62. Frances Yates, *Giordano Bruno and the Hermetic Tradition* (University of Chicago Press, 1964), 302.

63. Lovecraft, http://en.wikisource.org/wiki/The_Call_of_Cthulhu/Chapter_III.

64. Flusser, *Vampyroteuthis* [2012], 42.

65. Singleton, On Craft and Being Crafty, 115.

66. "The demonic predator's will-to-power" (for Flusser, *Vampyroteuthis* [2012], 53, 41): a "demonic predator" akin, in the tales of H. P. Lovecraft, to the *I.T.* or *Inuit Tornasuk* which was part of the mythic mix that culminated in the latter's Cthulhu, his version and vision *avant-la-lettre* of the colossal cybernetic cephalopod and of Flusser's Vampyroteuthis Infernalis (see http://en.wikisource.org/wiki/The_Call_of_Cthulhu/Chapter_II).

67. "The *incogitum hactenus* ['hitherto unknown'] of the hunter who is already there" (Negarestani, "A Good Meal").

68. Scholars have begun critical inquiry of the implications of interface aesthetics. "Just as literature has predominantly taken place in and around books, and painting has explored the canvas, the interface is now a central aesthetic form conveying digital information of all kinds. . . . It means that we should start seeing the interface as an aesthetic form in itself that offers a new way to understand digital art in its various guises, rather than as a functional tool for making art (and doing other things)"; Søren Pold, "Interface realisms: The interface as aesthetic form," 2005 (http://pmc .iath.virginia.edu/text-only/issue.105/15.2pold.txt).

69. Goffey, "Introduction," xvii.

70. Détienne and Vernant, *Les ruses de l'intelligence*, 34–52.

71. Jaron Lanier, "What cephalopods teach us about language," *Discover*, April 2006 (http://discovermagazine.com).

72. Flusser, *Vampyroteuthis* [2012], 19, 51–52. Détienne and Vernant, *Les ruses de l'intelligence*, 46, 51–52.

73. Détienne and Vernant, *Les ruses de l'intelligence*, 47, 45–46.

74. Ibid., 46.

75. Ibid., 47, 45–46.

76. Ibid., 46.

77. "The practice of concealing the identity when revealing it might be harmful." (Frank Herbert, *God-Emperor of Dune*, Ace Books, 1984, 215)

78. "Topic: The Proteus Effect," Virtual Human Interaction Lab project, Stanford University (http://vhil.stanford.edu/pubs/?ProteusEffect=yes).

79. Jaron Lanier, "You are not a gadget: A TEDxSF Talk," December 2010 (http://www.youtube.com).

80. Ibid.

81. "Weird: that which happens—fate, chance, fortune, destiny; [also] Fate, the Fates, Providence"—Wiktionary

82. Jaron Lanier, "A revelation! I've decided that the purpose of Virtual Reality is to turn humans into cephalopods," October 2006 (http://www.jaronlanier.com).

83. China Miéville, "M. R. James and the quantum vampire: Weird, haunto-logical, versus and/or and and/or or?" *Collapse* 4 (2008), 105 (http://weirdfictionreview.com).

84. Ibid.

18
To Make You Completely Present in the Moment

an interview with Scott Snibbe

Scott Snibbe is a media artist whose work engages users in creative interactions with interfaces of different kinds—some huge (airport instattations) and some really small (the screens of mobile phones). As a researcher, Snibbe explores engagements with technology that don't necessarily have a goal or purpose, but rather unfold unexpectedly, like events. Some of Snibbe's early interactive media projects from the 1990s have found new life in the form of apps. A designer and an entrepreneur, Snibbe founded and runs Snibbe Interactive and Scott Snibbe Studio, which specifically focused on production of original apps. His recent collaboration with Bjork on her *Biophilia* app album has made an important contribution not only to media art as such, but also to experiencing music. His game apps are different from what gaming is typically associated today—pervasiveness, intensity, and total consumption of the gamer. Snibbe's apps are instead slow, subtle, and meditative. In a sense, they actually push you to find new ways of getting in touch with all around you.

—Svitlana Matviyenko

Svitlana Matviyenko: As pieces of application software, apps apply the power of computing system for a particular purpose. Thinking of your projects, how do you see this "purpose"? How do your projects—such as *Biophilia* apps for Bjork or MotionPhone app—challenge or further develop the idea of an app?

Scott Snibbe: I've been creating a similar type of computer program as interactive audiovisual artwork for about thirty years. I was raised by artists, and when I got my first computer, an Apple II+, all it did when you turn it on was flash a cursor on an empty screen. So that type of computer felt like a blank canvas, and I started filling it with abstract art, animation, and generative sound.

In college, I worked in a computer graphics research lab—the only place where I had access to computers capable of interactive graphics—and I did more useful projects, like designing interfaces for movie special effects. However, I continued my private work on the side. One of my advisors said such work was "useless," so then I started calling these projects "useless programs" whose only purpose was to delight and tickle ones imagination and emotions. These programs were as useless as, say, a song, a story, or a movie.

For years I tried to convince various people that these programs had a market—not just to be shown in a gallery, but the same kind of market that songs have. We came close to a game deal with Sony in the 1990s but it never panned out. When the app store opened, that was finally a chance to release some of this work (Gravilux, Bubble Harp, and Antograph), without having to explain what it was or who the "market" is. And it turned out there was a paying audience for such programs.

In general, projects like these, and later *Biophilia*, change our understanding of an app from something useful, or a diversion, to something capable of sustaining emotional narrative experiences, and, in particular, ones that take interactivity beyond gaming.

SM: In our anthology, we suggest thinking of apps as a technique. Would you apply this definition to your apps?

SS: My work treats apps (or rather, more broadly interactivity) as a medium—one capable of the same expressive range in emotions and storytelling as movies, music, or literature. The apps I've created with my team and collaborators are meant to hold a place in culture similar to a book or a musical composition—something that expresses the human condition through interactivity. It's hard for me to understand apps as a technique—they represent an expressive palette, not necessarily a specific area of expertise. Movies and music aren't techniques, but expressive media.

SM: Among the affective, aesthetic, technical, social, and economical aspects of app-computing, which, in your view, are the most significant in terms of their influence on the popularity of apps? Are there any other aspects you would add to this list?

SS: The biggest aspect influencing the popularity of apps is the App Store itself—in particular, Apple's. The opening of Apple's App Store marked the first time that an individual software developer could release his software directly to a worldwide audience of millions, and also profit on that work. Other companies have copied this model, but not to the same effect. Android's store, for instance, allows instant publishing, so there's currently little curation and no quality control, so its harder to find an audience with the flood of pornography, viruses, and so on, each day.

SM: Initially, your apps were available only for the iOS devices. But I see Gravilux is already available for Android. What other factors apart from the

Figure 18.1
Bubble Harp, an app by Scott Snibbe.
Reproduced with permission of the
copyright holder.

new growing markets do you take into consideration as an app developer (i.e. programming language, regulations and requirements, audience, etc.)?

SS: We mainly take into account the quality of experience we can create and the audience on the platform, and for now always start on iOS because of the high quality of the experience and maturity of the market.

SM: On the one hand, mobile apps have become a major technique to operate our mobile devices. At the same time, the practicality of many apps is limited. Often, they sit on our touch-screens, handy and cute, without ever being used. In our project, we call these apps "charming junk." Where between sense and nonsense would you locate your apps?

SS: As I mentioned, my apps are useless by utilitarian standards. Their purpose is to expand a person's mind, and create an emotional resonance with image, sound, and interactivity. Many of them are meant to reflect one's mind back onto the screen—the most positive, beautiful aspects of one's mind. We're ordinarily cramming new information into our minds, which creates anxiety and craving—this is the effect your average email, news, and gaming app, though they are "useful." However, it's possible to create interactive apps that nourish our minds too. So that's where our apps stand on this continuum. Though it sounds a bit New Age, our apps are actually meant to provide some of the benefits of practices like meditation and yoga—to make you completely present in the moment, and to bring out the more positive aspects of your mind.

SM: In one of your interviews you said, "Listening to [Bjork's *Biophilia*] album without the apps isn't like watching Avatar without 3-D—it's like watching Avatar without the picture. The combination of the music and the apps [is] the full expression of Bjork's concept." Could you elaborate on that, focusing, if possible, on what you meant by "full expression"?

SS: The way people's brains work is that we fuse sensory phenomena into a simulated model of the world around us that appears only in our minds. Phenomena like music and color are *solely* psychological. They do not exist in the outside world, but are a radical interpretation of colorless and soundless vibrations of magnetism and matter. So, our brains are designed to fuse sense phenomena, not to isolate them. Listening to music without some sort of image accompaniment is actually nonsensical—and there is historical evolutionary evidence that movement and music are entirely fused sensually. It's a recent and unnatural phenomenon that people sit quietly and listen to music, or, that they do other things with music in the background. Music is meant to accompany dancing, movement. So, *Biophilia* is best appreciated as an app, because the visuals complete the sensorial whole. The concert is also a great way to experience it, though you can't explore a virus or dark matter in a concert hall.

That's the idea of the app, to provide a kind of alternative to the concert—a live interactive experience, but one that can leverage everything possible on a screen, from the abstract to the microscopic, gigantic, and invisible.

Providing sensory fusion is why long-playing albums (LPs) were so successful—they came with a beautiful work of art, liner notes, and a record that made you stay in one place to dance, lie down, or otherwise totally immerse yourself in. So this new album as app is a way to go back to our sensorial roots where music is interactively fused with image and movement.

SM: If you think of the most desirable app that has not been and possibly will never be designed, what would it be?

SS: An app to induce single-pointed concentration.

19

Nonlinear Music Navigates the Earth

an interview with Ryan and Hays Holladay (Bluebrain)

Bluebrain is a band currently based in Washington, D.C., where its two members, the brothers Hays and Ryan Holladay, were born in the early 1980s. The capital's marble monuments and grassy knolls had a profound effect on them as kids, and two decades later, they would "score" their city with an imaginative collision of composition and technology that was dubbed the world's first "location-aware album."

The Holladays' musical career first took shape during their college years in New York City. They formed a band called The Epochs, which released some recordings but eventually perished in Brooklyn's cannibalistic indie-rock jungle. When they regrouped in Washington in 2009 as Bluebrain, they didn't settle for gigging in the city's nightclubs and D.I.Y. spaces—they organized site-specific performances and happenings. Rather than albums and MP3s, they composed downloadable scores for various public spaces.

In 2011, the Holladays upped the ante with their first location-aware album, *The National Mall*. The duo had produced nearly three hours of music, all housed within a smartphone app that used Global Positioning System technology to trigger different segments of electronic soundscapes and string arrangements based on the listener's physical location on the National Mall. Walk one way and the tempo shifts. Walk another way and the melodies surge. Step off the Mall and the music stops cold. It sounds clever on paper, but when you're out there steering these plush electronic compositions with your footsteps, it becomes highly magical.

Since then, the brothers have composed and released location-aware albums for New York's Central Park (*Listen to the Light*) and the streets of Austin, Texas (*The Violet Crown*). Currently, they are completing one for what is perhaps the most breathtaking drive on the planet, California's Pacific Coast Highway. Each recording acknowledges the fact that digital portability has redefined the role that music can play in soundtracking day-to-day experiences. But Bluebrain's location-aware recordings also push the idea much further, exploring the role music can play as we actually navigate the Earth itself.

—Chris Richards

Chris Richards: Your "location-aware albums" have three main components: technology, space, and music. I'm wondering if you can put those chickens and eggs in order for us. Tell me how you conceived the idea for these apps. Was the idea to score a physical setting?

Ryan Holladay: The initial impetus wasn't to create an album as an app. Rather, the idea of using a smartphone application eventually presented itself as the best way to achieve this concept of geographically mapping music. When Apple opened up its development kit to outsiders, we saw it as the obvious tool for composing and presenting music in this new way that we had been talking about for some time. When Hays (my brother and the other half of Bluebrain) and I began this conversation of combining landscape with music, mobile apps hadn't really entered the picture yet. Our early conversations predated what we think of as a smartphone now. And many of the earlier projects and events that we did were circling around this idea of sound interacting with physical environment using much less sophisticated technologies. One of the first projects we did in this area was creating a musical accompaniment for the Smithsonian's Ocean Hall in the Museum of Natural History. But the only way we knew how to accomplish this was to create a score based on the length of time it takes for the average visitor to make their way through the exhibition. It was not "smart" in the sense that it responded to movement or allowed any sort of autonomy on the part of the listener. This was a static and linear piece that was intended to be used in a specific place and along a designated path, not unlike the work of sound artist Janet Cardiff. But with the introduction of apps came the ability to integrate user feedback just by their movement from one place on a map to another. This opened up the possibilities.

CR: One of the most courageous elements of your work has been your decision to make so much of it site specific. What was the motivation behind assigning these albums to a specific swatch of the planet?

Hays Holladay: I think one of the biggest misconceptions about technology, particularly with regards to art and music and digital media in general, is that the point is to constantly strive to make all content available everywhere at anytime to everyone. Remove all friction and allow content to reach as far as it wants to go. As a user of streaming video and audio services, I completely understand that desire, and that is certainly one of the great potential benefits of these emerging technologies and increasingly robust networks. I also believe, though, that beautiful things can happen when technology is used to limit our experiences with digital content using specific and intentional parameters. In the case of our work, what we're exploring is this idea of tethering sound to a defined physical space. And this, I think, has been the hardest thing for people to understand. We didn't want to create an album that could be listened to in your living room or a car. Yes, one can listen to an audio recording of harps anytime and in any place they want. But when this sound is triggered as you walk by waterfalls throughout the FDR Memorial on the National Mall, increasing in volume as you move closer, your brain makes this connection to the physical object and creates the illusion that these waterfalls are springing to life with these colorful sounds. It's that sort of discovery and association with your surroundings that help to make it a sort of surreal experience.

CR: That approach also excludes a lot of people from experiencing the work, though. Is there a way to create a location-aware album that's site neutral?

HH: We've talked about creating a work that would populate your immediate area using your current location as a starting point. In other words, musical elements and nodes would radiate out from whatever spot [in which] the user begins to use the app, spreading these elements over a span of a mile in all directions that could be explored in the same way as these site-specific app/albums. Though I think it would need to be done carefully to make sure the experience is still special and the placement of the music doesn't feel arbitrary. In Central Park, when you cross over the Bow Bridge into The Ramble and heavy drums begin to fade in, you understand what is happening as you're entering these woods and you know that someone is taking into consideration your surroundings with the sounds you're hearing. An iteration of this concept that could be experienced anywhere in the world would need some additional intelligence in order to have a similar effect.

CR: Plenty of musicians who still think in the framework of the traditional album take great care to get the track sequence right. For Bluebrain, instead of connecting your compositions in one linear chain, you have to the challenge of making them fit together like pieces of a jigsaw puzzle. How difficult is it to compose music for a location-aware album?

RH: In a way, the National Mall was the perfect first site [at which] to experiment with this concept, because of the physical arrangement of the park itself. While there are parts of the park that were designed to contrast with the formalism of "the Grand Axis," as it is sometimes called—the long stretch of the Mall that runs east to west from the Lincoln Memorial to Union Square is largely uniform in how it's laid out, section by section, punctuated by these

Figure 19.1
Transitioning between musical zones on the National Mall. Credit: Gabe Askew. Reproduced with permission of the copyright holder.

memorials and monuments. The National Mall Park is really a compilation [created by] multiple landscape architects and designers working within this very simple grid. The grounds surrounding the Capitol are the work of Frederick Olmstead. The paths circling the Washington Monument, the giant obelisk at the center of the park, were designed by the [Olin Partnership]. But while there are unique landscape ideas in various sections throughout the park, the overall framework of the National Mall Park is based on symmetry. That lent itself to coming up with a methodology to musically approach a physical terrain as [if] we were doing this for the first time. It felt a bit like we were playing with bumper lanes, because the park is so simple. There are parts where you can wander off, which we enjoyed playing with, but there is really only one way to walk from the Capitol Building to the Lincoln Memorial. You can't jump around or stray too far off course without leaving the Mall. Central Park, on the other hand, is essentially the vision of one person (Frederick Olmstead) who wanted it to be a place where you could get lost, a park designed with multiple paths to any given point. Putting this app

Figure 19.2
The start screen for *The National Mall*.
Credit: Brandon Bloch. Reproduced
with permission of the copyright holder.

together musically was much more difficult, and the decisions we made were less obvious and the topic of more disagreement and debate between us. Certain sections, like the Sheep Meadow, felt obvious, while others were more tricky and required us to make some decisions about where one melody ends and another begins.

CR: A lot of album-related apps that other artists have released have felt bogus to me. Like side orders. For you guys, the apps are the main course. The technology is the work and vice versa. Do you feel that others are harnessing this technology to its maximum capacity?

RH: When third-party developers were first allowed to start contributing their own apps for iOS, there was quickly an explosion in very innovative new content in areas that ranged from games to organizers to car-sharing services. And there were some incredibly inventive music apps, but they were more tools for artists and hobbyists to create with. It felt like artists were using the idea of an app the same that, say, CD-ROMs were used in the nineties. They were being treated as a way to promote an artist and traditional recordings.

Figure 19.3

Aerial view of the Washington Monument, showing paths designed by landscape architecture firm Olin. Credit: Olin Partnership. Reproduced with permission of the copyright holder.

Few artists were using these technologies to create entirely new kinds of works. And that's what we were most excited about. But it has also been the most difficult thing for people to understand about what we're doing. The *National Mall* app is not a bonus feature to a CD or LP release. The app is the work itself and the music can only be experienced with the use of the built in GPS functionality of the smartphone within the physical boundaries of the park. There will always be apps that show a band's tour dates, promote a CD, or offer other activities surrounding the artist's traditional work. We see apps as a new format with expanded tools with which to create entirely new kinds of works that can't be understood or experienced in any other way.

CR: We all carry an incredible amount of technology in our pockets these days, but do you think music consumers are still relatively conservative about how they experience music?

HH: Yes, but I think it's only because artists and developers are still thinking of apps as a way to add bells and whistles to this pre-existing model. Of
course there will always be a place for linear music in the way that we've all
grown up understanding. But I think there has yet to be a real recognition
on the content creation side of how these new tools can be used to change
how we approach recorded music. It reminds me a bit of how Bing Crosby
changed how the microphone was used in modern recording. Up until that
point, microphones had been seen as a way to capture a live performance. A
singer in the studio wouldn't really do very much different than if he or she
were performing in a concert hall, singing to a large audience, despite the fact
that there wasn't one in front of them. And much of the time that approach
still works in creating wonderful vocal recordings. But Bing Crosby showed
artists a different way by using the microphone as a way to sing very softly,
as if he were inches away from the listener's ear, amplifying it in the mix in
a way that wouldn't be possible in a live venue. It was [a] fundamental shift
in how performers thought about using a vocal microphone. I think there
are so many powerful tools contained in these tiny pocket-sized devices that
artists don't fully know what to do with yet, and so most artists aren't taking advantage of this expanded tool set and [are] trying to fit apps into an
older framework. There will always be a place for traditional, linear music, of
course, but I'm excited to see more artists begin to shift their approach and
integrate these things into the creation of their work and not as an after-
thought. I know it will happen—and it will be incredible when it does, as
songwriting and production are infused with the innovation that these new
technologies will allow.

Contributors

Christian Ulrik Andersen is an associate professor at Aarhus University in Denmark, where he is also chair of the Digital Aesthetics Research Centre, and a researcher at the Participatory Information Technologies Centre. He conducts research in digital art and culture, generally in relation to the practice of interface critique. Co-editor of *Interface Criticism: Aesthetics Beyond the Buttons* (Aarhus University Press, 2011), of a series of "peer-reviewed newspapers" (2011–), and of *A Peer-Reviewed Journal About . . .* (aprja.net), he is a frequent speaker at media art festivals and conferences.

Thierry Bardini is a professor in the Department of Communication at the University of Montréal. His research concerns the cyberculture, ranging from the production and uses of information and communication technologies to molecular biology. He is the author of *Bootstrapping: Douglas Engelbart, Coevolution, and the Origins of Personal Computing* (Stanford University Press, 2000), *Junkware* (University of Minnesota Press, 2011), and (with Dominique Lestel) *Journey to the End of the Species* (Éditions Dis Voir, 2011).

Nandita Biswas Mellamphy is an associate professor in the Department of Political Science at the University of Western Ontario, specializing in critical and radical political theory and the history of political thought from antiquity to post-modernity. She is also an affiliate member of the Department of Women's Studies and Feminist Research and has served as acting Associate Director of the university's Centre for the Study of Theory and Criticism. Her research interests are situated at the intersection of political theory, cultural theory, and Continental philosophy. Her topics of study include post-humanism, digital media culture, and the political dimensions of science fiction and neuroscience. Recently she held a visiting research fellowship at the Center for Transformative Media at the New School in New York. She is the author of *The Three Stigmata of Friedrich Nietzsche: Political Physiology in the Age of Nihilism* (Palgrave Macmillan, 2011). With Dan Mellamphy, she coordinates the annual Nietzsche Workshop @ Western. Her current research and teaching focus on the study of fear and terror as engines of globalization, particularly within the domain of what today is called "the war on terror." She has organized two international interdisciplinary conferences devoted to the study of war and the techno-politics of globalization, and has presented her work all over the world, most recently at the Center for 21st-Century Studies at the University of Wisconsin at Milwaukee. She has served on the editorial review boards of the *Intergenerational Justice Review* (Germany), the *Canadian Journal of Political Science*, the *Canadian Journal of Continental Philosophy*, Polity Press, and Palgrave Macmillan, and serves on the advisory board for Punctum Books.

Benjamin H. Bratton is a theorist whose work spans philosophy, art, and design. He is an associate professor of visual arts and the director of the Center for Design and Geopolitics at the University of California at San Diego. His research is situated at the intersections of social and political theory, computational media and infrastructure, architectural and urban design problems, and the politics of synthetic ecologies and biologies. His work focuses on the political geography of cloud computing, on massively granular universal addressing systems, and on alternate models of ecological governance. His recent publications include "What we do is secrete: Paul Virilio, planetarity, and data visualization," "Geoscapes and the Google Caliphate: Reflections on the Mumbai attacks," "Root the Earth: Peak oil apophenia," and "Suspicious images, latent interfaces" (with Natalie Jeremijenko). His book *The Stack: On Software and Sovereignty* will be published by the MIT Press.

Drew S. Burk is a cultural theorist who has translated works by such noted thinkers as Gilbert Simondon, Jean Baudrillard, and Paul Virilio. He is also the director of Univocal, an independent publisher of works in philosophy and theory located in Minneapolis.

Patricia Ticineto Clough is a professor of sociology and women's studies at Queens College and the CUNY Graduate Center. She is the author of *Autoaffection: Unconscious Thought in the Age of Teletechnology* (University of Minnesota Press, 2000); *Feminist Thought: Desire, Power and Academic Discourse* (Wiley-Blackwell, 1994), and *The End(s) of Ethnography: From Realism to Social Criticism* (Lang, 1998). Among the volumes she has edited are *The Affective Turn: Theorizing the Social* (with Jean Halley; Duke University Press, 2007), *Beyond Biopolitics: Essays on the Governance of Life and Death* (with Craig Willse; Duke University Press, 2011), and *Intimacies: A New World of Relational Life* (with Alan Frank and Steven Seidman; Routledge, 2013). Recently she has been creating performance pieces bringing together sound and images with theoretical and autobiographical discourses that also draw on ethnographic work in the Corona neighborhood of the Borough of Queens. Her forthcoming book is titled *The Ends of Measure*.

Robbie Cormier is a doctoral candidate in the Department of Philosophy at the State University of New York at Stony Brook. His work is primarily concerned with grafting insights from the theory of network automata onto fundamental ontology. His other research interests include theories of the subject, dystopian economics, physics, and technology.

Dock Currie is a PhD student in political science at York University in Toronto. His interests are in Situationist theory and praxis, post-phenomenology and the relation between social assemblages and ontology, post-structural ethics and embodiment, critiques of spectacular disciplinarity in the academy, and the philosophy and aesthetics of technology.

Dal Yong Jin holds a PhD from the Institute of Communications Research at the University of Illinois at Urbana-Champaign. He has taught at the University of Illinois in Chicago, at the Korea Advanced Institute of Science and Technology, and at Simon Fraser University. His major research and teaching interests are in globalization and media, new media and game studies, transnational cultural studies, and the political economy of media and culture. He is the author of *Korea's Online Gaming Empire* (MIT Press, 2010), *De-Convergence of Global Media Industries* (Routledge, 2013), and *Hands On/Hands Off: The Korean State and the Market Liberalization of the Communication Industry* (Hampton, 2011) and the editor of *The Political Economies of Media* (with Dwaye Winseck; Bloomsbury, 2011) and *Global Media Convergence and Cultural Transformation* (IGI Global, 2011).

Nick Dyer-Witheford is an associate professor in the Faculty of Information and Media Studies at the University of Western Ontario. He is the author of *Cyber-Marx: Cycles and Circuits of Struggle in High-Technology Capitalism* (University of Illinois Press, 1999) and a co-author of *Digital Play: The Interaction of Technology, Culture, and Marketing* (with Stephen Kline and Greig de Peuter; McGill–Queen's University Press, 2003) and *Games of Empire: Global Capitalism and Video Games* (with Greig de Peuter; University of Minnesota Press, 2009).

Ryan and Hays Holladay have worked together all their lives, most recently as the music and tech duo Bluebrain. "As Bluebrain, these brothers have brought an unrivaled energy and innovation to site-specific sound experiments, interactive concerts and film scoring." (Future of Music)

Recently they garnered attention for their exploration of location-based music composition, for which *Wired* dubbed them "pioneers." They have spoken about their work at companies and universities and have worked with institutions ranging from the Smithsonian to MTV. They have been featured in the *New York Times*, by the BBC World Service, in *The Guardian*, in the *Washington Post*, in *Rolling Stone*, in *Engadget*, and in *Fast Company*. In 2011 they were the subject of the *Music for Landscapes*, a short documentary produced by FCTN Creative. Ryan serves as the curator of New Media Art at Artisphere in Arlington, Virginia. Hays is the founder and chief engineer of Iguazu Sound in Los Angeles.

Atle Mikkola Kjøsen is a doctoral candidate in Information and Media Studies at the University of Western Ontario. His research interests are in Marxist value theory, new materialist communication and media theory, logistics and the circulation of capital, Artificial Intelligence's challenge to Marxist political economy, dromoeconomics, digital piracy and filesharing, and reality television.

Eric Kluitenberg is an independent theorist, writer, and curator on culture, media, and technology. He is the editor-in-chief of *The Tactical Media Files* (www.tacticalmediafiles.net), a research fellow at the Institute of Network Cultures at the Amsterdam University of Applied Sciences, and a lecturer in media theory at the Art Science Interfaculty in The Hague. Formerly (1999–2011) head of the media program of De Balie, a center for culture and politics in Amsterdam, he has lectured on media theory at a variety of Dutch academic institutions and has worked as a scientific staff member at the Academy of Media Arts in Cologne. His publications include *The Book of Imaginary Media* (NAI, 2006), *Delusive Spaces* (2008), *The Network Notebook Legacies of Tactical Media* (Institute of Network Cultures, 2011), *Techno-Ecologies* (RIXC, 2012), and *Open*'s theme issues on Im/Mobility (2011) and Hybrid Space (2006).

Lev Manovich is the author of *Software Takes Command* (Bloomsbury Academic, 2013), *Soft Cinema: Navigating the Database* (MIT Press, 2005), and *The Language of New Media* (MIT Press, 2001). He is a professor at The Graduate Center of the City University of New York and a director of CUNY's Software Studies Initiative and of the California Institute for Telecommunication and Information.

Vincent Manzerolle is a lecturer in the Faculty of Information and Media Studies at the University of Western Ontario, where he teaches courses on the political economy of information, mobile media, search engines and data mining, and media convergence. He has published articles on credit and payment technologies, consumer databases, mobile devices, apps, and media theory. A co-editor of *The Audience Commodity in a Digital Age* (with Lee McGuigan; Lang, 2013), he serves as a member of the editorial board of the open-access journal *tripleC: Communication, Capitalism & Critique.*

Svitlana Matviyenko is a media scholar who writes on psychoanalysis, topology, posthumanism, mobile apps, and networking drive. Her work has been published in *Digital Creativity*, in *(Re)-Turn*, in *Harvard Ukrainian Studies*, in *Krytyka*, and in *Kino-Kolo*. She serves as an associate editor of *(Re)-Turn*. She has curated several experimental dance performances at the Ukrainian Institute of America in New York and several exhibitions. Among the exhibitions she curated was The Imaginary App at Ontario's Museum London (with Paul D. Miller).

Dan Mellamphy is a visiting research fellow at the New School in New York, an adjunct professor of interdisciplinary theory and criticism at the University of Western Ontario, a co-founder and co-organizer of the annual Nietzsche Workshop @ Western (and the online Nietzsche Netwørk), and head of the online Centre for Peripheral Theory. He has served on the editorial review boards of *Symposium* (the peer-reviewed journal of the Canadian Society for Continental Philosophy), of *Prosthesis: The Graduate Journal of Theory and Criticism*, of *Helvete*, and of *Foucault Studies*, in addition to being a member of the advisory board of Punctum Books and a juror for AdeP Design Studio/ International Competitions in Architecture. He has published in *Foucault Studies*, in *Deleuze Studies*, in *Dalhousie French Studies*, in *Glossator*, in *Ozone*, in *Collapse*, in *Paideusis*, in *Janus Head*, in *Symposium*, in the *Canadian Review of Comparative Literature*, in *Modern Drama*, in *Leper Creativity: Proceedings of the Cyclonopedia Symposium* (edited by Edward Keller, Eugene Thacker, and Nicola Masciandaro), in *Alchemical Traditions from Antiquity to the Avant-Garde* (edited by Aaron Cheak), and in the forthcoming anthology *Marshall McLuhan's & Vilém Flusser's Communication & Aesthetic Theories Revisited.*

Paul D. Miller (a.k.a. DJ Spooky That Subliminal Kid) is a composer, a multimedia artist, and a writer. His written work has appeared in the *Village Voice*, in *The Source*, in *Artforum*, and in *The Wire*. Miller's work as a media artist has appeared in the Whitney Biennial, in the Venice Biennial for Architecture (2000), in the Ludwig Museum in Cologne, in the Kunsthalle in Vienna, in the Andy Warhol Museum in Pittsburgh, and in many other museums and galleries. His work *New York Is Now* was exhibited in the Africa Pavilion at the 2007 Venice Biennial and in the 2007 Art Basel show in Miami. His first collection of essays, *Rhythm Science*, was published by the MIT Press in 2004. He edited *Sound Unbound*, an anthology of writings on electronic music and digital media published by the MIT Press in 2008. DJ Spooky's film project *Rebirth of a Nation* was commissioned in 2004 by the Lincoln Center Festival, by the Spoleto Festival USA, by Wiener Festwochen, and by the Festival d'Automne à Paris. A DVD version of *Rebirth of a Nation* was released by Anchor Bay Films/Starz Media in 2008. In 2011, Miller released *The Book of Ice* (Thames and Hudson/Mark Batty), a graphic design project exploring the impact of climate change on Antarctica through the prism of digital media and contemporary music compositions; it was included in the 2011 Gwangju Biennial. Miller is currently a contributing editor to *C-Theory* and the arts editor of *Origin*, a magazine that focuses on the intersection of art, yoga, and new ideas.

Steven Millward is a tech blogger, a researcher, and an independent writer. Now based in China, he serves as a writer and an editor at Techinasia.com, focusing on Web news and startups. He also contributes to several culture and travel sites, to the British Broadcasting Corporation, to Voice of America, and to the Australian Broadcasting Corporation.

Anna Munster, a digital artist and a writer, has exhibited in Australia, in Japan, in the United States, and online. Her works include digital prints, multimedia works, and online works. She has written for the online *M/C Journal*, for *Photofile*, for *Australian Feminist Studies*, and for *Campaign*, and has published in various anthologies. She lectures on art and new media at the College of Fine Arts of the University of New South Wales. Her current projects include *Wunderkammer* (an "experimental interactive for CD-ROM" funded by the Australian Film Commission) and *hateSpace* (an online project about cyberhate).

Søren Bro Pold is an associate professor of digital aesthetics in the Department of Aesthetics and Communication at Aarhus University. His publications on digital and media aesthetics discuss topics ranging from the nineteenth-century panorama to the interface in its variant forms, including electronic literature, Net art, software art, creative software, urban and mobile interfaces, activism, surveillance culture, and digital culture. He took part in establishing the Digital Aesthetics Research Centre in 2002. In 2004 he co-organized the Read_me festival on software art. From 2004 to 2007 he was in charge of a research project titled The Aesthetics of Interface Culture, and from 2008 to 2012 he was research manager at the Center for Digital Urban Living. Currently he is leader of the research program in Humans and Information Technology and a researcher in the interdisciplinary research program in Participatory Information Technology. He has been active in establishing interface criticism as a research perspective. He co-edited the anthology *Interface Criticism: Aesthetics Beyond the Buttons* (with Christian Ulrik Andersen; Aarhus University Press, 2011).

Chris Richards is the pop music critic at the *Washington Post*. He covers White House concerts, D.I.Y. house shows, go-go, and Gaga. His work was included in the anthology *Best Music Writing 2011* (Da Capo, 2011).

Scott Snibbe is an artist, a filmmaker, and the founder of several companies, including Snibbe Interactive and Scott Snibbe Studio. Snibbe's installations can be found in the permanent collections of the Whitney Museum and the Museum of Modern Art, in science museums, and in airports. He has collaborated with musicians (including Björk) and filmmakers (among them James Cameron). Early in his career he helped to create the special effects software Adobe After Effects. *Biophilia*, on which he collaborated with Björk, is the world's first app album.

Nick Srnicek is a PhD candidate in International Relations at the London School of Economics. He is a co-editor of *The Speculative Turn: Continental Materialism and Realism* (with Levi Bryant and Graham Harman; Re.press, 2011) and a co-author of *Folk Politics* (with Alex Williams; Zero Books, 2014). He has published articles in *Collapse*, in the *Journal of Critical Globalisation Studies*, in *Pli*, and in *Symposium*.

Index

Plate 1

End of Water (EoH$_2$). The third of the "Apocalyptic Apps," it provides a detailed account of anthropogenic acidification and pollution of oceans and lakes and its catastrophic effects on aquatic ecosystems. The app maps measured pH and toxicity levels, linking them to the affected biota. Social media profiles are created for organisms at risk of extinction, so users can connect with them and write them thoughts, memories, and eulogies. Credit: Simone Ferracina.

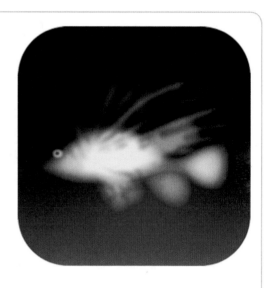

Plate 2

Wikilution, a network for the sharing and dissemination of information that can aid protests. There are three main components and layers of information to the app: an ongoing wiki collects literature and practical information that can contextualize and prepare newcomers to a protest, a "newsfeed" draws on media outlets to update protesters as events unfold, and finally a custom Google Earth interface allows protesters to log on, find each other, communicate, warn about sudden threats, and offer localizable medical and legal help. Credit: Alexander Chaparro.

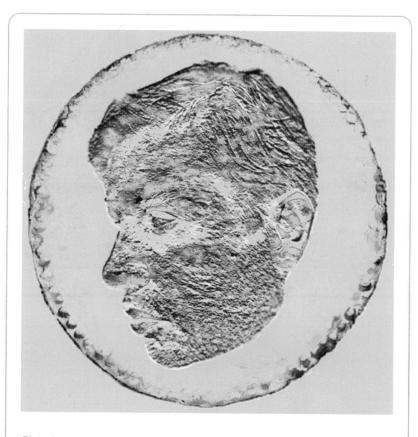

Plate 3

DOC-YOU-MINT. It allows a user to compile and mix original documentation by means of a mobile device. The parameters for the collected data are set by the user; a daily selfie, hourly GPS coordinates, weekly mobile screen captures, and nightly sky shots are some of the possibilities. Whatever one chooses to document, DOC-YOU-MINT will prompt an action ("photograph your window view now"), organize the gathered media, and "mint" a concise and moving picture (in the form of a slide show and/or an animated video) that can be shared in social networks. The prompt feature inherent in this app will guarantee the completion of said project(s). Credit: Vagner M. Whitehead.

Plate 4

Female Sexual Arousal. The design of this app was based on the most current scientific research examining physiological, affective, and contextual components of female sexual responsiveness and satisfaction. The app will generate a graph of sexual arousal based on Laser Doppler Imaging (LDI) technology, a multidimensional assessment tool of cues for sexual desire in women. LDI functions by measuring superficial changes in blood flow in the vulvar tissues resulting in visual cues such as the so-called sex flush, a red rash that begins in the stomach area, then spreads to the breasts and the neck. Credit: Jean-René Leblanc.

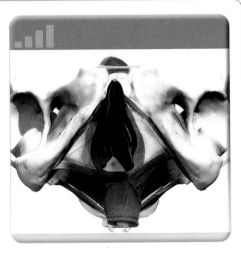

Plate 5

Borges. Your world—again! Trace your world, completely! With Borges, we realize a long-aspired ambition to create a complete, fully high-def remap of your personal geographic, social, and economic behaviors. The full potential of your self-traceability—realized! The application, always running once installed, continuously records you movements, environments and behavior. At the end of a long day, you can sit back and relive it precisely as it occurred, over and over. Quantified and qualified self, moment to moment, just as it happened. After a few months of using Borges, you won't know what world you're living in! Credit: Jamie Allen, Ishac Bertran, Ian Curry, Bernhard Garnicnig, Elena Gianni.

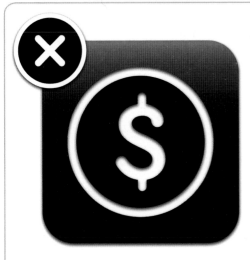

Plate 6

The Ultimate App—"the app that eats itself." The Ultimate App has the simplest function: to transact. One tap launches it, immediately initiating an in-session payment. Upon completion of the payment, the app elegantly closes itself. With seamless in-app payments, you can be finished using this app in seconds. No fuss, no muss—an app that performs its own finitude quicker than most. And, speed. The Ultimate App is quicker than any other app you've ever used. For the low per-use cost—only $0.99, €0.99, £0.99 (regionally). From engineering giant Claude Shannon's mind to your mobile device: pure potential, faster than the speed of life! Credit: Jamie Allen, Ishac Bertran, Ian Curry, Bernhard Garnicnig, Elena Gianni.

Plate 7

$upermark-it. In today's busy world, people often like to get where they are going and get there fast. Often time's mundane tasks like going to the grocery store can slow people down and cause frustration. With the $upermark-it app, these frustrations can be alleviated. Simply upload your grocery list, enter in the store you wish to shop and the app will generate a step-by-step map of where each item is located (the specific location on a shelf) to get you in and get you out as quickly as possible. No more searching for items or figuring what isle to go down next. The app does it all to help turn this often slow process, into a quick one! Credit: Matt Fenstermaker.

Plate 8

Song Catcher. This app cuts through the noises of our sweltering media ecology by locating, isolating, and inscribing truthful human expression. Whereas phonography-aided collectors of authentic folk songs c. 1933 were necessarily constrained by the indiscriminating openness of their cylinders, discs, or later tape (as Friedrich Kittler has more or less said, analogue sound recording lets it all in), *The Song Catcher* homes in on the being or becoming of what one (or many) really is (or are). The transmission of authenticity has long been recognizable by some on an affective level; an algorithm for increasingly inauthentic times, *The Song Catcher* finally allows for crisp, mediatized communion with the real. Credit: Henry Adam Svec, Tegan Moore.

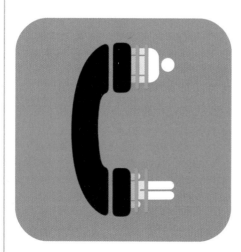

Plate 9

Telephort. Granted this app would render the entire public transportation sector obsolete as well as making cars and planes outdated. But how often have you thought that life would just be better if the commute didn't take as long as it does, or that the holiday would be better if the flight were shorter? If only you could teleport! Luckily there's an app for that! Telephort allows the user to type in an address that they want to go to. Telephort then physically moves the user from their current location to their desired destination, and it all happens through the app! Inspired by the mechanics of the 3D printer, Telephort uses similar but much improved technology to move the user from point A to point B. Credit: Christoffer Laursen Hald.

Plate 10

All-Purpose Reset Button. This is an all-purpose reset button that gives you an automatic do-over. It is useful for when you lose a game, have an argument, fail a test, or miss the bus. It's also great for getting to do something over again. To use the app, you open it, switch the lock, open the safety cover, and press the button. You will then feel like you are being pulled through a time warp. You will see images flashing by, and you have to keep your finger on the button until you get to the moment where you want to be. Then you simply take your finger off the button, and you will resume the position that you were in at that time. Credit: Isabel Higgon.

Plate 11

I Eye. This creative app will help you experience a new world that you haven't seen. Taking the place of your glasses, I Eye has the ability to correct your vision as well as fun features including night vision. You can use this useful and fun app when you feel bored or you have to find something lost in the night without any light. Credit: Michelle Kim, Suzie Kim, and Claire Cho.

Plate 12

Weather Changer. Have you ever felt too hot or too cold, or in the mood for rain or snow? Ever wanted to change the weather with your finger? Well, now you can. All you have to do is click on the season you want, then choose the exact temperature and how you want the atmosphere to be. It's as easy as that and only takes a few seconds for complete comfort. Credit: Nika Maklakova.

Plate 13

Situationiste. Choose your destination. Get lost. Exploiting the navigational dependence humanity has developed with GPS, Situationiste fragments the everyday conceptual anchor via a localized psychogeography. The result is a global deconstruction of place. Once activated, the app produces a micro-macro transference mapping across the threshold between the immediate and remote. The user—now virtually lost—finds itself immersed in an alien architecture, a topologically equivalent landscape. New York now reads as a geographically isomorphic selection of Barcelona or Sapporo. A grid is a grid is a grid is a grid. Credit: Katrina Burch, Lendl Barcelos, Michael O. Vertolli.

Plate 14

Mirage app is an augmented-reality-based 4D fine art installation. By democratizing the nature of art into a social experience that allows for the creation of non object oriented art across mobile and Web-based platforms, it represents a disruptive step in the evolution of art in the twenty-first century, utilizing the app framework to provide technological transparency while delivering 4D-based content that is both interactive and shareable across the spectrum of popular social media. Credit: Raymond Salvatore Harmon.

Plate 15

iLuck. This app uses GPS, which first determines the location of the user. Then it places four-leaf clover markers where luck could be located. When approaching each marker, the program automatically changes the course to another location, so the iPhone user begins an endless wander in different directions. At the end, rather than trying to find his own luck, using his own intuition, he finds himself stupidly walking around with his overpraised guiding device. Credit: Yana Krachunova (a.k.a. PixelDelay).

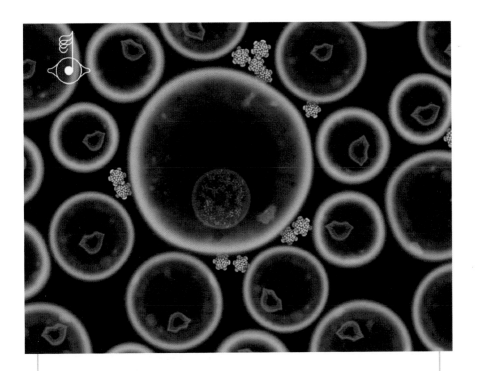

Plate 16
"Virus," from the "album cover" for *Biophilia*. Credit: Björk, Scott Snibbe.

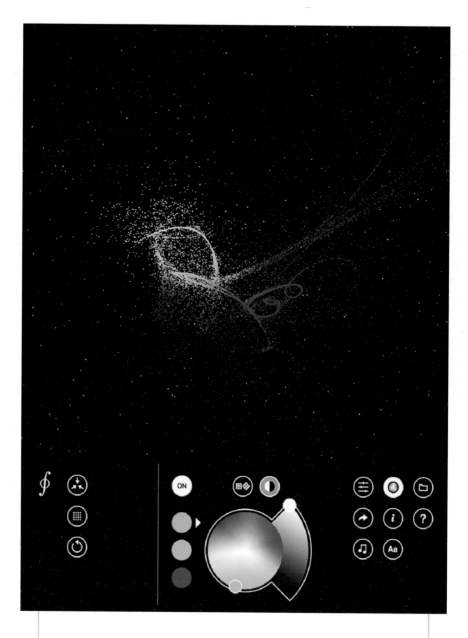

Plate 17
Gravilux. Credit: Scott Snibbe.

Plate 18
"Cosmogony," from the "album cover" for *Biophilia*. Credit: Björk, Scott Snibbe.